VIOLENT

APPETITES

VIOLENT APPETITES

HUNGER IN THE

EARLY NORTHEAST

Carla Cevasco

Yale
UNIVERSITY PRESS

New Haven & London

Published with assistance from the Annie Burr Lewis Fund.
Published with assistance from the foundation established in memory of
Philip Hamilton McMillan of the Class of 1894, Yale College.

Yale University Press books may be purchased in
quantity for educational, business, or promotional use.
For information, please e-mail sales.press@yale.edu
(U.S. office) or sales@yaleup.co.uk (U.K. office).

Printed in the United States of America.

Library of Congress Control Number: 2021943740
ISBN 978-0-300-25134-0 (hardcover : alk. paper)

A catalogue record for this book is available from the British Library.

This paper meets the requirements of ANSI/NISO Z39.48-1992
(Permanence of Paper).

10 9 8 7 6 5 4 3 2 1

For my parents

CONTENTS

CONTENTS

ACKNOWLEDGMENTS

Writing a book that has reciprocity as one of its main themes, I am humbled by the labor and care with which other people have supported this project.

I learned much of what I know about writing from my undergraduate professors at Middlebury College, especially David Bain, Robert Cohen, Bill Hart, Brett Millier, and Amy Morsman.

The Harvard American Studies program was the first home for this project. The "Four Js"—Joyce Chaplin, Jill Lepore, Jane Kamensky, and Jennifer Roberts—shepherded this project, and me, with grace and wit. I was privileged to be part of the American Studies community, including Colin Bossen, Holger Droessler, Marisa Egerstrom, Amy Fish, Katherine Gerbner, Balraj Gill, Kyle Gipson, Brian Goodman, Andrew Jewett, Theresa McCulla, Dan McKanan, Zach Nowak, Arthur Patton-Hock, Eva Payne, Sandy Plácido, Scott Poulson-Bryant, Evander Price, Whitney Robles, Laurel Thatcher Ulrich, and Tom Wickman. I was especially lucky to be part of a phenomenal cohort: Christopher Allison, John Bell, Dan Farbman, and Rebecca Scofield. Special gratitude to John, Whitney, Zach,

Chris, and Rebecca, both for reading parts of this book multiple times, and for their friendship. Other dedicated readers of this project were members of the Harvard Early America Workshop, including Jennifer Chuong, Alicia DeMaio, Marion Menzin, Julie Miller, Peter Pellizzari, Shuichi Wanibuchi, and Luke Willert. Students in my History of Hunger class helped me to think through the larger arguments of this book.

The Department of American Studies at Rutgers University–New Brunswick has been as supportive a place as any junior faculty member could ask for. My thanks to my colleagues, especially Sylvia Chan-Malik, Jeff Decker, Nicole Fleetwood, Allan Isaac, Maria Kennedy, Olga Lozano, Lou Masur, Ben Perolli, Jimmy Sweet, Andy Urban, and Colin Williamson. Members of my writing group have kept me accountable over the years; thanks to David Dreyfus, Erica Edwards, Anette Freytag, Diane Fruchtman, Bice Peruzzi, and Charles Senteio, among others. I benefited from the mentoring of the Rutgers University Faculty Development Program for Early Career Excellence under the guidance of Bernadette Peters and Beth Tracy; my thanks also to my coach, Lisa McGahren. At Rutgers, it is my honor to teach the best students in the world, many of whom are first-generation students, BIPOC, and/or queer. Their passion and brilliance give me faith that a better future is possible. I hope that they learn from me even a fraction of what I learn from them. I am privileged to work at a university with one of the strongest faculty unions in the United States; Rutgers AAUP-AFT and the Coalition of Rutgers Unions fight tirelessly for the rights of Rutgers workers, including myself.

A number of scholars in the broader Early American Studies and Food Studies communities have supported and offered feedback on this project in many ways, including: Jenny Anderson, Virginia Anderson, Kathleen Brown, Emily Contois, Rachel Herrmann, Elizabeth Hoover, Joanne Jahnke-Wegner, Julie Kim, Michael LaCombe, Andrew Lipman, Hailey Negrin, Cristobal Silva, Kelly Watson, Ashley Rose Young, and Anya Zilberstein.

Several institutions funded this project over the years: the John Carter Brown Library; the Winterthur Museum and Library; and at Harvard, the Charles Warren Center for Studies in American History, the Department of History, and the Graduate Student Council. The Rutgers Center for Cultural Analysis provided a fellowship in the Medical Humanities Seminar, led by Ann Jurecic and Susan Sidlauskas, whom I thank along with the other seminar participants for their intellectual community.

No writing of history is possible without archives, libraries, and collections and the people who work at them. I thank the staff at the American Antiquarian Society, the British Library, Historic Deerfield, Houghton Library, the John Carter Brown Library, the Massachusetts Historical Society, the Massachusetts State Archives, Schlesinger Library, the Wellcome Collection, and the Winterthur Museum and Library, as well as the staff at Rutgers and Harvard libraries, especially the Rutgers librarians who made my access to physical and digital collections possible even during the COVID-19 pandemic.

Many audiences offered feedback on this project over the years. I extend my gratitude to the attendees of the American Studies Association annual meeting, the American Historical Association annual meeting, the Amsterdam Symposium on the History of Food, the Boston University American and New England Studies Program Graduate Conference, the Colonial Society of Massachusetts Graduate Student Forum, the Columbia University Seminar on Early American History and Culture, the Huntington Library "Empowering Appetites" conference, and the "Cannibalism in the Early Modern Atlantic" conference at the University of Southampton.

At Yale University Press, Adina Berk, Joyce Ippolito, and Ash Lago kept this project moving through the publication process, and Eliza Childs thoughtfully edited the manuscript; I thank them all for their labor in the midst of the COVID-19 pandemic.

There are not enough words to express my gratitude to my partner Alex, as he keeps our little family together in so many ways. But suffice it to say that without his love and care I would not have been able to write this book, for which he also made the map.

This book is dedicated to my parents, Elaine Morley and Peter Cevasco, who nourished my love of food and my fascination with early American history, and thus set this project in motion long before I ever conceived of it.

Portions of chapter 3 are revised from: Carla Cevasco, " 'Nothing which hunger will not devour': Disgust and Sustenance in the Northeastern Borderlands," *Early American Studies* 19, no. 2 (2021): 264–93.

Portions of chapter 1 are revised from: Carla Cevasco, "Hunger Knowledges and Cultures in New England's Borderlands, 1675–1770," *Early American Studies* 16, no. 2 (2018): 255–81. ©2018 The McNeil Center for Early American Studies. Reprinted with permission of the University of Pennsylvania Press.

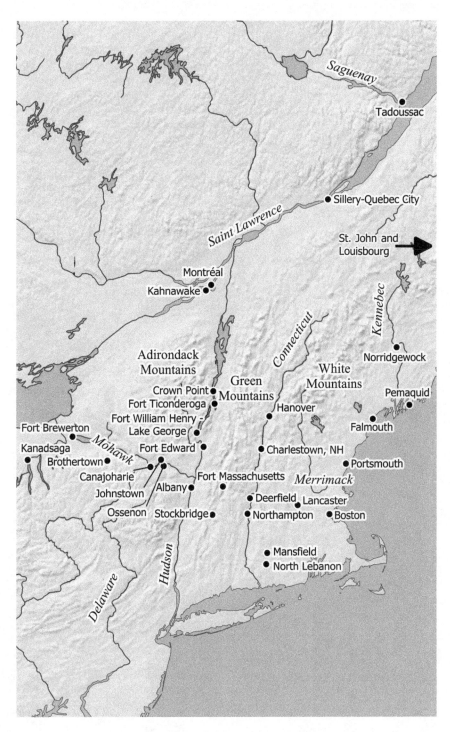

Important places in the northeastern borderlands mentioned in the text. Map by Alex Oberg.

INTRODUCTION

The Problem of Hunger in Early America

When the Presbyterian missionary Samuel Kirkland sat down to his first full British meal in several months in April 1765, he could not restrain himself. Over the winter, Kirkland had been adopted into a Seneca family, which included his older brother Tekânadie, Tekânadie's wife, and their children. Alongside the rest of their community in Kanadasaga, in what is now called the Finger Lakes region of New York, the family had recently resettled as refugees from the Seven Years' War. The disruptions of the war and a failed harvest the previous summer meant that the community suffered a late spring food shortage. As the hungry season wore on, the family traveled to a British fort to ask for food assistance. Six days of travel brought them to Fort Brewerton, where Kirkland left the family to camp outside the fort while he went up to meet with the commanding officer.[1]

Noticing that Kirkland was emaciated, the officer offered him the leftovers from his dinner, "a bowl of rice soup" and part of "a leg of mutton or venison." As the missionary ate, he later recalled, "my appetite soon became raging," and he attacked the food on the table: "I cut one slice after another of the flesh & felt as if I should soon devour all that was

1

brought . . . and not be satisfied." Watching Kirkland stuff himself, the officer told Kirkland, "with a very pleasant air," that since he had been "next to a state of starvation" for so long, he should pace himself, lest he make himself ill. To this "extraordinary kindness and great politeness," Kirkland responded rudely, "with some *warmth*." Unhinged by his hunger, he imagined that his host "grudged the food." "*Sir I am willing to pay you for what I eat*," Kirkland snapped (though he would later recollect "I had not a farthing"). The officer patiently told Kirkland that "he would feed me with pleasure, . . . if it would do me no injury," but that he was acting on Kirkland's behalf. Finally, Kirkland "*dropped* my *knife* and *fork* & come to *myself*." He expressed gratitude to the officer for the meal.[2]

The officer promised to send food to Kirkland's Seneca family, who were waiting, "hungry," on the shores of the lake outside the garrison. Within a few hours, the overstuffed Kirkland vomited up "my excellent dinner" before returning to apologize to the officer for his "ingratitude." The officer told Kirkland that the incident did not afford him the "*least disgust*" but filled him with "compassion" for Kirkland's suffering.[3]

When Kirkland recorded this episode more than three decades later, he could not remember whether he ate venison or mutton. The "violence of my appetite" had blotted out the specifics of the meal, but he vividly remembered his hunger, disgust, and shame. Meanwhile, the suffering of the Seneca family down on the lake shore remained, in Kirkland's narrative at least, unspoken and unseen.

Born in 1741 and educated at Eleazar Wheelock's Moor's Indian Charity School and Princeton, Kirkland became a missionary to Kanadasaga at age twenty-four. In the first few months of his missionary career, Kirkland learned about Seneca culture from his adoptive family, while contributing to the turmoil of a community battered by colonialism and famine.[4] He kept a journal of his experiences, only to destroy it later and then rewrite it in 1800 in the last decade of his life. Even recalling events from a thirty-five-year distance, Kirkland's memories of his early missionary experiences were not just embarrassing but visceral, disgusting, and disturbing.

Kirkland's anecdote about his violent appetite was one of many such narratives of uncontrollable hunger in early America. The account of the tense meal at Fort Brewerton described not just Kirkland's physical and psychological responses to famine but the larger contexts of a hungry and disordered place and time. It was the story of one example of social collapse—a guest being rude to his host, a relation neglecting his family. It was the story of scarcity and displacement—of the Seneca, already refugees from a colonial war, forced to travel to British authorities to ask for food aid. It was the story of the cultural arm of colonialism—a British missionary attempting to convert the Seneca to Christianity and also transform the ways they ate and lived. It was the story of colonial violence on scales large and small—from the British military occupation of Seneca lands, to Kirkland's mission, to his disregard of his starving Seneca family. And it was also the story of Indigenous survival—of a Seneca family trying to endure hunger and trying to teach a British colonizer how to do the same.

Kirkland called his hunger "violent." But he did not see his mission or his treatment of his adoptive family in the same light. How could hunger be violent in early America? How did hunger intersect with other forms of violence, such as colonialism? And how did people survive hunger's violence?

This book tells the story of how people experienced, used, succumbed to, and survived hunger across cultures in northeastern North America in the seventeenth and eighteenth centuries.[5] The era saw a long, messy period of endemic violence between the end of early French and English colonial efforts (approximately 1630) and the beginning of the Age of Revolutions (approximately 1770). The lack of food fundamentally transformed power relations in the borderlands of the northeast, where Indigenous peoples and French and English colonists brought their understandings of hunger to bear on a rapidly changing world. It was a world in which colonists tried to claim supremacy over Native peoples while often failing to feed themselves. It was a world in which Indigenous peoples fought the colonial invaders' attacks on their food sovereignty, suffered scarcity, and adapted and carried on ancestral foodways.

Demonstrating how colonists struggled to survive scarcity, while Native peoples weathered hunger by leveraging traditional knowledges, rewrites the history of colonization. In the northeast, colonists remained vulnerable in the face of Native resistance, even deep into the late eighteenth century. Colonists believed that their foodways were superior to those of Native peoples. Yet the invaders often faced fears of food shortage well into the late eighteenth century, even if they were not always aware of how much their food scarcity jeopardized the colonial project. Where scholars have tended to highlight the power of colonialism to dispossess Indigenous peoples, this book uses hunger to expose the precarity of colonial survival and the strategies of resilience that Native peoples used to endure both scarcity and colonial invasion.

Indigenous peoples thrived in landscapes—their homelands—that colonists found challenging and deadly. They did this, especially in the more northern regions, by maintaining a fundamentally different relationship to their lands than did the agriculture-dependent colonizers. In traditional foodways across the northeast, Native women cultivated productive farms and foraged an extensive array of wild plant foods. Native men hunted and fished a variety of proteins. People traded and gifted food throughout the region. These flexible means of subsistence often insulated Native communities from crop failures in a way that was not available to colonists or other Europeans across the Atlantic. At the foundations of Native food systems lay understandings of reciprocity, of humans living among and responsible to other beings in a vital world. Colonialism may have challenged Native foodways, but these traditions of subsistence remain powerful even today, having helped Indigenous communities survive centuries of conquest.

Food scarcity played a critical role in shaping settler colonial projects in North America. English and French colonists brought their own ideas about hunger from across the Atlantic. The invaders clung to their ideas even when exposed to radically different understandings of hunger among Native peoples. Although settlers undertook colonization in the interest of material gain—exploiting land, people, and other resources—they rationalized the invasion on cultural grounds, deriding Indigenous bodies as weak, savage, and incapable of properly feeding themselves.[6] While colonists constructed racial and bodily difference between themselves and Native peoples, they were correct that Indigenous peoples did have different conceptions of hunger and the body, and different means of surviving scarcity. As a result, Indigenous peoples experienced hunger differently than did colonists: less likely to face it and more likely to survive it.

Even while arguing for the continuity of Indigenous resistance, it is important to emphasize that Native peoples bore the brunt of violent change during the early centuries of colonialism. Seeking to expand their empires, colonizers worked to subjugate and dispossess Indigenous peoples, not just through the formalized violence of war but with the slower, subtler violences of missionizing, environmental degradation, and trade.[7] Colonists dislocated Native peoples' established ways of managing seasonal scarcity, forcing them from their homelands, disturbing networks of trade and alliance, destroying crops and stores, and disrupting cycles of planting, harvesting, foraging, fishing, hunting, and preserving. As colonists invaded, their prophecies about Native poverty and hunger became self-fulfilling. Nevertheless, Native peoples showed extraordinary resilience in the face of food scarcity, war, and displacement, marshalling sophisticated systems of hunger knowledge and maintaining food-based rituals throughout the centuries. If colonialist violence took the form of hunger, then surviving it formed an important front of Indigenous resistance.

Rather than an economic or political history of hunger in early America, this book is a story of how people defined hunger and how they lived through it. Emphasizing the cultural impact of hunger does not mean that hunger in early America was necessarily imaginary or metaphorical. Much of the hunger described here was very real, and certainly the archive describes instances of what can only be called starvation. However, the rhetoric of starvation and of deadly food shortage appears much more often than evidence of the phenomenon itself, especially when colonists wrote about themselves. As a work of cultural history, *Violent Appetites* examines the power of colonists' beliefs in their own vulnerability to hunger, even if that vulnerability was at times more imagined than real. Such ideas about hunger would reverberate for generations in colonial mythologies.[8] In early America, as in our own time, authoritarian power structures saw certain peoples' hunger as more important or real than others.[9] How these beliefs formed, and how they made the world around them, is the subject of this book.

Many Words for Hunger

In a story about how people defined hunger, each other, and themselves, my own choice of words matters. The setting of this book is the northeastern borderlands, the region of North America that encompasses present-day New England, upstate New York, Quebec, and the Maritime provinces. The term "borderlands" encompasses the shifting, overlapping, and intermingling of peoples and cultures that occurred in this area. To avoid privileging colonial American or Canadian national narratives over Indigenous ones, I have adapted the terminology of the "northeast" or "northeastern North America" rather than national titles, while recognizing that these terms remain colonial nomenclature. By any name, this region formed the front lines of pivotal conflicts between Indigenous peoples and British and French invaders throughout the seventeenth and eighteenth centuries.[9]

Throughout the text, the terms "Indigenous" and "Native" appear interchangeably. When possible—which is not always, given the tendency of colonial sources to refer generically to "Indians"—Native peoples are identified by their specific tribal affiliations. When discussing alliances and linguistic or cultural groups more broadly, the text uses more general terms, such as "Haudenosaunee" or "Wabanaki." The text refers to the Europeans as colonists or invaders. When referring to colonists of a specific national or imperial identity, the book uses "French" or "English" (pre-1707) or "British" (post-1707) as appropriate, while acknowledging that these labels, too, threaten to gloss over a vast array of experiences based on region, class, gender, and so forth.[10]

In addition to naming the actors in this story, *Violent Appetites* also names a variety of their experiences. Colonial writers sometimes used the word "hunger," but I use it as an umbrella term for a variety of words they likewise employed, including "appetite," often meaning a particular taste for something; "gluttony," an over-the-top hunger that was one of the seven deadly sins in Christian traditions; "famine," the widespread hunger that affected an entire population; "dearth," the day-to-day scarcity experienced by the poor; "starvation," or the risk of death from hunger; and other words referring to a shortfall in food, such as "want," "lack," or "scarcity." Colonial authorities were particularly concerned about what they saw as excessive appetites, as in the British physician John Harris's definition of "intemperance": "inordinate appetite, and immoderate desire, and use of meat and drink" leading to "Gluttony, and Drunkenness."[11] These different words might have different cultural or political valences. But there are also many reasons to be skeptical of colonizers' invocations of hunger, or other names for it. *Violent Appetites* weighs the specific terminology that colonial sources used against other readings of the evidence. Such analysis is necessary because colonial writers tended to under- or overestimate Indigenous hunger as it suited their needs; so, too, did colonial sources attach different levels and meanings to various colonial hungers. In some places and times colonists were certainly dying of hunger, as they often claimed, but in other places and times they were simply exaggerating. Ascertaining how and why these narratives were recorded in these ways is crucial to the story of early American hunger.

The Indigenous peoples of the northeast also had their own names for hunger with their own meanings, and they used them differently depending on the audiences they addressed and the circumstances they navigated. An eighteenth-century French-Wabanaki dictionary demonstrated that hunger was a complex concept in Wabanaki cultures and languages at that time, with a multiplicity of words and phrases pointing to a variety of bodily experiences and communal performances of scarcity. One could be hungry, very hungry, or constantly eating. But one could also experience "walking" or "canine" hunger, or be crying from hunger. One could be hungry because one had eaten certain foods but not others: "I am hungry because I have not eaten meat or fish, but I have eaten a lot of corn." One could state how one had not eaten for a long time and list the number of days without food: "I can go a long time without eating . . . one day . . . two days." Reflecting Wabanaki norms of reciprocity, hunger was not only an individual but a social act, in which people could hunger for one another or make someone else hungry. In the 1730s, one Jesuit missionary reported returning Wabanaki hunting bands greeting priests with " 'We are dying of hunger.'" The multifaceted experiences of Wabanaki hunger gave rise to a dense hunger vocabulary, hinting at varieties of hunger that might not have existed in the conceptions of European colonists.[12]

Food scarcity was also of crucial importance in Haudenosaunee or Iroquoian languages. A translation manual assembled by French Sulpician missionaries translated common Catholic prayers and liturgies into Haudenosaunee languages, but it carefully conjugated only a handful of Haudenosaunee verbs. All of the conjugated verbs related to eating or feeling hunger. Similarly, though not as plentifully as the Wabanaki dictionary, a French-Wendat dictionary compiled by a French missionary in the 1640s listed a number of verbs for types of eating, including to eat everything, to eat too much, and to taste. For the missionaries who assembled such translation manuals and dictionaries, it was just as important to be able to communicate about food as it was to instruct Indigenous peoples in matters of the soul.[13]

Whatever words they used, colonial and Indigenous peoples recognized that hunger posed particular risks to society and culture, a phenomenon I call "the problem of hunger." As this book will demonstrate again and again, hunger unraveled the social fabric, whether widespread hunger threatened to topple institutions or individual hunger drove people to kill and even eat family and friends.

The variety of names for hunger reveal that it is both a physiological experience and a shifting cultural concept across time. The notion that hunger is culturally constructed might seem foreign in our own era: in present-day classifications, hunger might be categorized as a shortfall of calories or specific nutrients ("hunger" or "malnutrition"), or it might mean not being able to rely on one's next meal ("food insecurity"). These measures, while ostensibly objective or quantitative, instead reflect contemporary Western cultural imperatives. Often, people's hungers do not fit these categories at all: for example, the absence of a particular staple, even in the midst of plenty, might leave people feeling like they are starving.[14]

Violent Appetites also introduces two related terms, "hunger culture" and "hunger knowledges." Hunger culture is the way that different cultures conceptualize and experience hunger. Hunger knowledge is a subset of hunger culture that encompasses the ways that people respond to and survive hunger.[15] Indigenous and colonial people used various strategies to survive in a world of cultural continuity and rapid, violent change.

Recognizing that knowledge took many forms and was produced by many people, *Violent Appetites* defines "knowledges" capaciously. This expansive definition falls in line with scholars of science and medicine in early America, who have examined the collision of Indigenous, West African, and European knowledge systems in the midst of slavery and colonization. This far-reaching definition recognizes physical or tacit practices, such as belt-tightening to lessen the sensations of hunger, as forms of knowledge alongside conventional Western understandings of intellectual and cultural history. As Europeans invaded Indigenous lands, they struggled to fit North America and its peoples within categories of knowledge

8

that existed back in Europe. Networks of White, wealthy, male natural philosophers and patrons raced to catalogue unfamiliar peoples, plants, animals, and more in the so-called New World. They attained this knowledge through marginalized interlocutors and laborers—women, poor people, and people of Indigenous or African descent—in exchanges that were rarely egalitarian. Across differences in language, culture, and power, Europeans misunderstood, obscured, and exploited Indigenous knowledges. However, Native peoples had their own sources of power during these exchanges, sharing some knowledges with colonizers and refusing to reveal others.[16]

While in this book I describe hunger culture and hunger knowledges as they existed in a specific place and time, these terms have a much broader relevance to the study of hunger. Across history, people have faced hunger often deployed against them as a weapon of oppression. Hungry people have responded with fortitude and ingenuity, creating and passing down knowledge systems in order to endure. Because these are knowledges produced by poor, marginalized people, they are not often celebrated for what they are: tremendous achievements against the odds. But they are knowledges that desperately need recognition as the world faces the many crises of the twenty-first century.

The World of the Northeastern Borderlands

The Indigenous northeast before colonization was a dynamic place of shifting political and cultural forces and of great ecological and climactic variation. The homelands of Algonquian-speaking peoples in what is now southern New England offered bountiful agricultural lands and coastal territories, and large webs of kinship and alliance. Further inland, in what is currently upstate New York, the Haudenosaunee Confederacy, or the People of the Longhouse, united Mohawk, Oneida, Onondaga, Cayuga, and Seneca peoples (and after 1722, the Tuscaroras to the south) around the principles of peace, or Gayeneshagowa. Speaking a related language, the Wendat lived to their north, in the present-day upper Great Lakes and St. Lawrence region. To the east lived the Wabanaki Confederacy, or the People of the Dawnland, an Algonquian-speaking alliance formed in the early seventeenth century out of nations whose homelands stretched between what is now called the Atlantic coast and Vermont. Abenaki, Norridgewock, Penobscot, Kennebec, Maliseet, Passamaquoddy, and M'ikmaq people all were part of the Confederacy at some point in its history. In the subarctic north lived the Algonquian-speaking Innu people. Long before colonizers invaded, these nations traded and treated, made alliances and war, and lived in reciprocity with their lands. Estimates of Indigenous populations before the colonial invasion vary widely, but the Native peoples of eastern North America certainly numbered in the millions, vastly outnumbering the first colonial outposts.[17]

A few colonial expeditions entered the region's waterways in the sixteenth century, but in the late sixteenth and early seventeenth centuries, first French and then English colonizers began to occupy the Native northeast in greater numbers. The earliest of both empires' colonial efforts failed—French invaders founded Fort Charlesbourg-Royal in present-day Quebec in 1541 and abandoned it by 1543; English colonizers founded Roanoke in present-day North Carolina in 1587 but had vanished by the time a relief mission arrived in 1590. By the beginning of the seventeenth century, however, both France and England had established what would become permanent outposts: the French Port-Royal, in what is now Nova Scotia in 1603, and the English Jamestown, Virginia, in 1607. From these tiny footholds, the colonizers tried to carve colonial spaces out of Native territories.

The English dreamed of finding an Eden in North America. They did not find it. They struggled to recreate England in the so-called New World. During the initial English colonization efforts in the early seventeenth century, constant violence, disease, hunger, and other forms of suffering proved deeply destabilizing to English bodies and minds. These early sufferings would come to define the mental world of English colonial culture, even as they threw the viability of the entire colonial project into doubt. Colonists' visions of imperial control wavered in the face of North American realities, both the land and its peoples.[18]

English colonial efforts would have failed without the intervention of Indigenous peoples, who were far more populous and knowledgeable about how to survive in North America. Through superior numbers, diplomacy, warfare, and cultivating English dependence, eastern Native peoples maintained strategic advantages over the colonizers for decades. But,

[handwritten annotation: Indigenous people were a help to colonies]

most scholars of early English colonization have argued, this dynamic shifted before the close of the seventeenth century. The invaders' diseases, violence, and enslavement took a deadly toll on the Indigenous peoples of the east. More and more colonizers crossed the Atlantic and built larger, more permanent outposts. New England became a prosperous center of agriculture and shipping. Shaking off their tenuous beginnings and concealing their dependence on Native peoples, the colonizers began to thrive.

For a long time, scholars argued for the stability and cohesion of New England's small towns from the late seventeenth through late eighteenth centuries, especially compared to the far more chaotic colonization of the Chesapeake that unfolded to the south. More recent scholarship, however, has questioned this narrative of New England as placid and plentiful colonial center. Colonial violence upended the worlds of both colonial and Indigenous peoples. Far from a homogenous world of successful Puritans, New England's communities were home to marginalized peoples, free and unfree, of Indigenous and African descent. The vision of New England that emerges from these histories is much more embattled, within and without, than earlier scholars had determined.[19]

Rather than orderly and peaceful, New England in the eighteenth century remained in many ways just as precarious, at least in its understanding of itself, as it had been at its origins. The suffering of early colonists cast a long shadow on those that came after. The fragility of the colonial enterprise persisted far beyond the seventeenth century—both in its material conditions and in the imaginaries of colonial people. Indeed, eighteenth-century New Englanders remained deeply anxious about the stability of their communities, seeing enemies both within and outside their borders.

They had every reason to be anxious, because they were invading Indigenous lands, and they were not the only trespassers. English and British colonists lived in a time of nearly constant borderlands violence with Indigenous peoples and the French, for whom colonization had proceeded in a different rhythm than that of the English. Both empires had accelerated their efforts at establishing colonies in the early seventeenth century, but the material similarities between New England and New France largely ended there. French invaders never traveled to New France in the same numbers as did the English: in the 1770s, an estimated 90,000 colonizers lived in Canada, in contrast to over half a million colonists who inhabited New England at the time. Most colonizers in New France wanted to make their fortunes and return to France as soon as possible, rather than trying to remake French society in a new place. As a result, the French colony struggled to achieve demographic stability with a population consisting largely of single men, unlike the entire family units that transplanted to New England. In the seventeenth century, the French government even encouraged intermarriage between French colonial men and Native women. This policy, which ultimately failed, represented a much more assimilationist approach to colonization compared to the English.[20]

New France pursued assimilation with Indigenous peoples through other means. Until they achieved the population density needed to till enough land to practice agriculture in earnest, French colonists adapted to Indigenous ways, even as they dreamed of the new landscape they would create. In the seventeenth century, the invaders optimistically believed that they could "cultivate" eastern Canada in the image of agrarian France. By the eighteenth century, however, they were forced to recognize that France and New France did not share the same climate and could not support the same plants or agricultural practices. As a result of these environmental factors, New France never became an agricultural exporter like New England. Instead, New France's main extractive industries were fishing and fur trapping. French invaders in these industries found themselves completely dependent upon the knowledges of Indigenous peoples, from the technologies of snowshoes and traps, to the navigational and environmental knowledge, cultural awareness, and language skills that Indigenous guides provided to fur trappers. These trappers, or *coureurs de bois*, became the most extensively integrated into Indigenous communities compared to the majority of colonists, often by marrying Native women in order to gain kinship access to Indigenous exchange networks. Most French colonists interacted with Native peoples in other ways, through the contexts of missionizing, slavery, and the urban fur trade. Despite these long, extensive, and intimate colonial entanglements with Native peoples, some scholars have been quick to dismiss the continued presence and importance of Indigenous peoples in eastern Canada, with one historian erroneously concluding that Indigenous peoples "receded into the shadows" upon the advent of European colonization.[21]

But to consider only colonial aspirations provides an incomplete and misleading portrait of the early northeast. Contrary to the fantasies of many colonial historians, Native peoples did not quietly disappear from the northeast in the seventeenth and eighteenth centuries. From the beginnings of the colonial invasion in the early seventeenth century to the American Revolution and beyond, Indigenous peoples carried out resistance—whether armed or otherwise—to the colonial trespassers in their territories. Many of these conflicts intersected with disputes between the British and French empires over what they perceived of as "control" of the North American continent. In much of the northeast, however, the idea of colonial supremacy over Indigenous peoples or their lands remained an illusion for much of the eighteenth century. The British and French empires needed Native alliances, intelligence, and martial strength to make war against each other. In turn, Indigenous peoples used their political and military prowess—and their knowledges of their homelands—to maintain their sovereignty against the colonial invaders as they played rival empires off of each other. But the violence of invasion also upset balances of power within the Native world, leading to violence between Native polities.[22]

Nearly constant warfare, with violence between declared wars, persisted throughout the seventeenth and eighteenth centuries. It is impossible to overstate the impact of this violence on Indigenous and colonial peoples: in the words of one historian, "communities, colonies, and nations struggled for survival, one generation after another." In four global conflicts that tore through the northeastern borderlands—King William's War (1688–97), Queen Anne's War (1702–13), King George's War (1744–48), and the Seven Years' War (1757–63)—the British and French empires wrestled over colonial spaces around the globe, while Native peoples took advantage of these disputes in order to resist colonial incursion. This period also saw more localized borderlands conflicts, including Father Rale's War or Dummer's War (1722–25), and Father Le Loutre's War (1749–55). In the seventeenth century, Native people and colonists clashed in the Pequot War in 1637 and in King Philip's War (1675–78). Between declared wars, violence still flared. Living with decades of constant war and violence profoundly affected the peoples of the northeastern borderlands.[23]

One of the main interventions of this book is to argue that colonial vulnerability, particularly with regards to food, continued deep into the eighteenth century in the northeast. Another intervention is to argue that hand-in-hand with this colonial precarity went Indigenous survival and resistance to colonial invasion. Indigenous peoples in the northeast would continue to use hunger knowledges to their advantage for generations after this study ends.[24] Colonists' belief in their vulnerability, meanwhile, persisted long after the reality of it. These myths of settler precarity are just as dangerous as myths of Indigenous disappearance. Narratives of colonial vulnerability—even and especially when this precarity was not based in fact—resemble narratives that continue in many dangerous forms in American culture. Dominant or powerful groups have frequently relied on fears of marginalized peoples to consolidate power and quell internal dissent. In our own time, myths of White male fragility have been used to justify further oppression of many of the most vulnerable people in the United States. As the stuff of life and a vital ingredient in cultural belonging, food is a powerful way to examine such inequalities.

Food and Hunger in Early America

The Indigenous peoples who faced colonial invaders in the seventeenth and eighteenth centuries had spent generations honing their subsistence systems to their environments. Although colonists would not necessarily see it as such, Indigenous peoples obtained not just sufficiency but plenty in their traditional foodways. The wide-ranging climates and geographies of the northeast produced varied foodways and knowledges throughout the region. Algonquian-speaking peoples in what is now southern New England, as well as Haudenosaunee peoples inland and the Wendat around the Great Lakes, combined extensive agriculture with hunting, fishing, and foraging. The longer growing seasons in these areas enabled a greater reliance on agriculture than for peoples in harsher climates. Women and children cultivated the Three Sisters, or corn, beans, and squash. They also foraged for wild foods and encouraged their growth through management of the landscape, such as controlled burning of underbrush and targeted foraging techniques. Men hunted in the winter and fished at other times of the year. Preservation methods, such as drying and fermenting, stretched food supplies across seasons.[25]

Harsher climates demanded more intricate seasonal patterns of subsistence. In the Dawnland, Wabanaki communities maintained cycles of sea-

Indians,
Many Methods
for
food

sonal movement between inland and coastal territories. In the spring, with a community's winter stores exhausted, the men caught river fish, then dried them to last throughout planting season. After the women cultivated their farms and made sure that their crops were established, the community moved to the coast for a few months, to live off of fish and shellfish there before returning inland to harvest their crops in late summer and early fall. In late fall, they moved to the coast again to catch large fish as well as sea birds and other game. In midwinter, family hunting bands traveled deep into the forested north to hunt large game, most importantly moose; men killed game while women processed it. Wabanaki people kept dogs as livestock, a mobile source of protein. Throughout the year, Wabanaki women foraged wild plant foods—tubers, nuts, berries, fungi, and greens. To the north, into the subarctic, the Innu faced an even colder climate and a shorter growing season, with the balance shifting more toward wild food provision rather than agriculture, though corn continued to be a staple even in these regions.[26]

Into this world of Indigenous foodways, colonists brought their own ideas about food, many of which were disastrously ill-suited to North America. As one scholar has described it, early English colonization quickly devolved into a "creation story from hell." The invaders' foodways were especially hellish. Early seventeenth-century colonists faced "seasons of misery," resorting to cannibalism at Jamestown, suffering famine at Plymouth, starting a resource war with the Pequot, and stealing food from Indigenous peoples throughout the period. The invaders survived only with the aid of Indigenous peoples. The power dynamics of the interactions that saved early colonial outposts from starvation were very complex. In some cases, Native people offered gifts or exchanges of food, agricultural instruction, and other forms of support to colonists, whom they saw as potential trading partners or allies, and in some situations perhaps as political tributaries. In other cases, colonists stole from Indigenous food caches or requisitioned food by force, often expecting Indigenous people to become *their* tributaries or enslaved people. In times of environmental pressures, such as the years of drought and agricultural shortfall that plagued the Powhatan Confederacy during the Jamestown invasion in the early 1600s, colonial incursion and exploitation of Indigenous food resources stoked the flames of violence.[27]

Colonists destroyed Native (ask Rabbit)

Any tribe Rely they

Nevertheless, when it came to sustaining themselves, Native peoples maintained the upper hand over the newcomers. Their many generations spent perfecting the best means of extracting food from their homelands had led them to develop flexible subsistence methods that could adapt to seasonal variation, warfare, and other kinds of change. Indigenous people who interacted with early colonists were acutely aware that the newcomers did not necessarily bring these same skills or knowledges, especially in an unfamiliar landscape. Native people used colonial hunger to their political advantage, whether they liberated colonists from starvation or recognized it as a useful ally in driving out the invaders.

Indigenous peoples and colonizers faced the possibility of hunger in part because the invasion of North America took place against a backdrop of environmental crisis around the world. From North America to Europe and beyond in the seventeenth century, the Little Ice Age brought famine, war, and violent political transformations. The Europeans who colonized North America struggled with new climates, especially the colder than usual winters of the northeast of the continent, and learned only slowly from Indigenous adaptations to severe winter conditions.[28]

Changing environments proved particularly destabilizing to colonizers' understandings of their bodies. Early modern Europeans believed that the outside world had an effect on the body through forces they rather confusingly called "non-natural": air, food, exercise, sleep, the emotions, and excretion. For colonial invaders steeped in these environmental theories of the body, colonizing the Americas presented an unnerving possibility: that in a new environment, colonists would be transformed, potentially into Indigenous peoples themselves. By the eighteenth century, these colonial fears had begun to dissipate, particularly in light of colonial epidemics and the resultant Indigenous depopulation, with colonists instead becoming convinced that *their* bodies were the most suited to flourish in North America. Nevertheless, colonists remained attentive to the ways that different foods affected them physically, and they associated different foodways with different peoples. Native peoples likewise understood the body as inextricably entwined with the outside world and feared that radical environmental change—such as dispossession—might wholly change people, physically and spiritually. In the collision of peoples, bodies, and foodways from North America, West Africa, and

Europe, early America served as a crucible for constructions of race, gender, sexuality, and Indigeneity.[29]

Putting their anxieties aside, the growing numbers of colonists brought with them insatiable appetites. They began to thrive on the corn that Native peoples had taught them, however willingly or unwillingly, to grow. The colonists learned to adapt some of their agricultural practices to new lands and climates. When they had sufficient food, New Englanders adhered to a fairly traditional English seasonal subsistence diet, based on grains, meat and fish (for those who could afford them), vegetables (primarily in warmer months), milk and cheese, with beer to drink. Although the poor fared better nutritionally in New England than across the Atlantic, many households still may have faced some form of food scarcity, or at least a lack of food choices, in late spring, after winter stores ran out and before summer crops could be harvested. In the seventeenth and eighteenth centuries, wealthier colonists would have eaten much more meat than their poorer neighbors and would have replaced the dense rye and cornmeal bread called "Rye and Injun" with refined wheat bread as their staple. In New France, colonists appropriated some Indigenous foodways to French methods and tastes. The French quickly adapted to eating squashes, Jerusalem artichokes, beans, strawberries, and maple sugar, which simultaneously fulfilled familiar niches in the French food landscape and were easy to grow or extract in the climate of New France. Nevertheless, as in France, grain remained the center of New France's political economy of food.[30]

From the end of the seventeenth century through the eighteenth century, scholars have tended to argue, colonial food supplies stabilized and colonists began to dismantle Native food sovereignty in the northeast. Evidence suggests that the Wabanaki and Haudenosaunee suffered from food scarcity at various points in the eighteenth century as a direct result of colonial disease, violence, and other disruptions. Moreover, colonists perceived Indigenous peoples as hungry, their bodies weak and starving, their foodways and land use deficient. Ideas about Indigenous poverty proved to be crucial justifications for colonization. Even scholars who have emphasized Indigenous defenses of food sovereignty point to its eventual decline by the nineteenth century, in the face of relentless colonial pressure, including the use of imperial antihunger policy to suppress Native resistance.[31] Yet in spite of these attacks on Native food sovereignty and sovereignty more broadly, Indigenous nations have endured in the northeast. Many of their early subsistence methods and hunger knowledges remain in use today, practiced throughout the generations and revitalized alongside broader cultural revitalization efforts. In the twenty-first century, Indigenous peoples continue to defend their food sovereignty.

By analyzing perceptions about both Indigenous and colonial hunger, and the ways that these perceptions created the colonial northeast in the seventeenth and eighteenth centuries, this book places scarcity at the center of the early American story. In their quest to justify settler colonialism, French and British narrators tended to describe Indigenous or colonial hunger however best suited colonial agendas. Indigenous peoples, meanwhile, understood their own bodily and cultural experiences differently than did European writers. These facts invite scholars to consider hunger critically, as a site of the contested construction of Indigenous and colonial bodies in early America. Hunger was both a bodily experience and a culturally mediated condition. Moreover, while the United States has throughout its history envisioned itself as a nation of plenty, hunger must be seen as a fundamental part of early American history and the larger American story.[32]

Hunger is an altered state. It can sharpen the senses or fracture the mind. It is clear, from social science research on hunger, that extreme hunger destroys bodies and communities. Used as a weapon, or resulting from environmental catastrophe, hunger can destroy entire populations and cultures. Under the threat of famine, people will at first become more intent on sharing or traveling far and wide to find food. As famine sets in, people withdraw to their family units, hoarding food and sharing only with their closest relations. Finally, hunger destroys all sense of social responsibility; even close family members will fight each other to the death for food as society completely collapses. The possibility of such collapse haunted Indigenous peoples and colonists throughout early North America, and it happened again and again.[33]

Archives and Methods

The field of food studies has tended to emphasize plenty rather than scarcity, but the history of hunger offers much grimmer antecedents. Throughout modern history, scientists have carried out the physiological study of hunger on marginalized populations, often under coercive or violent conditions. Over the past few decades, scholars have called for more attention to hunger in the humanities and social sciences and have theorized its lack of emphasis within the academy, declaring that "the history of hunger is for the most part unwritten. The hungry rarely write history, and historians are rarely hungry." In recent years, the field of hunger studies has focused on policy solutions to food scarcity in the present day. Historians, meanwhile, have begun to tackle hunger as a historical subject in various times and places, including early America.[34]

The nature of hunger presents an archival conundrum to historians. The very people most likely to experience hunger were the least likely to leave written sources in their own words or to have their traces preserved by archivists. Scarcity makes the archive, accompanying and exacerbating other forms of oppression that were directed, in early America as now, at the poor, women, queer people, Indigenous peoples, and people of African descent. Following scholars of archive theory in and beyond early American Studies, I have adopted a critical stance toward the archive. The disparities and miscommunications in the circulation of knowledge in this period have influenced the archive in ways that leave a variety of ethical challenges to historians. Scholars of negotiations across power differentials tend to be attentive to silences in the archive, seeking out ways to overcome these silences. But there are some situations that do not call for this approach. Non-Native historians like myself must respect the places in the archive where Indigenous peoples were protecting their traditional knowledges from colonial intrusion. In the task of sorting out these kinds of silences from the silences about marginalized peoples that are prevalent in an archive largely compiled by wealthy men of European descent, I have relied on frameworks from scholarship by Native scholars and others who study early American colonial encounters.[35]

Violent Appetites interprets a broad variety of colonial sources in order to approach hunger and peoples' experiences of it from many angles. Religious documents, including sermons, devotional texts, litanies, and prayer books, illuminate the rituals and rhetoric of food, hunger, and the body. Recipe books have much to tell historians about food and medicine and, read against the grain, can also speak to scarcity. Medical and scientific texts reveal the medicalization of eating and hunger. Captivity narratives, missionary accounts, provincial and military records, and letters and diaries provide a sense, however incomplete, of colonial policies and colonial and Indigenous experiences of hunger in the borderlands.[36]

Each of these bodies of sources presents its own range of challenges, which will be considered throughout this book. Broadly speaking, I interpret my sources through some rather old-fashioned methods within the field of American Studies. Thick description, originally borrowed from cultural anthropology, is the practice of exhaustively describing and then interpreting behavior to learn about culture. "A good interpretation of anything," wrote Clifford Geertz, who developed the concept, "takes us into the heart of that of which it is the interpretation." Rather than the heart, this book will take us into the stomach of what it interprets, through anecdotes and case studies that immerse the reader in intense bodily experiences. Mindful of the ways anthropology has furthered imperial projects, I use thick description in concert with theory from Indigenous scholars. Close reading as a method was first developed by Southern literary scholars in the mid-twentieth century with an explicitly White supremacist agenda. Recent generations of American Studies scholars have rehabilitated the methodology by placing the close analysis of texts within a variety of historical and theoretical contexts. Engaging with these histories, the literature scholar Kyla Tompkins suggests the term "promiscuous reading" to encompass interpretations that combine an emphasis on language with "literary and historical" method, as well as insights from other fields, including ethnic studies and queer studies.[37]

Theories and methods from Native American and Indigenous Studies as well as early American Studies have helped me to interpret the deliberately patchy and opaque colonial archive. Drew Lopenzina's concept of "unwitnessing" explains that "to maintain the ideological framework of the colonial endeavor the evidence of the senses had to be rhetorically undone." To address colonial silences and misrepresentations, this book whenever possible compares colonial sources against other period European sources, or contemporary botany, anthropology, and environmental studies, in order to, in the words of Joyce Chaplin, "achieve reasonable hypotheses about what occurred" and "turn down the background noise" of colonial rhetoric. Upstreaming, or the practice of reading later documents against seventeenth- and eighteenth-century sources, can illustrate the persistence of Native traditions over time. Indigenous scholars, the descendants of this book's historical subjects, have placed their peoples' histories in living cultural and linguistic contexts, notably Lopenzina, Lisa Brooks, Vera B. Palmer, Robin Kimmerer, and others cited throughout these pages.[38] I am aware that as a non-Native scholar researching Native histories, I am writing about bodies of knowledge and histories of trauma that do not belong to me. I am also writing about how colonizers oppressed Indigenous peoples and rationalized that oppression, a legacy with which I must contend as a settler scholar, living and working on stolen land. I am deeply indebted to the work of the Native scholars cited here; any errors are mine alone.

Like many works of history, *Violent Appetites* uses small pieces of evidence to make big claims. I pay close attention to individual experiences because hunger is, at its most basic, a totally intimate and personal sensation: the pangs of an empty stomach. Many of these sensations multiplied add up into culture, which is to say that the individual experiences described here can be understood as distillations of broader cultural essences.

Kirkland's individual experiences, his famished eating, his rudeness to his host, and his disregard of his hungry Seneca family were not the worst manifestations of what hunger made people do in the early northeast. Violent appetites drove colonizers to eat human flesh, steal food from children, and invade a continent. Indigenous peoples marshalled generations of foodways to resist colonization. Everyone hoped that they could avoid hunger. Everyone, one way or another, had to confront it and hope that they would survive.

CHAPTER ONE

TAKE A HITCH UP IN MY BELT

Hunger Cultures and Knowledges

Near Kanadasaga in 1765, a Seneca girl of "6 or 7 years old" became lost in the forest after wandering away from a hunting party. The child knew what the forest offered for food. As Samuel Kirkland recorded, she lived for two weeks off of "deer's legs" hunters left behind, as well as "white oak acorns" and "winter greens" she foraged. The fare was paltry—when rescuers found her, the girl was "nearly exhausted" with hunger—but the child's knowledge of wild foods saved her life.[1]

Taken captive by Native people near the Susquehanna River in late 1763, the teenaged British colonist Isaac Hollister, alongside a fellow captive, stockpiled ears of corn and cornmeal cakes and plotted an escape. The two set out in March 1764 and within a week had exhausted their stores. Lacking the Seneca girl's knowledge of how to live off the land, they starved. The situation became so desperate that Hollister's companion proposed a cannibalism pact: "He told me, that *if he died first, he would not have me afraid to eat of his flesh, for I am determined . . . to eat of yours, if you should die before me.*" Accordingly, when his companion died, Hollister sliced "5 or 6 pounds" of flesh from the corpse, but he hesitated to eat it. Soon afterward, a group of Seneca captured Hollister.[2]

Four decades earlier, ten Wabanaki guides led the Jesuit missionary Sébastien Rale on the run from English soldiers whom they feared would kidnap the French priest. They made their way through the late winter woods from their coastal fishing grounds toward the inland village of Norridgewock. When food ran short after a few days, they foraged the tender layer of new growth beneath tree bark, large white mushrooms, and a bitter lichen called rock tripe, which when boiled made "a very dark and disagreeable porridge," Rale wrote. The priest claimed that he "risked dying from hunger and misery" on this journey. But his letter is silent as to whether his Wabanaki guides, who had managed to find food all around them, had experienced hunger themselves.[3]

Hunger pushed all of these people to physical extremes, but the knowledges of the Seneca girl and the Wabanaki guides, as opposed to the ignorance of Rale and Hollister, made the difference between life and death. These experiences demonstrate that hunger in the northeastern borderlands was both a physiological drive and a signifier of rich cultural meaning. The physiological reality of hunger produced cultural coping measures, or hunger cultures—the different forms in which people experienced and conceptualized hunger. Hunger cultures varied depending upon the communities that created them. An important subcategory of hunger culture was hunger knowledges, the coping strategies that communities developed to help them survive the material reality of hunger.[4]

Colonists and Indigenous peoples brought different cultural understandings of hunger, and ways of navigating it, to their experiences of scarcity. Region, cultural background, gender, class or other social status all affected individuals' unique encounters with hunger. Indigenous peoples made knowledges rooted in the lands they came from. Nevertheless, throughout the experiences of French and English colonists, and Algonquian and Haudenosaunee peoples, hunger cultures and knowledges shared the same broad contours within cultural groups. But between cultures lay vast differences. In the northeastern borderlands, the colonial newcomers struggled to make sense of hunger as well as Indigenous approaches to it.

As the French and English invaded the northeast, they brought their own hunger cultures and knowledges into contact with Algonquian and Haudenosaunee ways of understanding and managing hunger. In their homelands, French and English people tried to solve dearth through policy and scientific innovation, struggled to understand hunger as a medicalized condition, and spun poems and tales out of scarcity. Largely spared the famine that wracked France and the rest of the continent throughout much of the early modern period, the English confronted hunger as an unfamiliar adversary in New England. Meanwhile, French colonists struggled to adapt their understandings of hunger, based largely on peasant experiences of dearth and famine, to the Indigenous communities they observed. European cultures and knowledges mostly proved a poor fit for the landscapes of northeastern North America.

In the borderlands, colonists would find themselves in close contact with sophisticated Native cultures of hunger across many nations. Unlike Europeans who struggled to fit hunger into their worldviews, Wabanaki, Haudenosaunee, and other northeastern Indigenous peoples viewed hunger as an inevitable part of a cycle of seasonal subsistence. They mobilized reciprocal relationships to acquire and share food, and they developed nimble and adaptable ways of managing scarcity. Indigenous hunger knowledges included foraging for wild foods, implementing medical and bodily practices, and using humor as a psychological coping mechanism.

Despite encounters with Indigenous hunger cultures and knowledges, colonial invaders rarely recognized the value of these traditions, even as colonists survived because of Indigenous ways of managing hunger. The larger French context of famine made French colonists interpret Indigenous hunger as mere poverty, while British colonists minimized Native hunger or failed to ascribe its absence to Indigenous knowledges. The narratives of Mary Rowlandson in King Philip's War, Sébastien Rale in the leadup to Dummer's War, and Samuel Kirkland in the aftermath of the Seven Years' War demonstrate how much colonists relied upon Native hunger knowledges and how colonial violence taxed but did not completely overwhelm the deep wellsprings of Native traditions. Again and again, colonists survived food shortage because of Native hunger knowledges. Nevertheless, because of their differing hunger cultures, colonists only rarely recognized the power of Native ways of living with scarcity.

English Hunger Cultures

Although famine reared its ugly head in England in the late sixteenth and early seventeenth centuries, and widely publicized "starving times" winnowed down the first inhabitants of Jamestown and Plymouth, the English who colonized North America did not identify theirs as a culture of hunger from the mid-seventeenth to mid-eighteenth century.[5] The dearth of dearth in this period created a uniquely English hunger culture, a hunger culture that was unfamiliar with hunger and had a paucity of hunger knowledges. These characteristics of English hunger cultures and knowledges developed at the confluence of political, economic, religious, and medical contexts in the early modern period. In the colonial invasion, English colonizers' unfamiliarity with hunger would mold their responses to scarcity and to Native hunger knowledges.

The problem of hunger had tremendous influence in English politics throughout the medieval and early modern eras. Fearful that famine would lead to food riots and other forms of rebellion, elites sought to alleviate food scarcity by prosecuting food hoarders, regulating pricing of such staples as wheat, bread, and ale, banning grain exports, and encouraging grain imports. Those in power justified such measures with a paternalistic rhetoric of protecting the common good. Such policies faced multiple challenges, including the difficulty of ensuring adequate provisioning of urban centers, inflation overwhelming regulations on bread pricing, and working-class resistance.[6]

Throughout this period, people at all levels of English society understood food supplies in terms of unequal, hierarchical dependencies. A series of patriarchal relationships structured the entirety of society, with the Christian God, kings, political elites, and male heads of household dominating and protecting those below them. Within the food system, peasants held responsibility for producing food through their agricultural labor, and elites held responsibility for ensuring that the common people had enough to eat through proper food policy. In times of famine, local elites were supposed to distribute grain stores to the peasantry on behalf of the king. But in the late Tudor period, a series of food crises in the 1590s and 1620s threatened to destabilize both the food system and the political system. As enclosure increasingly forced peasants off the land and the Little Ice Age caused a string of failed harvests, the poor found themselves without enough to eat. Within the hierarchical ordering of society, dearth, or the food scarcity experienced by the poor, signified that the political elites had failed in their duty to provide for their dependents. The peasant classes rose up to demand food.[7]

These crises helped usher in a new era of food stability in England. In response to peasant uprisings, elites revised antifamine policies to help the hungry in more direct ways than regulation of pricing or exports. Local authorities began to distribute food aid and created work programs intended to enable the poor to earn money for food. Around the same time, innovations in agricultural technology enabled a more stable food supply for the population. As a result of these two factors—more effective anti-hunger policy alongside technological innovation—England did not see widespread famine or food rioting from roughly 1650 to 1730 or 1740, the era when many colonists made the crossing to the American colonies. After 1740, market transition, population growth, and a plateau in gains from agricultural technology created a large population of urban, landless, hungry workers. In an era which has been called the " 'golden age' of food riots," British peasants again marshaled the "politics of provisions" to protest grain exports and demand access to food. Elites pursued colonization schemes in part to defuse the potentially explosive food politics at home, hoping that hungry peasants would find something to eat in North America. However, the colonists who invaded America between the mid-seventeenth and mid-eighteenth century carried with them the more placid legacy of the hundred years of relative plenty that preceded this riotous age. Where English society had long punished hoarders and gluttons, early fantasies of colonization promised abundance to all.[8]

However, the same agricultural "improvement" that had stabilized the English food supply in this period would ironically leave the English ill-prepared to feed themselves in North America. Over the course of the early modern period, the agricultural economy of England dramatically transformed away from subsistence farming. A variety of technological innovations, such as new systems of crop rotation, enabled massive increases in agricultural productivity. But political factors like enclosure also played a role, increasing yields on consolidated farms but destroying rural communities and shunting peasants to urban centers. The move toward a surplus agricultural economy and an urbanized population increased reliance on the monoculture of cereals.[9] Overall, the increased agricultural productivity of the early modern period helped to fend off mass hunger, but the focus on grain production resulted in a monotonous diet composed primarily of grains, especially for the poor. Fewer people retained the agricultural knowledge of subsistence farming or foraging from earlier times. Reliant on the cultivation of a select few crops and focused on monoculture, many English colonists would struggle to adapt to new subsistence conditions in the so-called New World.

Even with an increasingly stable food supply, many English households would have experienced some degree of seasonal scarcity in late spring, after winter stores ran out and before summer crops could be harvested. This scarcity might have taken the form of either an actual shortage or a lack of food choices. The poor would have felt seasonal shortage most acutely, but even the menus listed in recipe books aimed at wealthy households reflected seasonal variations in diet. The February and June dinner menus from Penelope Bradshaw's 1754 cookery book *The Family Jewel* showcased different foods depending upon the season, from preserved fruits in the winter to fresh strawberries in the summer. Familiar with their own seasonal rhythms of plenty and scarcity, colonists would nevertheless not necessarily understand the seasonal variations of Indigenous diets.[10]

Beyond the political, economic, and agricultural realms, English hunger culture had deep roots in religion. The Christian calendar of fasts in the spring and thanksgiving feasts in the fall likely had its origins in the realities of seasonal access to food. But religious understandings of food shortage ran much deeper. The English saw their hierarchical ordering of society and the food system as divinely ordained. So, too, did they understand hunger as a form of divine punishment and its absence as an example of divine providence. Protestants of all denominations in early modern England agreed that those who hungered had attracted God's wrath via sin. Hunger was both the problem and, in the form of religious fasting, the solution. Rituals of fasting and repentance formed a crucial individual and societal response to an angry God. Although fasting exposed even England's wealthiest to hunger, this type of hunger culture emphasized regular, predictable fasting over irregular, unpredictable scarcity.[11] Religious fasting made meaning from a specific kind of intentional hunger, but the hunger culture and knowledge of fasting did not tidily encompass other experiences of scarcity, as English colonists would come to recognize.

While the early modern English made sense of hunger in their religions and politics, they had little to say about it in their medical literature. There were several possible reasons for this absence. Medical authorities now know that starvation causes a wide spectrum of effects on the body, many of which could be mistaken for other illnesses. Moreover, medical authorities of the early modern period, writing for the amply-fed elite audiences who could afford to buy books, were more concerned with the health effects of *too much* food rather than the lack of it. In the rare event that writers acknowledged the possibility of unintentional hunger among their readers, they dismissed it as unusual and temporary. The writers of early modern English medical manuals did not consider starvation to be a medical problem.[12]

Semi-starvation and starvation cause a broad swath of physiological and psychological effects, as the body slowly consumes itself in order to stay alive. In a symptom that may have confused early modern medical authorities, semi-starving and starving people suffer from diarrhea and other gastrointestinal distress. In terminal starvation, when the digestive system ceases to function, this diarrhea becomes bloody, which is also a signature symptom of dysentery. Since "irregular and ill dyet" and the "Bloody Flux" frequently occurred together, as the German army physician Raymund Minderer noted, some starvation deaths in the early modern period may have been incorrectly recorded as dysentery. When observers did not recognize the varied symptoms of starvation or semi-starvation, hunger disappeared beneath other diagnoses.[13]

In early modern England, hunger constantly appeared in medical texts, but it was hunger leading to gluttony that largely concerned these elite, male writers. Physicians agreed that overeating was a major cause of illness. After all, gluttony was one of the seven deadly sins, and as the physician John Harris warned in *The Divine Physician*, "Diseases are the interests of Sin." The writers of medical manuals therefore advised their readers to restrain their appetites. "Meat and Drink . . . taken in too great measure . . . may be the occasion of many diseases," wrote the German physician Daniel Sennert, published in England in 1658. Gluttony posed a particular danger within the physiological understanding of the time, which revolved around the circulation of the four humors—blood, phlegm, black bile, and yellow bile—throughout the body. Attention to the "non-naturals," or external factors including food, drink, retention, and excretion, constituted an important part of what would today be called preventative medicine. Consuming more food than necessary led to blockages in the flow of humors or could cause "the imperfect Concoction of food," in Harris's words, resulting in the formation of harmful compounds called "crudities." These conditions wreaked havoc on health, which relied upon the proper balance and smooth flow of liquids in and out of the body. Physicians thus prescribed fasting, arguing, like the self-help writer Thomas Tryon, that "a little *gentle Hunger*" would clear "superfluous Matter" from the digestive system. In addition, medical practitioners recognized specific, pathological forms of overeating, such as the "Doglike appetite," which caused its sufferers to "devoure in meate without measure" before "vomiting like dogges," as described by the physician and surgeon Philip Barrough. Across these texts, gluttony troubled medical writers far more than hunger.[14]

In a world where people constantly risked lapsing into gluttony, *lack* of hunger likewise raised concern. Medical writers identified several types and causes of loss of appetite. Sennert offered many humoral reasons why a patient might lose his or her appetite: because "many crude and watery humours compress the mouth of the stomach"; "because concoction and distribution is hindred in the stomach"; or "because aliment abounds in the body" due to ineffective excretion. Like Sennert, Barrough agreed that physiological defects, humoral imbalances, or sickness could result in a loss of appetite. The physician Peter Shaw wrote that a patient might experience "anorexia," or a long-term distaste for food, "from hard drinking, great heat, a fever," or "consumptions." Medical writers agreed that lack of appetite did not spontaneously occur in a healthy person but rather could be linked to hangovers, hot weather, sickness, or physiological dysfunction. To "provoke appetite againe," Barrough prescribed a diet of "diverse" foods "after the daintiest fashion." While the physician and herbalist Nicholas Culpeper blamed "variety of meats" and "curiously and daintily dressed" foods for gluttonous excesses, Barrough harnessed the appetite-stimulating powers of tantalizing nibbles to encourage those who had lost their hunger to find it again.[15]

Although they expended many words on gluttony and lack of appetite, medical authorities only rarely acknowledged that people might be hungry simply because they lacked enough food to eat. Any lack of food was seen as an anomalous, impermanent circumstance. Soldiers, with their frequently "irregular diet," might starve one day and stuff themselves the next. In his manual on military medicine, translated into English in 1674, Minderer offered up ways to assuage hunger and thirst, while warning soldiers not to eat "unwholesome" food even if they were very hungry. For soldiers forced to "stand some hours in battail," Minderer prescribed the herbs *Carlina* and *Imperativa,* which soldiers could suck on to stave off hunger and thirst. Minderer cautioned soldiers that no matter how hungry they felt, they were not to eat tainted food likely to cause illness: "stinking Venison, rotten cheese, musty bread." For Minderer, hunger's main threat to soldiers lay in spoiled foodstuffs, not starvation. Like Minderer, medical authorities in early modern England concerned themselves far more with overeating than not eating enough or at all.[16]

English Hunger Knowledges

Early modern English hunger culture interpreted episodes of hunger as anomalous within a well-ordered hierarchical society. Outbreaks of hunger would be unusual and brief, so long as agricultural laborers produced increasing amounts of food and elites produced benevolent policy to distribute it, and so long as people fulfilled their religious obligations and did not give in to gluttony. This understanding ensured, in the seventeenth and eighteenth centuries, that the breadth of hunger knowledge remained small. One avenue of hunger knowledge took the form of the detailed regimens of religious fasting used to draw God's favor to a hungry community (see chapter 2). Otherwise, only a handful of English writers proffered ways to cope materially or psychologically with the effects of unexpected hunger. Like the rest of English society, the production and spread of hunger knowledge reflected hierarchical divisions of class and gender. Hunger knowledge generated by elite men would be of only limited use to the rest of the population. Many of the producers of English hunger knowledge were the women who grew, gathered, cooked, and compounded the foods and medicines that sustained households, but their hunger knowledges did not always enter the world of print. Popular oral and print culture, meanwhile, wrestled with the daily reality of hunger for the poor.

In the realm of material hunger knowledge, the search for edible substitute foods fascinated the scientist and inventor Hugh Platt. Writing in the famine-plagued 1590s, as elites scrambled to address widespread scarcity, Platt experimented with finding cheap, portable substitutes for staple foods. His work ostensibly targeted the poor, as well as soldiers and sailors, groups who might experience temporary hunger. The book *Sundrie New and Artificiall Remedies against Famine* considered "all manner" of possible foods "out of which [one] might by any probabilitie draw any kind of sustenance." However, Platt did not consider *all* potential famine foods to be suitable, and he confined himself to foods that were "most plentifull in their quantitie, least offensive in their nature and most familiar with our soile and bodies." In other words, Platt was most interested in foods that were abundant, not totally abhorrent, and suited to English soil and stomachs—rather an optimistic purview in times of scarcity and of limited use to English colonists in the coming decades.[17]

Because famine threatened England as a result of failed grain harvests, many of Platt's suggestions focused on bread, a staple of English diet. He offered numerous substitutes for wheat, barley, or rye. Platt advised boiling "Beanes, Pease, Beechmast, Chestnuttes, Acornes" in several changes of water to remove their "ranknesse." Dried and ground into meal, these substitutes could be made into bread when grains were scarce. Other potential bread ingredients included lentils, pumpkins, and leaves from such trees as apple, pear, oak, and beech. Platt tried making bread from wheat straw but found it too "browne" and "grettie" to eat. As this failure suggests, Platt's alternatives could not make perfect replacements for grain, and he acknowledged that substitution would not please every palate. If the "color, tast, or savor" of substitute foods "happen to offend," Platt recommended that cooks render them more palatable with herbs, spices, and other flavorings, from wine to honey, saffron to cinnamon.[18]

Platt published *Remedies against Famine* when many of the poor in England faced devastating scarcity, yet there was something more than a little utopian to his experimentation: if people were so poor they had no wheat, they probably had no saffron to improve the taste of their substitute bread. But among his famine foods, Platt also recorded (though noted he had not tried) grimmer concoctions than nuts and honey. A man could live by eating "a fresh turfe or clod of earth" once a day, or by "sucking of his owne bloud" or drinking "his owne urine," Platt's sources claimed. Unlike Platt, the desperately hungry may have resorted to these measures, and worse.[19]

While English men regarded food shortage with anxiety and offered only limited hunger knowledge to overcome it, English women had deeper wellsprings of hunger knowledge, born from lifetimes of household management. The intermixing of medicinal and culinary preparations in women's recipe books attested to the wide breadth of knowledge that many women maintained. This female knowledge, often passed through families and communities and down the generations, served as a bulwark against possible hunger and a font of popular medicine. Across social strata, women sustained their households with food and medicine. Elite women understood themselves as upholding the religious and social order through the proper distribution of food to their families, servants, and other beneficiaries. Further down the economic ladder, working-class women's critical roles in provisioning their families and protecting household assets made them key participants in the crowd actions that accompanied food shortage. Ann Carter rallied a group of female food rioters in Essex, England, in 1629 with the cry, "I will be your leader for we will not starve"; authorities would soon execute her for her role in the protests.[20]

English peasants saw more plenty than their continental counterparts, as England, somewhat uniquely within Europe, avoided famine between the mid-seventeenth and mid-eighteenth century. The result was a scarcity of hunger in English art and culture of the early modern period. It is no coincidence that English fairy tales were not nearly as bleak as French ones, which abounded with hungry wolves in grandmothers' clothing. Moreover, the English had few in the way of hunger jokes, which would have enabled them to laugh at hunger. A 1706 pamphlet entitled *The London Apprentices Complaint of Victuals: Or, A Satyr against Hunger* offered a rare example of English hunger-based humor from the period. In rhyming couplets, a speaker identified as "a Prentice that is troubled with a Stingy Mistress" bemoaned his constant hunger, describing in detail the agony of his innards, the "Griping Pains which with'reth all my Guts." The outside of his body also showed the effects of starvation, rendering him "a Skeleton of a Creature." Hunger sapped the apprentice's strength, and near the end of the poem, the speaker claimed that "my enervate Hand / So weak is grown, scarce can my Pen command." While the speaker's litany of corporeal suffering was melodramatic, he accurately described hunger's toll upon the body.[21]

Midway through the poem, the speaker identified the cause of his hunger, blaming the topsy-turvy gender relations of the household in which he apprenticed. The mistress, who was "despotick" in addition to "Old and Ugly," wore the "Breeches" in her marriage, while her "foolish" husband was "baffled by a Petticoat." The bullying wife forced her husband to be a *"Miser,"* leaving the apprentice to implore, "Heavens snatch me from this Hunger-starving Brood." In the end, the *Complaint of Victuals* satirized only the tyranny of women who browbeat their husbands and starved their apprentices. Hunger itself remained deadly serious, as well as gendered and classed. The miserly mistress of the poem embodied male fears of women's control over food resources within domestic spaces.[22]

The relative lack of hunger in England from the mid-seventeenth to mid-eighteenth centuries created a hunger culture adapted to plenty, which resulted in a paucity of useful hunger knowledge. This hunger culture and knowledge, forged in times of abundance, would face very different circumstances across the Atlantic. The Edenic rhetoric of exploration and colonization prepared colonists for plenty in the New World; the scarcity they found shocked them. In the borderlands, English colonists encountered hunger as they had not known it before. The very detail with which they described hunger suggested that they met scarcity as an unfamiliar adversary.

French Hunger Cultures

In their hunger cultures, the French shared a great deal with the English, including gluttonous elites and political questions about how to manage scarcity. Unlike England, however, France continued to face

33

famines regularly throughout the eighteenth century, as the result of specific economic, political, and technological factors. Whereas English landless workers rallied behind food politics, in France starving peasants revolted most dramatically against scarcity and inequality. Constant tension over hunger kept French elites uncomfortably aware of their hungry counterparts in the working classes, but it did not force these elites to develop rich and resilient hunger cultures. Instead, French hunger cultures and knowledges largely categorized hunger as the province of the poor. French elites, like their English counterparts, struggled to produce useful hunger knowledge, even in the face of tremendous scarcity. As a result, French colonists brought with them a conception of hunger as poverty, a restrictive lens through which they would view Native people's hunger cultures and knowledges in North America.

As in England, the French depended economically and calorically on grains, and the government regulated the pricing and production of cereals. French society hinged on the patriarchal responsibilities of the king toward his subjects, including the duty to ensure an adequate food supply. In turn, authorities hoped, the general population would yield to the hierarchy that guaranteed them subsistence. French officials recognized that they could not maintain power over the common people unless the populace had enough to eat. Rather than actively distributing food, however, these officials worked to regulate commerce, leaving direct food aid to religious and medical organizations. The majority of antihunger policies concerned Paris and other large urban centers, as their dense populations could—and did—foment uprisings much more efficiently than peasants dispersed in the countryside. Despite the monitoring of grain markets and bread pricing, however, regulation struggled to keep pace with the vagaries of climate, epidemics, demography, and inequality. In the short term, the consequence would be famine. In the longer term, it would be revolution.[23]

Where England largely escaped famine by the 1620s, hunger exacted a gruesome toll in France throughout much of the seventeenth and eighteenth centuries. A famine in 1693–94 killed one million people, or 6 percent of the country's population; another famine in 1709–10 took half a million lives. Famine hit the grain-growing regions of the country hardest, as these areas had the least varied diet and were the most dependent on grains; when harvests failed, disaster followed. Hunger also worked in deadly tandem with disease, whether by weakening the body's immune system or by forcing starving people to eat tainted food likely to cause illness. The practice of transporting grain to famine-afflicted areas could not always overcome bad weather, poor harvests, war, and an overall lack of infrastructure for the relief of the poor. An increasingly varied agricultural economy and improved distribution networks, not major changes in grain markets or policy, eventually lessened the mortality rate of famines by the second half of the eighteenth century. Nevertheless, France suffered frequent mass starvation events for a century and a half longer than did England, and inequality continued to grow.[24]

Throughout the early modern period, the prevailing religious understanding of hunger in France, as in England, saw famine as a sign of God's displeasure. An anonymous guide from 1545, entitled *Very Useful Advice against Famine*, warned its readers that "the famine imminent not only in France, but in all the neighboring countries" was "divine punishment." As in biblical times, God manifested displeasure against "arrogant, disobedient people [who] transgressed his commandments" with "famine, disease, or war." "We must humiliate ourselves, and demand pardon from God for our sins," the author exhorted readers.[25]

But by the late eighteenth century, such religious justifications could no longer prop up the hierarchical ideal of a dutiful king and an obedient populace. People at all levels of society increasingly suspected aristocrats and the government of a "famine plot" to starve the masses.[26] A combination of climate events, stagnant agricultural technology, radical shifts in economic policy, widening inequality, and a surge in poverty eventually produced the French Revolution. For the French people who colonized northeastern North America before 1763, France's long legacy of famine and inequality would cause them to understand hunger as a product of class.

Famine also left its mark on French medicine, where hunger was much more visible than in the English medical literature. Manuals such as *The Charitable Remedies of Madame Foucquet*, by a philanthropist who ran charitable hospitals in Paris in the seventeenth century, offered detailed instructions for making and distributing "soups for the poor." Hospitals and religious orders offered food aid, though care providers disagreed on how best to feed the poor and the ailing. One doctor in Nîmes complained that, far from being in danger of starving to death, the patients in his hospital were fed too much for their health. By contrast, Sidoine-Charles-François Séguier de Saint Brisson's 1764 *Philopénes, or the Regime of the Poor,* critiqued how the nuns at religious hospitals regimented the sustenance of the needy, decrying charitable "meals too light to appease hunger." The regulations of hospital charity, moreover, served other forms of oppression, as the French government leveraged the medical establishment against Roma, Protestants, and other marginalized people throughout the early modern period.[27]

In a time of epidemics and famines, the staggering mortality rates animated medical discourses around food. Medical authorities produced a flood of guides written both for elites providing care to the impoverished countryside and for the poor caring for themselves. While paternalistic in tone, these manuals acknowledged the toll of hunger upon the poor of France. And yet, as in England, these texts tended to emphasize balancing one's diet rather than addressing a shortfall in food. Among French medical writers, gluttony remained of primary concern, even for patients who were obviously starving. A royal physician warned patients to "nourish" themselves only with enough food to "maintain and repair [their] vitality," lest overeating and impaired "Concoctions" make "the Stomach, like the Intestines, fol[d] back with Crudities," causing "an infinity of Diseases." Even for patients clearly suffering from food shortage, medical authorities warned against the perils of overeating.[28]

But crucially, unlike English medical writers, French authorities specifically identified starvation or lack of food as a cause of disease. Assessing the high rates of illness among the poor, the popular physician Paul Dubé blamed "the improper practice of the things non-natural," singling out "the poor substance and quality of foods and the inequalities of their usage, which arise because [people] have them sometimes in abundance, and frequently suffer from dearth." Unpredictable food intake led to the formation of obstructions and crudities in the body, meaning that the poor "had a very high necessity for purgative remedies," which Dubé recommended. He also noted that the poor were likely to suffer from "a lack of appetite or disgust" after eating "bad foods." For Dubé, even the starving might lack appetite or need to purge obstructed humors from their bodies—ailments that similarly plagued wealthy, gluttonous patients. While Dubé warned against eating too much and then too little,

Henry IV's physician Nicolas Abraham de la Framboisière explicitly linked dire health effects to starvation alone. Of convulsions caused by "inanition," Framboisière declared, "when it is confirmed, it is incurable." Framboisière's acknowledgement of starving patients set him apart from English physicians who barely conceded the existence of hunger. The greater populations of starving peasants in France caused elites to write hunger into the medical literature, whereas it was largely absent in the equivalent English-language publications of the time.[29]

French Hunger Knowledges

The omnipresence of famine in France in the seventeenth and eighteenth centuries created distinctive hunger knowledges. As food scientists searched for alternative staple foods, poets decried hunger and peasants told tales of scarcity and plenty. French hunger knowledges arose from a society that grappled constantly with hunger, unlike England's dearth of dearth. Yet French hunger knowledges faced many of the same challenges as English ones: most of the recorded knowledge came from elite sources, and elites failed to develop realistic solutions for scarcity. As a result, French hunger knowledges, like their hunger cultures, by and large categorized hunger as a problem facing the poor, a perception that French colonists would bring with them across the Atlantic.

As in England, many French producers of hunger knowledge focused their efforts on finding substitute staples for cereals. Like Hugh Platt's research in England, these efforts revealed elites to be deeply out of touch with the realities of grain-dependent peasant life. The manual *Very Useful Advice against Famine,* whose subtitle promised a "regime of health for the poor," exhorted wealthy readers to "help the poor." But the advice the book contained would not have been particularly useful to starving readers. One chapter compared which kinds of foods, including different varietals of wine, were more nourishing than others. The author recognized that bread was the "principal and most accustomed food of the poor" but suggested meat stew as a substitute for staple grains. Of course, in the midst of catastrophic grain shortage, starving French peasants were not deciding between claret or white wine, or which meat to put in their stew. These recommendations, while well-intentioned in scolding wealthy readers "not to let the poor die of hunger by our greed," nevertheless demonstrated how elite authorities on hunger knowledge did not comprehend the actual hardships of starvation.[30]

Other reformers offered alternatives to staple grains. For example, the agronomist Antoine-Augustin Parmentier lobbied for the French to accept potatoes in place of the more traditional starches of wheat or rye. The easy-to-grow crop caught on quickly with the peasantry, but the upper classes took more convincing. In such works as his 1773 *Chemical Analysis of Potatoes*, Parmentier argued that potato starch could make "light and pleasant" bread. While his efforts led Louis XVI to wear a potato flower in his lapel at court, the French were particularly reluctant to accept potato starch in place of other grains in baking. The tubers finally became popular across classes after the Revolution, when Republicans adopted potatoes as a patriotic yet frugal food in times of famine.[31]

The political upheavals of early modern France, and the famines that resulted from them, also made their way into the cultural production of the period. A satirical poem, *The Discount on Bread in Burlesque Verse*, written in the midst of a series of civil wars between the aristocracy and the crown, described conditions in Paris, where rebels against royal authority had blockaded themselves in the spring of 1649. The speaker described Lenten meals in the besieged city, in which "one eats flesh / because bread is too expensive," as well as other siege foods, such as "dogs" "cats," "slippers," and "books." Unable to afford bread, besieged Parisians had to violate Lenten regulations against eating meat—alongside other taboos against eating pets, footwear, or reading material. With the insurrectionists and the royals having signed a peace treaty and the siege completed, the speaker imagined a "usurious" baker who "does not want to bake bread anymore / because there is less gain / and schemes against abundance / striving to restore indigence." Like the English apprentice's lament, *The Discount on Bread* satirized the grim subject of hunger, but the French poem also instructed its readers with a kind of hunger knowledge—that not just pets but shoes and leather book bindings could serve as food when there were no other options.[32]

While political upheaval forced hunger into the lives of literate Parisians like the poet of *The Discount on Bread*, the vast majority of France's hungry were poor. Many historians have concluded that European peasants in the

early modern period faced a harsh landscape of poverty, hunger, and, con-
sequentially, demographic collapse. From this hungry world grew both terrible and wonderful tales of food, a type of hunger knowledge that enabled
peasants to process the scarcity around them. French peasants told cruel
fairy tales, in which wicked stepmothers cast out children as burdensome extra mouths to feed and witches fattened up these same children for cannibalistic ends. But the peasantry also daydreamed of the Land of Cockaigne,
where the houses were built of food and friendly roasted pigs offered up
slices of themselves to hungry travelers. Fairy tales enabled peasants to grap-
ple with and imaginatively triumph over a landscape of deprivation. Poor
people used fairy tales to instruct each other about how to survive, unlike the
utterly unrealistic remedies to famine that wealthy observers proposed.
Famine and dearth accompanied political strife in France, but they were also
the day-to-day conditions of the poor. The French parallel between hunger
and poverty, like the English lack of understanding of scarcity, would follow
colonists across the Atlantic to their encounters with Indigenous hunger cultures and knowledges.[33]

Native Hunger Cultures

The agricultural revolution in England and France held out the promise
of steady, monotonous diets based on wheat, barley, and rye. Political systems in these nations depended on the elites' ability to distribute large quantities of grains, lest a hungry populace challenge their authority. Fighting
hunger, and its destabilizing effects, was largely a question of producing and
transporting ever more grain to meet the needs of a growing population.

Although Native hunger cultures likewise developed out of reciprocal relationships, reciprocity played a much broader role across Indigenous political,
economic, and environmental systems. Reciprocity—to other people and to
the rest of the nonhuman world—governed how Native peoples responded
to hunger, whether food shortage resulted from war or from normal seasonal
rhythms. While Native women farmed much of their communities' food in
the form of staples like corn, beans, and squash, Indigenous foodways as a
whole encompassed a far wider range of foods than the grain-dependent
European diet. The resultant Native hunger cultures were tremendously
nimble and resilient in times of scarcity.

Across the Native northeast, different nations experienced seasonal scarcity to different degrees based upon their geographies and subsistence patterns. Because the Wabanaki and Innu inhabited more unforgiving northern environments with shorter growing seasons, they often relied more heavily on wild foods than did their neighbors to the south and west. The Haudenosaunee and the Algonquian peoples of southern New England lived in milder climates with longer growing seasons, could farm more intensively, and faced less extreme possibilities of seasonal food shortage. While colonists often suggested that Indigenous peoples were constantly starving, the Native peoples of the northeast found plenty in landscapes that colonists would find challenging. They did so using traditions of reciprocity and deep understandings of their ancestral environments.

Like colonists, Native communities had protocols for responding to hunger. As in English and French hunger-relief policies, exchanges of food could reinforce hierarchies of dependence. But crucially, unlike colonists, the Native peoples of the northeast also had food distribution traditions that were based less upon exploiting dependence and more upon reciprocity. They often described these relations using the metaphor of "the common pot," which the Abenaki scholar Lisa Brooks has defined as "that which feeds and nourishes" relationships throughout Native spaces. The common pot was an explicitly gendered understanding of environment, labor, family, and community: "Women are the creators of these vessels; all people come from them, and with their hands and minds they transform the bodies of their animal and plant relatives into nourishment for their families." This same philosophy underpinned a political ethic. Indigenous peoples of the northeast understood that everyone in the same geography shared the same resources and would therefore suffer the same consequences of war, environmental degradation, greed, and hunger.[34]

The common pot informed responses to hunger within and across communities and nations. Communities shared food with those around them to endure both seasonal scarcity and the hunger borne of war. Wabanaki family moose-hunting bands would redistribute meat to bands that had not had successful hunts. Leaders gave away food to support their communities. This ethic of sharing food resources generated resilient ties between families, communities, and nations, bonds that leaders like the Wampanoag saunkskwa Weetamoo would draw on when making use of

Narragansett allies' food supplies during King Philip's War. The common pot included everyone, which meant that throughout the early colonial period, Indigenous peoples shared their food with colonists—both willingly and unwillingly. Burdensome mouths to feed, by turns ignorant and covetous of the landscape's bounty, Europeans took advantage of the generous, communitarian spirit of the common pot.[35]

Unlike colonists, the Native peoples of the northeast had hunger cultures that explicitly accepted some degree of hunger as a normal part of seasonal living. Before and throughout the colonial invasion, Native people reciprocally shared food resources, working to protect their communities from the destructive effects of hunger. Indigenous acceptance of hunger gave rise to a vast array of hunger knowledges, offering adaptable and resilient ways to respond to the inevitability of food shortage. These strategies for withstanding scarcity, developed in Native political and environmental worlds, would also give them huge advantages over colonial adversaries when faced with hunger.

Native Hunger Knowledges

Based upon their familiarity with some form of seasonal hunger, the Indigenous peoples of the northeast developed a broad array of measures for coping with hunger. These strategies included not just ways of acquiring and consuming food but also ways of managing hunger's effects on the body and the mind. Northeastern Indigenous peoples had superior hunger knowledges that involved a wide range of practices varying across nations and landscapes, including botanical knowledges, medical and bodily practices, and psychological practices. Native peoples foraged a variety of wild plants, gorged or tightened their belts, and made jokes about hunger as a means of staving off its terrors. Forged for coping with seasonal and situational food shortage, hunger knowledges would become essential to Native survivance once the colonial invasion began.

An important form of Native hunger knowledge was the practice of eating a wide range of wild foods. Many of these foods, like maple sugar, were staples of Indigenous diets, but Native botanists drew on a broad array of wild plants that grew even broader in times of scarcity. Tubers were an important food source: the English captive Mary Rowlandson wrote that the Wampanoag and their allies foraged "ground nuts," a staple tuber for many northeastern tribes; "artichokes," likely sunchokes; "lily roots," a relative of onions; and "ground beans," a bean-like plant with underground seeds. Other English captives reported that nuts and berries, including acorns, blueberries, huckleberries, and bilberries, accompanied greens like purslane. Captives described Indigenous peoples eating various parts of trees, including bark and "touchwood"—the rotten wood used for starting fires—"fried in bear's grease." Elizabeth Hanson, a captive of the Wabanaki in the 1720s, remarked upon eating "the Bark of some Trees" and reported that her daughter was "forced" by scarcity to eat nothing else "for a whole Week"; Stephen Williams, likewise a Wabanaki captive in 1704, also noted eating "bark of trees," and Rowlandson expressed amazement that her captors would eat "the very bark of trees." French missionaries reported the Wabanaki foraging for rock tripe, a bitter lichen, along with "the inner coat or second bark of trees" and "tree buds"; they wrote that Haudenosaunee people derisively called the Wabanaki "*Rontaks,* that is to say, *Tree Eaters.*"[36]

Colonists' lists of the many different plants that Native peoples foraged do hint that as resources dwindled, foragers' search for wild plant foods became more challenging. Plant adaptations to climate or predators meant that some foods needed extra preparation to make them edible. The fibrous textures of wood and bark meant that they had to be fried or boiled before consumption, though even with cooking, they probably remained fairly indigestible. Wild plant foods are often bitter, likewise necessitating extra culinary labor: for example, acorns contain toxic quantities of tannic acid and require thorough soaking before eating. Proper preparation could render some of these foods edible but not always pleasant to eat. And in the end, the rewards of such effort could be meager. Besides nuts, most foraged plant foods would have been relatively low in calories, making it difficult to meet the energy needs of people walking all day or carrying heavy loads, especially in cold temperatures. With each individual food contributing only scant calories or nutritional value, foragers gathered an increasingly wide variety of foods over increasingly large areas, which was a significant time investment. Nevertheless, although foraging and preparing wild plants could present a variety of challenges, botanical knowledge offered Native people a large array of foods in times of plenty and scarcity. Such a varied diet was far less vulnerable to environmental or political disturbances than the grain-based agricultural systems of England and France.[37]

Beyond ensuring resilience through eating a variety of foods, Indigenous botanists also carefully monitored and maintained wild food resources. Indigenous foragers have described an unwritten code of ethics governing the harvest of wild plants, norms that likewise reflected the reciprocal spirit of the common pot. Plants were (and still are) seen as animate members of the family of all beings, subject to the same reciprocity that bound together human relationships and deserving of respect in the processes of harvest and consumption. Foragers were supposed to ask permission of plants before harvesting, to leave behind enough of what they harvested for other human and nonhuman foragers and for the health of the plant community itself, and to offer a gift in exchange. Moreover, foraged foods, like other resources, were to be allocated in reciprocal ways among human communities. True knowledge of wild plants encompassed not just knowing the locations of wild plants or the physical tasks of picking and preparing, but also the rituals and ethics surrounding the harvest and sharing of specific plants.[38]

Indigenous women supplied much of the food in their communities, through farming and foraging; nevertheless, Indigenous botanical knowledge crossed lines of gender and age. The Mohegan missionary Samson Occom recorded herbal recipes that he had learned from a male healer for a number of ailments, including digestive complaints: a treatment for "collick" consisted of a "hand full of each" of "Elder Root & Sweet farm Root," boiled; "Indian flax R[oot]" was "good for Bloody flux" (dysentery). Young children also knew herbal lore, as in the case of the Seneca child whose hunger knowledge permitted her to survive on acorns and wild greens after becoming separated from a hunting party. Not all botanical knowledge circulated, however. Certain forms of plant knowledge were sacred or otherwise secret in nature. Passed down through families and communities, these knowledges usually remained opaque, often purposefully so, to colonial observers.[39] Ideas of reciprocity among people, and between human and other-than-human beings, informed the vast body of Native plant knowledge.

Knowing what to consume was only one part of hunger knowledge. Grappling with hunger also entailed adapting to the body's responses to want and plenty. The Wabanaki could alternate between feasting and fast-ing, in customs that Europeans routinely criticized. Some of these feasts and fasts had ceremonial purposes, but the Wabanaki also adapted their routine meals to uneven food intake. Comparing Wabanaki foodways to French ones, Rale wrote, "Their meals are not regular, as in Europe." Instead, he explained, "they live from day to day. When they have food they take advan-tage of it, without concerning themselves about whether they will have enough to live on in the following days." Hanson similarly observed of her captors, "When they have plenty, [they] spend it as freely as they can get it." Instead of parceling out their food so that it would last a long time, they ate it all at once. Hanson complained that "they live, for the most Part, either in Excess or Gluttony and Drunkenness, or under great Straits for Want of Necessaries." What Rale and Hanson saw as a lack of self-control or an inability to plan for the future was in fact cultural and metabolic adaptation to periods of scarcity. While Rale and Hanson concluded that Wabanaki people who did not eat for days must have been starving, because colonists experienced hunger under those circumstances, it is instead very possible that fasting Wabanaki people did not feel the sensations of hunger in the same ways. Wabanaki moose hunters, who boiled moose bones to render every last ounce of fat, could go long periods without meals because of the satiating qualities of their almost all-fat diet. These practices, while not legible to European observers, made the Wabanaki far more capable than colonists of withstanding periodic scarcity.[40]

Beyond feasting and fasting practices, the Wabanaki also used a specific medicinal plant to help them overcome hunger. Jesuit missionaries noted Wabanaki peoples' "devotion to tobacco." While "men, women, and girls" all smoked, it was "the hunters" who were "sadder than everyone else" if they lacked for tobacco. Hunting took place in deep winter, when other food supplies ran short, and tobacco's appetite-suppressing qualities would have been useful to the Wabanaki in that season, helping them to weather periods of scarcity between kills.[41]

Senecas, too, adapted their bodies to the rigors of food shortage. Samuel Kirkland recorded the specific bodily practices that his adoptive Seneca family used in times of hunger. The Seneca employed a series of strategies to keep the digestive system functioning smoothly when food was short and meals intermittent. In times of feast and famine,

Kirkland's brother Tekânadie explained that the Seneca drank liquid bear fat to "to open the *outer door*" and stave off constipation. Ignorant of this practice, Kirkland suffered "a severe *cholick*" until his adoptive grandmother counseled him to drink one and a half gills of bear grease, which brought him relief. In particularly lean times, when there was no choice but to wait for food that might be days away, Tekânadie advised Kirkland "to take a *hitch* up in my belt, every day or two," only to loosen it "when I came to set before a large Kettle filled with good broth." Kirkland reported that he "had found great advantage" with this practice, which allowed him to lose "a little flesh" but retain "a high state of health" despite hunger.[42]

Cultivating psychological resilience was also a key part of coping with hunger, and Native hunger knowledges encompassed psychological coping strategies alongside bodily practices. A common strategy was making jokes about hunger. The English, however, rarely laughed at these hunger jokes. Rowlandson suspected a trick when she asked one Indigenous man for news of her son, and he responded that he "did eat a piece of him, as big as his two fingers, and that he was very good meat." Though Rowlandson felt "discouragement" at the possibility of her son's cannibalistic demise, she took some solace what she called her captors' "horrible addictedness to lying." What Rowlandson saw as cruel deceit was more likely a joke at her expense. Similarly, Hanson claimed that her Wabanaki "master" threatened to cook and eat her baby, telling her that "*when it was fat enough, it should be killed, and he would eat it.*" He asked for "a Spit . . . to roast the Baby upon," then unwrapped the child and looked it over, only to decide "*it was not fat enough yet*" to eat. Hanson thought the man was only trying to "aggravate and afflict me." Like the exchange Rowlandson recounted about her son, this threatened baby-eating can be read as a joke Hanson did not understand. An emaciated Kirkland faced a gentler hunger joke from the Seneca, when young men teased him "that I was so light and spry I could run *like a deer*—and before the wind I should scarcely touch the ground." From Kirkland's contention that he remained in "good spirits," it seems that he was somewhat unique among colonists in understanding humor's ability to make hunger bearable.[43]

From eating a variety of wild plants, to drinking bear grease, to making jokes about hunger, Native hunger knowledges helped their users to weather the physical and psychological hardships of scarcity. Although these strategies were initially developed to endure periods of scarcity brought about by war, weather events, or the seasons, they would prove to be critical to Native survival during colonization, when colonial and Indigenous hunger cultures and knowledges would collide.

Negotiating Hunger Cultures and Knowledges

The colonial invasion of North America brought the distinctively English, French, and Indigenous hunger cultures and knowledges into contact with each other. As captives of Native war parties or missionaries to Native communities, English and French colonists were forced to confront the differences between their own hunger cultures and knowledges and those of Native peoples. Three colonists' narratives reveal how their authors viewed these differences: Mary Rowlandson, an English minister's wife taken captive by Wampanoag and other allied nations during King Philip's War in 1675/6; Sébastien Rale, a French Jesuit missionary to the Wabanaki village of Norridgewock in the 1720s; and Samuel Kirkland, a Presbyterian missionary to the Seneca town of Kanadasaga in the mid-1760s. All three were elites of their time—two missionaries and the wife of a minister—and their understandings of Native hunger reflected their privileged positions within colonial society.

The accounts of Rowlandson, Rale, and Kirkland all point to the ways that colonists and Native peoples negotiated hunger cultures and knowledges throughout the seventeenth and eighteenth centuries. Native approaches to hunger adapted to seasonal and climatic variation as well as to changing politics and war. The colonial invasion both revealed the resilience of Native hunger cultures and knowledges and placed new burdens on Native survival strategies as the decades passed. Colonists alternated between misunderstanding and marveling at Native approaches to hunger, sometimes rejecting and sometimes adapting to Native ways of overcoming scarcity.[44]

A party of Wampanoag, Nipmuc, and other allied Indigenous peoples took Mary Rowlandson and several of her children captive from Lancaster, Massachusetts, in February 1675/6 during King Philip's War. Rowlandson witnessed Indigenous resilience in enduring hunger as a captive of the powerful Wampanoag saunkskwa Weetamoo and her family. Rather than recognizing this resilience, however, Rowlandson interpreted it as evidence of God's wrath against colonists. As a Puritan, Rowlandson conceptualized her captivity as a spiritual trial and her own hunger as God's judgment, a forced fast. During her captivity, Rowlandson lurched from one debasement to another in her desperation to "satisfy my hunger." Rowlandson may well have exaggerated the threat of starvation to herself and her captors, for what she saw as a barren landscape actually offered something of a paradise for its original inhabitants. Weetamoo's party traveled through the Connecticut River valley, an expanse of rich alluvial land that supported Indigenous agriculture, grain storage, settlement, and trade on a vast scale. Colonists and Native peoples would fight and die over these fertile fields for generations.[45]

But instead of focusing on the evidence of flourishing Native agriculture that surrounded her, Rowlandson's account emphasized Native gathering and hunting. Near the end of her food-obsessed narrative, Rowlandson listed some of the array of foods that her captors foraged and hunted, in addition to provisions that they captured from the English. The party ate tubers, "nuts and acorns," and "several other weeds and roots, that I know not." They boiled "old bones" to release marrow, fat, and insects and drank the broth, and they hunted and consumed a broad array of animals: "horse's guts, and ears, all sorts of wild birds . . . bear, venison, beaver, tortoise, frogs, squirrels, dogs, skunks," and "rattlesnakes." This adaptability of food resources, in a winter landscape that Rowlandson mistakenly saw as barren, gave Native peoples such a tremendous advantage in war it could only be God's doing, she concluded. "I can but stand in admiration to see the wonderful power of God, in providing for such a vast number of our enemies in the wilderness, where there was nothing to be seen, but from hand to mouth," she wrote. "The Lord feeds and nourishes them up to be a scourge to the whole land." By crediting Indigenous survival wholly to divine influence, Rowlandson's account tried to render Native hunger knowledge invisible.[46]

Rowlandson claimed that she never saw Native people in danger of starvation. Despite the fertility of the river valley around them, however, the party's food supply does seem to have been under pressure. The sheer breadth of foods that they ate and the timing of their journey in late winter and early spring, a season when food supplies would have usually been tight, both suggest scarcity. Moreover, at this point in the war the English had adopted a policy of destroying Indigenous corn plantings in the hopes of starving out their enemies: "It was thought, if their corn were cut down, they would starve and die with hunger." Despite this policy, Rowlandson insisted that she "did not see (all the time I was among them) one man, woman, or child, die with hunger." But people *had* died to ensure food supplies to the alliance. A Wampanoag expedition led by the sachem Canonchet undertook a dangerous journey from the Connecticut River to Narragansett territory to retrieve corn stores for Weetamoo's group. Canonchet sacrificed himself to allow a female relative of Weetamoo's husband to escape; this woman carried twelve quarts of corn back to Weetamoo's party. Nourishing the community came with deadly costs in the midst of war but also drew on powerful Native networks of reciprocity and alliance.[47]

Rather than ascribing these extraordinary feats of survival to Native hunger knowledges—farming, hunting, foraging, and activating political alliances—Rowlandson saw it as God's will. Indigenous peoples, with their astounding ability to survive in a seemingly harsh landscape, could only be God's punishment to colonists. Rowlandson did not see Native hunger around her, only her own, and she interpreted Native strength, survival, and sacrifice as just another form of divine retribution for her fellow colonists. Yet even as Rowlandson discounted Indigenous hunger knowledges, her descriptions of Native foodways testified to their ingenuity.

Like Rowlandson, the French Jesuit missionary Sébastien Rale undertook a journey through what he saw as an unforgiving environment, led by Wabanaki guides. Rale had founded a Jesuit mission in the village of Norridgewock, in what is now Maine, in the 1690s. Throughout his career, Rale worked to strengthen ties between the Wabanaki and the French, which made him a target of English raids multiple times between 1705 and the raid that killed him in 1724. As described above, Rale and his guides fled from English soldiers before the start of Dummer's War in the early 1720s. Their journey took them through a late winter landscape in which the lakes were just starting to thaw. After exhausting the supplies they carried, they killed and butchered a dog and foraged lichen, mushrooms, and oak bark to eat on their journey. When they arrived back in Norridgewock, Rale hurried to his wigwam and ate plain dry cornmeal, "raw as it was," because he was so hungry. The people of the village, meanwhile, prepared him a hearty meal of corn porridge, bear meat, acorns, a cornmeal biscuit, and a roasted ear of corn. When he asked them why they had made him such a "fine feast," they told him, "You haven't eaten for two days, and we wish to God that we could very often regale you in this way."[48]

Like Rowlandson, Rale interpreted his experience of hunger and Wabanaki hunger through his own colonial perspective. In a letter to his brother, Rale described the journey and the meal, explicitly comparing Wabanaki understandings of the situation to his own. He called the Wabanaki who prepared his food "these poor Savages" and told his brother, "The meal that they made me, however frugal and unappetizing it may appear to you, was, in their opinion, a veritable feast." Placing Rale's experience in the context of Wabanaki hunger knowledges and cultures, however, significantly changes the meaning of both the journey and the meal. It is unclear whether Rale and his guides were truly in peril of "dying from hunger and misery" as Rale claimed. Where eating dogs would have seemed like the height of extremity for European observers, Wabanaki people kept dogs as livestock, taking advantage of their adaptability as a mobile protein source in exactly the kind of situation Rale described. Wabanaki languages included a specific word for the ability to withstand a two-day fast, suggesting that such an occurrence would not have been as much of a shock or hardship to Rale's Wabanaki guides as it was to the priest. Viewed within the context of the norms of Wabanaki subsistence, the journey of Rale and his guides becomes far less of a life-or-death affair than Rale perceived.[49]

Rale interpreted Wabanaki hunger culture and knowledges through the lens of French hunger culture. He came from a medical tradition in which, according to Paul Dubé, alternating between feast and famine wreaked havoc on one's health: Dubé wrote that the poor had a dangerous pattern of eating "sometimes in abundance" and "frequently suffer[ing] from dearth." In the fruits of the resilience and generosity of the Wabanaki guides and villagers, Rale instead saw something "poor," "savage," "frugal," and "unappetizing." Like French peasants, in Rale's view, the Wabanaki suffered under poverty, a poverty that both French and English colonists ascribed to all northeastern Indigenous peoples.

Ignoring the possibility that Native practices might be an adaptation to resource scarcity, colonists would ultimately use this "poverty" as a major justification for displacing Native peoples from their lands—and for ignoring the knowledges that led Native peoples to live in these ways in the first place. Rale's poverty-focused view of hunger obscured the ways that the Wabanaki found subsistence and even plenty in their landscape.[50]

At first glance, Samuel Kirkland's journal of his first posting in a Seneca village seems to offer a largely sympathetic view of Native hunger. His detailed descriptions of his adoptive family's hunger knowledge reveal a level of respect for Seneca traditions that is rare in many other colonial accounts. However, Kirkland's journal also demonstrates how much colonialism brought hunger to the Senecas and how even their well-established systems of hunger knowledge could not necessarily protect them from the health effects of starvation.

Kirkland arrived to Kanadasaga in February 1765, and by March the village had fallen into late-winter scarcity, exacerbated by crop failures the summer before. "Provisions are exceeding scarce," Kirkland recorded. With no seed to plant in the spring and winter game sparse, "The appearance of things at present seems to threaten a famine among the Indians the ensuing season." Kirkland tracked food scarcity in the community through hunger's toll on his own body. In March, he described himself as "emaciated" with "some loss of bodily strength."[51]

Although Kirkland was sympathetic to Seneca hunger, his journal nevertheless focused on his own physical experience, viewing his adoptive family from a distance. The food shortage eventually became so severe that in April, Kirkland, Tekânadie, and the rest of the family began to travel from fort to fort to beg for food. As an English missionary, Kirkland received extra food from British military officials he encountered on their journey, but even with aid the rest of the family continued to suffer. Kirkland's sister-in-law fell ill with a fever and cough. An Oneida woman, Sally Montour, "urged her in the most pressing manner" to stop nursing her toddler, lest she develop "consumption"; Tekânadie's wife refused to wean her child. She died a few weeks later, her illness no doubt worsened by hunger. Describing her last days, Kirkland enumerated his sister-in-law's qualities, calling her "remarkable for her patiences" in the face of starvation, travel, and illness. But he did not record her name, or comprehend her centrality within her family in a matrilineal society. Although Kirkland showed some understanding of Seneca hunger cultures and knowledges, he came from an English hunger culture that, like French hunger culture, struggled to process scarcity. This colonial gap in knowledge would have dire consequences, both for themselves and for Native people.[52]

Raised in the plenty-minded hunger culture of mid-seventeenth- to mid-eighteenth-century England, generations of English colonists and their descendants did not recognize the utility of Native approaches to hunger. Colonial hunger cultures struggled to make sense of scarcity and largely failed. Although French hunger culture struggled more consistently with scarcity in a period of relative plenty for the English, the French emerged from this struggle with only one way of conceptualizing hunger, as the burden of the poor.

As a result, colonial hunger cultures and knowledges consistently overlooked or misinterpreted Native ways of managing hunger. The invaders remained convinced that their ideas about hunger were superior. Colonists disregarded Indigenous hunger knowledges, either by minimizing Native hunger entirely or by stereotyping Native people as constantly starving. Denying Indigenous hunger knowledges was part of a larger colonial project to racialize and demonize Indigenous peoples. But in one way the colonists were correct: Native peoples *did* experience hunger differently than colonists, as a result of unique Indigenous hunger cultures and knowledges. Such hunger cultures and knowledges arose from familiarity with hunger and attempted to overcome it through such practices as foraging, belt-tightening, joking, and sharing food with others.[53]

In spite of their superior hunger knowledges, Native people still did face hunger, a hunger that arose not from laziness or poverty, but from adaptations to resource scarcity and colonial upheavals. In the face of colonial invasion, Indigenous hunger knowledges did not completely shield their practitioners from starvation or hunger-related illness. The invaders introduced new challenges for Native subsistence, rattling alliances and hierarchies; disrupting seasonal cycles; stealing or destroying food caches, agricultural fields, and hunting and fishing territories; or in other ways jeopardizing Native access to food. Nevertheless, Indigenous peoples and cultures survived scarcity where colonists could not because of the flexibility of Native hunger knowledges.

The outcome of negotiations over hunger in the northeastern borderlands elevated European colonists' understanding of hunger as anomalous over Native peoples' acceptance of hunger as routine. But what
would a borderlands hunger culture have looked like? The way Kirkland
laughed at Seneca hunger jokes indicated the possibility of a hunger culture that could bridge Native and colonial experiences of hunger. This
type of borderlands hunger culture might have arisen on an individual
level in cases like Kirkland's. Indeed, since the beginning of colonization,
certain invaders had learned how to discard their European assumptions
and embrace Indigenous ones in order to survive in a new environment.
Kirkland's ability to do so, however temporarily, enabled him to weather
a period of food scarcity among his Indigenous hosts far more gracefully
than either Rowlandson or Rale.[54]

But colonists had stark limits on their willingness to adapt to Native ways.
The violences of colonization, war, and captivity—the very circumstances
that made privileged English and French colonists encounter hunger—also
prevented them from adopting Indigenous hunger cultures and knowledges.
Instead, they rejected these ways as they rejected Indigenous ways more
broadly. As Londa Schiebinger has argued, "Ignorance is often not merely
the absence of knowledge but an outcome of cultural and political struggle."[55] The extraordinary cross-cultural circumstances of captivity, missionizing, or war rendered English and French hunger strange, temporary, and
anomalous to colonists. Native peoples, by contrast, knew how to live with
hunger.

Hunger knowledge operated in the northeastern borderlands in much
the same way as the common pot: Native people were willing to share
what they had with European colonists, but colonists had little or nothing
to offer in return. The violence of settler colonialism obscured Native
hunger knowledges as it displaced Native bodies. The colonial dismissal
of Indigenous ways of living with scarcity would cast a long shadow on
both Native peoples and colonists as they confronted a hungry world.

Surrounded by the possibility of scarcity, colonial invaders and
Indigenous peoples tried to make sense of the violence of the colonial invasion. The intentional hunger of religious fasting, and its counterpart,
ceremonial gluttony, provided a particular form of hunger knowledge that
made hunger into meaning. Across the borderlands, people offered up rit-

uals of eating or not-eating, using the power of their empty stomachs to direct divine wrath against their foes. Just as colonists disregarded the utility of Native hunger knowledges, so too did they try to dismiss the power of Indigenous religious fasts and feasts. Indigenous peoples resisted by continuing their own practices and at times adapting colonial ceremonies into their belief systems. But just as colonists found their scanty hunger knowledges inadequate to surviving in Native spaces, so too did colonial fasts and feasts fail to allay colonists' fears that their God had forsaken them in this new land. Meanwhile, Native people would keep finding ways, old and new, to endure hunger.

CHAPTER TWO

GOVERN WELL YOUR APPETITES

Fasting and Feasting

"If we *change* or renounce our religion," Onoonghwandekha warned his community, the Seneca would become "a *miserable abject people.*" He pointed to other Native nations to the east who had already taken this path. Converting to Christianity, abandoning their traditional ways, these Native peoples made brooms to sell to the colonists "to buy a loaf of Bread" or became agricultural laborers like "*mere women.*"

It was February 1765, and Onoonghwandekha, a leader of the Seneca at Kanadasaga, addressed his community in a moment of crisis. A foreign visitor had come and brought death with him. Samuel Kirkland had arrived to Kanadasaga only a few weeks earlier. He moved into the home of a chief who died mysteriously within days. Not only was the timing of the man's death suspicious, but Kirkland had examined and touched the corpse, stoking fears of witchcraft. A council convened to discuss Kirkland's fate.

In his speech, Onoonghwandekha argued that Kirkland, "the *white man* we call our Brother," brought a "dark design" to the community. Accepting the missionary and the "*white people's Book*" he offered would jeopardize everything the Seneca held dear. Onoonghwandekha reminded his listeners that the god Thaonghyawagon, "*Upholder of the Skies,*" had already given the Seneca a holy book of their own, inscribed "in our heads & in our minds." In the "*ancient customs,*" the Seneca honored Thaonghyawagon through "*religious feasts*" and offerings. These rituals arose organically out of the rest of Seneca ways: women planting and harvesting and deliberating, men hunting and fishing and making war.

Onoonghwandekha knew from the example of converted Native peoples to the east that Kirkland's mission, and the larger colonial ambitions it symbolized, threatened to change not just the "*ancient customs*" and "*religious feasts.*" He feared that Seneca ways, already battered by years of colonialism and war, could collapse. Giving up feasts for Thaonghyawagon in favor of Christianity could be the death of Seneca culture, Onoonghwandekha declared: "*All all* will be gone."[1]

Eight years earlier, on the day of the annual fast in May 1757, the Anglican minister Arthur Browne delivered a similar warning to his congregation at Queen's Chapel in Portsmouth, New Hampshire. His sermon addressed Isaiah 1:20: "*For if ye be willing and obedient, ye shall eat the good of the land; but if ye refuse and rebel, ye shall be devoured with the Sword:* for the mouth of the Lord hath spoken it."[2] Even as the congregation fasted, Browne's choice of biblical passage invoked consumption: *eating* the good of the land or facing a *devouring* sword in the words from the *mouth* of the Lord.

Browne titled his sermon *The Necessity of Reformation, in Order to Avert Impending Judgments.* It certainly seemed as though judgments were impending: Browne spoke to the congregation as the British military suffered one defeat after another in the Seven Years' War. For Browne and many of his listeners, these military disasters indicated God's displeasure with the British colonists. Unless his community stamped out their sins, Browne warned, God would defeat the British forces, and "our rights, religion and properties will be blasted and defeated." If the French won the war and spread Catholicism through the land, Browne reminded his listeners that they would face "a *famine, . . . not of bread, nor a thirst for water,* (altho' these also may befall us) *but of hearing the word of the Lord.*" British Protestants under French Catholic rule would *maybe* go hungry, but their souls would *definitely* starve.[3]

By fasting and attending worship services on this day of the annual fast, Browne's congregation made the first step toward gaining God's forgiveness and averting a terrible Catholic future for their community. But Browne demanded more of his listeners, calling for a spiritual solution in corporeal language. Believers must examine themselves for sin: "Let every one of us then descend into his own breast," Browne declared, to search for "what darling lust is nourished there." Such lust brought God's judgment down on the community and had to be destroyed. "Let us bring it instantly forth and slay it before the Lord," Browne proclaimed. Violent times called for stern measures against the weak body and sinful heart.[4]

Onoonghwandekha and Browne both saw their communities as vulnerable to being devoured by their enemies. The colonial invasion threatened the Senecas' lives, lands, and traditions. Warfare with Indigenous nations and the French threatened British colonists' bodies, souls, and colonial project. The violence sweeping through the northeastern borderlands placed everyone and everything in peril. But ritual could create certainty where uncertainty loomed. Drawing on older traditions to face new challenges, authorities like Onoonghwandekha and Browne used ceremony and rhetoric to try to keep their communities in line, in hopes that they could form a united front against their many external enemies. The "body politic" was more than a metaphor: it was a practice that disciplined individual bodies in order to make the communal body whole. In the words of the anthropologist Mary Douglas, "strong social control demands strong bodily control."[5]

There was no more effective demonstration of bodily control than rituals of feasting and fasting, an important facet of colonial and Indigenous hunger knowledges. Observers of these rituals believed that fasting in the correct ways with the correct intentions weaponized hunger to direct divine wrath against one's enemies. Such communication with the divine was key, because the conflicts of the northeastern borderlands were at least in part religious wars between British Protestants, French Catholics, and Indigenous believers, some of whom were also Christian. These were wars not just for land and power but for souls.[6]

Across colonial and Native communities, people made meaning out of hunger using rituals of fasting or feasting. The conventions of the Protestant or Catholic communal fast illuminated French and British ideas about food's role in social control and fasts as a means of directing God's wrath against one's enemies. Both Protestant and Catholic beliefs about fasting remained relatively steady over the early modern period, until the First Great Awakening began to challenge the institution of the communal fast in the colonial northeast. The Wabanaki war feast offered an alternative method of bodily mortification, carrying on traditions throughout the colonial invasion; some Wabanaki also observed Catholic fast days. Although certain missionaries recognized Wabanaki expertise at fasting, colonists did not recognize Wabanaki feasts as the product of self-control, instead arguing that these ceremonies showed Native bodies' inability to be disciplined. By contrast, French accounts of the fasting of Mohawk Catholic converts in the late seventeenth century revealed that colonists also saw Native bodies as overly amenable to mortification. The Mohawk who participated in these rituals of repentance sustained longer traditions of mourning and women's spiritual leadership in their communities. Finally, the lives of two ministers, Jonathan Edwards and Samson Occom, demonstrate how the institution of Protestant fasting evolved in the context of colonialism in the late eighteenth century. While Edwards encouraged believers to turn away from the communal fast toward an individual relationship with God, Occom and other Christian Native peoples of southern New England turned to fasts and related rituals of repentance to preserve and create communities during periods of intense colonial pressure.

Ceremonial feasting and fasting constituted particularly important kinds of hunger knowledge. In the eyes of their practitioners, these rituals could change the world. In order for these ceremonies to be effective, believers had to observe the rituals correctly and maintain faith in their ability to draw divine favor. This second task became increasingly difficult throughout the seventeenth and eighteenth centuries, an era that challenged the meanings of ritual feasting and fasting across cultures. For colonists, the colonial invasion's violence imperiled Christian ceremonies by calling their very effectiveness into question. Despite decades of adherence to rituals of bodily mortification designed to turn away godly wrath, communities still faced bloodshed throughout the period, leading even religious authorities to express frustration with the rituals' seeming lack of efficacy. While British and French leaders felt that their rituals were under attack, Native communities faced the violence of colonialism and the risk of cultural genocide. With remarkable resilience, Native people endured

decades of violence and assimilation, both by continuing traditional practices and by incorporating aspects of colonial ceremonies. In the end, the
bloodshed in the borderlands constantly tested Native and colonial communities' ways of making meaning out of bodily suffering.

Colonial Feasts and Fasts

In 1707, John Williams returned home to Deerfield, Massachusetts from
a harrowing ordeal of captivity and loss and published the best-selling account of his tribulations, *The Redeemed Captive Returning from Zion*. His narrative began with a warning: "The History I am going to Write, proves,
that Days of *Fasting* and *Prayer* without REFORMATION, will not avail, to
turn away the Anger of God from a Professing People."[7] Williams lived in
a world in which people fasted and prayed in attempts to turn God's
wrath from their communities. But Williams's own devastating experiences drew the power of these same rituals into question.

Throughout early modern Europe and the North American colonies,
many if not most Christians believed that religious fasting could change
the world. Their conviction rested upon the foundation of providentialism,
a particularly widespread belief in the seventeenth century, when ordinary
people and leaders of most denominations saw tangible evidence of God's
will all around them. In a providential world order, Christians understood
God's providence as being revealed through unexpected or confounding
occurrences. Military defeats or victories, natural disasters or good harvests, outbreaks of disease or good health, all indicated God's pleasure or
displeasure with a community or nation. So, too, could more local or domestic events, such as birth defects or a farm animal behaving strangely,
demonstrate God's attitude toward certain individuals' souls. In a world of
trials, many ordinary believers sought a sense of agency. They placed great
faith in the efficacy of religious fasting and described it in clear-cut terms.
A Massachusetts colonist named Lawrence Hammond noted in his diary
that with a drought threatening, several Boston area congregations kept a
day of fasting and prayer on May 3, 1688. At the bottom of the page,
Hammond later drew a pointing hand (a symbol called a manicule) and
wrote, "Note that ever since the fast on May 3d much raines hath season-
ably & mercyfully fallen ... praised be God." While such thinking was

common across denominations in the early seventeenth century, by the mid-seventeenth century it had begun to fall out of favor with Anglicans, who blamed Puritan providentialism for the uprisings that culminated in the English Civil War. Puritan elites, by contrast, continued to interpret the world through the lens of God's providence at least until the beginning of the eighteenth century, when they, too, began to turn toward the ostensibly more rational vision of the world promised by the Enlightenment. Nevertheless, the idea that God would signal his intentions via dramatic events would recur in the sermons of many denominations well into the eighteenth century and in the folk beliefs of everyday people far beyond that.[8]

The power of religious fasting played an important geopolitical role in the embattled northeastern borderlands, where colonialism made the extraordinary commonplace. As colonists invaded Indigenous peoples' homelands and Indigenous people resisted, the resulting waves of violence created plenty of fodder for New England's Puritan providential interpreters. Faced with such persistent evidence of God's wrath, colonists responded by declaring days of fasting and repentance. Religious authorities believed that these rituals could turn the tide of war. In the late seventeenth century, the horrific violence of King Philip's War struck Puritans as particularly potent evidence of God's rage, an embarrassment to a people who had used utopian rhetoric in their founding of a separatist religious polity. After the war, ministers would argue that English colonists were victorious in King Philip's War only because of divine intercession.[9] If days of repentance could assuage God's anger, the English believed, then fasting was a critical spiritual weapon against Indigenous and Catholic French enemies. In return for proper displays of penitence, God granted miracles. Or so fasting communities hoped.

The claims that fasting could turn away God's fury were crucial to its significance as a social and political institution. Many people who fasted and engaged in rituals of penitence, and the authors of the multitude of devotional manuals that offered instructions of how to do so, believed in the capacity of the fast to hold back the tide of God's wrath. Yet for Protestants, and especially Puritans, such claims collided with the central Puritan doctrine of predestination. According to Puritan beliefs, God had already decided on the fate of every soul. Acts of fasting and engaging in penitence, no matter how strictly they adhered to biblical regulations, could not in fact change God's mind about someone's fate. In the words of Lewis Bayly's foundational Puritan text *The Practice of Piety,* "We may escape the *Judgment of the Lord;* not for the *Merit* of our Fasting (which is none) but for the *Mercy* of God." Nevertheless, Bayly assured his readers, "No Child of God ever *conscionably* used this holy Exercise, but in the end he obtained his Request at the Hand of God." But fasting "*conscionably*" was a very difficult task. According to Puritan authorities like Bayly, only a small number of those who fasted and prayed were truly repentant, limiting fasting's efficacy. Angered by insufficient fasts, God would continue to withhold his mercy.[10]

This conundrum bedeviled religious authorities. How could ministers or priests be absolutely certain that their charges were carrying out all of the required duties of the communal fast—not just its outward signs, abstaining from food and going to worship services, but the grueling internal work of examining one's soul? Amid violence in the borderlands, like Williams's capture at the hands of French, Wabanaki, Mohawk, and Wendat raiders during the 1704 raid on Deerfield, worshippers began to wonder: Could God have forsaken them? Would fasting be enough to turn away God's wrath?

Despite such uncertainty, fasting was a crucial facet of European hunger knowledge. Proper adherence to fasting protocols, authorities argued, could make the difference between life and death for entire communities. But fasting was also a fundamental component of Christian devotion, so common in early modern Europe that it would have been a routine part of everyday life. To be Christian was to fast, on certain days, in certain ways. These practices of intentional hunger gave meaning to empty stomachs. The act of abstaining from food served as the centerpiece of a whole series of other practices and beliefs undertaken individually and communally. Throughout the Reformation era and the First Great Awakening, however, denominational divisions led to very different understandings of the components and purpose of fasting, even if these differences were in the end more rhetorical than practical.[11] For Catholics, and for many Anglicans, the communal fast was simply part of these churches' political and religious authority. Fasting took place as a communal event, centered around the Eucharist or communion. Puritans shared the communitarian vision of fasting, but they emphasized the fast's ability to control the individual body and the body politic.

Across denominations, fasting held a wealth of meanings and took a number of forms. Fasts took place at the individual, household, congregational, and national level. Religious authorities' capacious definitions of fasting suggest that the word "fast" was far more elastic in early modern Europe than in our own time, part of a larger culture of Christian asceticism. In a time when gluttony stood in for many other kinds of sin and the stomach played almost as large a role in moral life as the soul, fasting served as an important instrument of social control. Bringing communities together over and over on certain days or at certain times of the year, fasts sought to control the rhythm of the seasons. They also served as a first line of defense against threats to the community, like disease and violence. But, more important, these rituals sought to control the body and the soul, regulating not just food, but sleep, sex, and the senses. On the most intimate level, feast and fast days were supposed to dominate the soul with acts of prayer, reflection, and repentance.[12]

Fast days aligned with seasonal cycles of food scarcity, with the long Lenten fast falling in the lean days of late winter and early spring. For those routinely exposed to scarcity, fast days could help them to conserve food resources and to imbue physical suffering with religious meaning. For those who did not routinely face hunger, fasting was their only taste of it. The elite Anglican writer Robert Nelson's *Companion for the Festivals and Fasts of the Church of England* reflected that among its many purposes, fasting enabled its practitioners to "better guess at" the "Miseries" and "Inconveniences" facing those in poverty. "Charitable Relief," accompanied with "fervent Prayer," helped to make the gesture of the fast "acceptable to God," Nelson noted.[13] But the privileged readers of devotional manuals like Nelson's faced hunger only intentionally, in the form of the religious fast. The hunger knowledge of religious fasting could not encompass the messy realities of the day-to-day scarcity that poor and marginalized people faced.

Across early modern Europe and its colonies, days of feasting and fasting marked the seasons of both Protestants and Catholics. The Church of England's calendar of feast and fast days required its members to feast or fast 195 days of the year, with fast days outnumbering feasts three to one. This schedule simplified the even more complex Catholic calendar, which included dozens of feast and fast days but also many days of abstinence, which meant abstaining only from meat. Catholics and, by the late seventeenth century, Anglicans had the opportunity to take communion once a week or even more often. Accounts of Catholic saints sometimes described them miraculously surviving on a diet of the Eucharist alone.[14]

By contrast, Puritans sought to distance themselves from a calendar of such frequent observances by restricting their feasts and fasts to only a few days per year. Plymouth Colony fasted three days for every feast. In New England, fast and feast days were supposed to be declared only when necessary, but the observances became increasingly routine by the late seventeenth and early eighteenth centuries. Try as they might to avoid the Catholic and Anglican calendars, Puritans often still mirrored them, declaring fast days in the meager springtime months and days of thanksgiving after harvest in the autumn. They also declared special fast days in response to events such as droughts, epidemics, earthquakes, or attacks from Indigenous or French raiders.[15]

Like the timing of fast days, the language of proclamations of these days tended toward the formulaic in Massachusetts. Proclamations listed the visible signs of God's mercy or displeasure, set a date for a day of thanksgiving or fasting and prayer, enumerated topics for prayers, either begging God for lenience or expressing thanks, and briefly instructed ministers and individuals about their responsibilities for the day. A broadside proclaiming a fast day in May 1691 noted that the province suffered under *"many & heavy Judgments of Heaven"* because of the sinful behavior of its inhabitants, which were *"provocations"* to God. The proclamation enumerated the many *"matters that call for most Earnest SUPPLICATION unto GOD,"* particularly the ongoing King William's War with *"FRENCH and INDIAN Enemies."* Next, the proclamation instructed individuals and ministers about their tasks on the fast day: the "several Ministers and Assemblies" would enact the fast in their communities, and no one could engage in "Servile Labour" on the day of the fast. If these efforts were successful, God might see fit to *"bring us up again from the Depths of the Earth."*[16]

Despite their weighty rhetoric, the proclamations made use of the same template over and over, with official records hinting at the repetitiveness of these declarations. Resolving to declare a day of fasting in August 1701, the

Massachusetts Governor's Council noted several incidents of "awfull providence," including the deaths of the governor and lieutenant governor, and "the blasting [of] the fruits of the Earth." The resolution ended, however, with the reminder to append "such other things as the Hon[ora]ble Council shall see cause to add." Similarly, an April 1704 resolution to set days of thanksgiving noted only "various Occasions" of God's providence, "which It is left to the Hon[ora]ble Board to Enumerate."[17]

Calvinists, Anglicans, and Catholics all observed a highly codified practice of fasting at specific times of the year. Beyond their strict calendar, fast days called for a comprehensive program of physical and mental control. Although Protestants often complained about Catholic superstition and laxity, there were more similarities than differences between Protestant and Catholic fast day regulations. While various denominations of Protestants and Catholics disagreed over the exact details of these practices, the goal remained the same: bodily and spiritual submission. In the words of Nelson, public fasting was an act of "Obedience that is due to our lawful Superiors," meaning civil, religious, and divine authorities. But true obedience proved elusive. In spite of the many devotional manuals that laid out strict guidelines for fasting, the lived reality of fast days often fell short of religious authorities' expectations.[18]

It was difficult to live up to authorities' requirements, because fasting could be grueling work. Puritans and other Calvinist writers described a practice of fasting that entailed far more than simple abstention from food. The Sandemanian minister Samuel Pike's *Public Fasting* offered a comprehensive guide for individuals' responsibilities during a fast. He urged "all serious Christians" to go to public worship and prayer on fast days. While these public aspects of the fast were important, domestic tasks formed the foundation of an effective fast. Pike noted that fast participants must abstain from sin, labor and other "secular Employments," "even your *ordinary Food*," and sex. Fasting persons should instead devote their energies to such activities as "Bible study," "solemn Meditation and serious Consideration," "humble Confession and Supplication," and "Conversation with each other upon suitable Subjects."[19]

Anglican devotional manuals presented a less severe vision of fasting. It was true, wrote the Arminian Anglican bishop Simon Patrick, that "a *compleat* and *perfect* Fast consists in total abstinence from all Meat and Drink until the Evening: and then also in Eating and Drinking sparingly, and that of the meaner sort of Food." However, Nelson's *Companion for the Festivals and Fasts of the Church of England* noted that while fasting "in a strict Sense" meant "a *total Abstinence*" from food and drink, a looser definition of fasting might instead entail abstinence from "Flesh and Wine" or "deferring eating beyond the usual Hours," in a manner "that afflicts us."[20]

Catholic writers described the physical and mental work of fast days in similar terms but with key differences. Instead of the complete abstention from food that some of his Protestant counterparts urged, the English Catholic convert John Gother told his readers "To eat but one Meal a day," abstaining both from meat and "Whit-Meats." The lone meal of the day should not "provoke to Gluttony" with "choice and expensive" foods; instead, a fast day meal needed to complement the general theme of "Fasting and Mortification." The fasting person must not "gratify, when it is a time to punish" fleshly appetites. Unlike Pike's comprehensive bodily definition of fasting, Gother's focused simply on abstention from food, not from all bodily needs and pleasures.[21]

Whether they ate on fast days or not, the inner work of fast days— prayer and reflection—united Catholics and Protestants. Nevertheless, Gother's rhetoric about this inner work was gentler than that of some of his Protestant contemporaries. To Gother, the fast day demanded that the faithful "keep a more than ordinary Watch on the Soul" and focus, "as far as Circumstances will permit," on "Praying, Reading, and doing good Works." A fasting person "ought to consider himself as an Offender, who is to make Atonement for his past Sins and sue for Mercy," Gother wrote. Gother's mandates, to "consider" oneself a sinner, to devote oneself to prayer only "as far as Circumstances will permit," compared rather tepidly to Arthur Browne's call that sinners reach into their hearts and slay their desires before the eyes of God.[22]

The way that writers argued repeatedly and vehemently for the necessity of not eating on fast days suggests that it might have been, ironically, one of the most violated provisions of fasting. Religious authorities insisted that not-eating served vital spiritual purposes. A fasting person's hungry body served as a "Token of our Humiliation before GOD." "We are Sinners before the Lord exceedingly," Pike scolded readers, and the act of fasting demonstrated "that we have forfeited the very Food we eat" by repaying God's beneficence with sin. Moreover, Pike argued that those experiencing the "deep Concern and Grief" that came with acknowledging their sinful natures would lose their appetites anyway. From this lost appetite for food arose a hunger for God.[23]

Despite the emphasis on bodily mortification, however, fasting did not necessarily entail a complete abstention from food. Calvinists, Anglicans, and Catholics disagreed about what level of abstention constituted true fasting. For some, the fast day diet might have included fish, beans, vegetables and fruits, and grains, but not meat or other animal products. The French physician Nicolas Andry's 1710 *The Lenten Diet* urged its readers to eat only "lean foods," such as "grains, greens, fruit, and fish," rather than meat. As a material expression of the complexity of Catholic regulations for fasting, *The Lenten Diet* presented a whopping 564 pages of instructions for the proper observance of Lent. Calvinists, by contrast, believed in fasting more austerely, aspiring to deny themselves all food on fast days, although those incapable of going twenty-four hours without eating, such as children, pregnant or nursing people, or the ailing, were given more leeway. The Anglican Patrick made similar allowances for those of delicate constitutions; while "imperfect," wrote Patrick, a fast of "abstinence from some kind of Food, which we most love; or in feeding sparingly of any kind" could do the trick, so long as this partial abstention would "afflict" the fasting person, bodily affliction being the true goal of fasting. As a Catholic, Gother likewise allowed exceptions to fast day rules "for particular Reasons" (which he did not list), in which case certain fasting individuals might "have leave to eat Flesh at Dinner."[24]

Beyond these guidelines, however, lay a great deal of ambiguity. The pre-reform Catholic Church's dispensations for eating certain forbidden foods on fast days frustrated many, even within the church. Gother chided Catholics who ate "Fruit betwixt Dinner and Collation, as if this did no injury to the Fast." Patrick likewise decried those who canceled out their abstemious day with a "Luxurious Supper," or who on a fast day simply replaced their customary meals with "another kind of Diet." These practices, Patrick insisted, were "no more Fasting, than *change of Apparel* is going naked." The Puritan minister Nicholas Bownde similarly dismissed Catholic fasts as too lax, complaining that Catholics equated fasting with skipping the light evening meal, "so that they held it a very good fast, if a man went to bedde supperlesse upon their fasting daies." With the material boundaries between an acceptable and an insufficient fast so contested, it seemed in some ways that intention mattered more than action.[25]

As much as they warned readers not to forget the physical tasks of the fast, religious writers also inveighed against shirking the mental and spiritual work of fasting. Would-be fasters frequently fell short in their devotions: "There are certainly great Abuses in the keeping of Holy Days and Fasts, such as are very provoking to God," noted Gother. Protestant fast day sermons frequently cited Isaiah 58–59, which read in part, "Is it such a Fast that I have chosen . . . wilt thou call this a Fast, and an acceptable Day to the Lord?" This passage warned that fulfilling the physical requirements of fasting, but not making a true reformation of one's behavior, would fail to attract God's mercy. Sermons from around New England stressed the importance of the true fast. The Boston Puritan Benjamin Colman decried the "monstrous Iniquity" and "Hypocrisie" of assuming that fasting and "Shews of Devotion" alone were evidence of the people's "Righteousness." In Connecticut, another Puritan minister, Marston Cabot, preached that those who would "affect a gloominess of Countenance, Speech and Behaviour" fasted only for their own vanity and "not unto God." In Portsmouth, New Hampshire, Browne quoted from a different verse of Isaiah to underline the grave consequences of refusing to fast: "*If ye refuse and rebel, ye shall be devoured with the Sword*" of God's judgment. Yet as writers stressed the dire necessity of mental and spiritual participation in fast days, their choice of biblical language veered back toward the alimentary: those who did not apply themselves to the spiritual task at hand risked being "*devoured with the Sword.*" The body, which fasting was supposed to hold at bay, crept back into fast day rhetoric all the same.[26]

The many rules for fasting all served a common purpose, of disciplining the earthly body for the sake of the immortal soul. Ideas about bodily suffering for spiritual purposes were in flux in Reformation-era Europe. Many Catholic writers of the period saw physical suffering in the image of Christ as an important part of devotional practice, arguing that one's spiritual life was rooted primarily in the body. Protestant reformers such as John Calvin, by contrast, argued that bodily pain only offered a means of practicing the mental discipline necessary for authentic spiritual participation. This spiritual participation, in the eyes of many Protestants, entailed mental but not physical anguish. These two views coexisted uneasily in the religious landscape of early modern England, and individuals' beliefs and practices often differed substantially from the ideals laid out in treatises.[27]

In spite of evolving and divergent ideas about bodily suffering, the Protestant and Catholic writers of fast day manuals were united in insisting that the body had to be prepared for the meditative tasks of fasting and prayer. Over and over again, writers described this preparation in disciplinary terms. Devotional manuals repeatedly cited Paul in 1 Corinthians 9:27, "I keep under my body, and bring it into subjection." As Patrick wrote, "by bringing the Body into subjection, it helps *to raise* our Minds to Heavenly thoughts." Abstaining from food punished the "animal frame" until it became "subservient to the Frame of the Mind" of humiliation and repentance, in the words of Pike. It was necessary to "*subdue* our Flesh to the Spirit," said Bayly. The flesh needed to be "chastened," "afflict[ed]" and "ke[pt] under," and the "animal Appetites" forced "into Subjection," Joseph Sewall preached to the governor and other Massachusetts officials in 1740. Fasting enabled the "*Mortification* of fleshly Lusts, Appetites, and Inordinate Passions," wrote Colman, echoing Bayly's words that fasting "mortifie[d] the *Flesh*." Gother vividly described these principles for his Catholic readers in a section of his catechism entitled "Of Self-Denial." Believers must "kee[p] a strict Watch" and set "a Guard" upon themselves, in order to "brin[g] them into the Subjection to the Will of God." "All is to be kept in Government," Gother elaborated, before listing the governed parts: "the Understanding, the Will, the Memory, the Heart, the Affections, the Desires, the whole List of Passions, the Eyes, the Ears, the Tongue, the Taste, the Hands, the Feet." Believers had to monitor their entire bodies and souls against sin, just as they would be monitored by earthly and spiritual authorities. Afflicted, chastened, subdued, subjected, subservient, mortified, guarded, governed: the unruly body threatened the spirit and needed to be tamed. In a hierarchical society, the body needed to learn its place like everyone else: "Govern well your appetites," warned one Massachusetts fast day sermon in 1727.[28]

The administration of fast days mobilized the entire hierarchy of society. A king, governor, or other governing body proclaimed a fast day. Proclamations instructed religious authorities in their duty to implement

the ritual in their communities. Ministers and priests crafted special sermons or homilies. Worshippers turned out to services to hear the words
of their religious leaders and demonstrate their spiritual commitment to
their communities. They also mortified their bodies by denying them of
food, sleep, and sex. Those who participated in fast days helped to make
and reinforce social hierarchies of gender, class, and power.

Fast day sermons preached on the eve of sending English colonial soldiers off to war emphasized the proper roles and behaviors for different
groups in society. In the case of fast day sermons aimed at soldiers, ministers both instructed men of the proper performance of masculinity and
hinted at the ways that wartime could destabilize society as a whole.
Following the outbreak of Dummer's War between the Wabanaki
Confederacy and Britain in 1722, Benjamin Wadsworth led a fast day service in Boston for Massachusetts soldiers. He reminded his listeners of
Deuteronomy 23:9, "When the Host goeth forth against thine enemies,
then keep thee from every wicked thing." He exhorted both soldiers and
those who remained at home to be extra careful to avoid sin during the
heightened stakes of wartime. Wadsworth noted that war disrupted society
and brought its own "peculiar danger" of people "Indulging themselves in
vicious practices." Soldiers faced the greatest moral hazards "if we fight
against Men with our Bodies, and against GOD by our *Sins.*" Meanwhile,
those on the home front also bore spiritual responsibility for soldiers' well-
being, lest civilians "expose and hazard [soldiers'] welfare by our own wick-
edness." Finally, Wadsworth placed the eruption of war into a context of
God's continued wrath against "a *professing* but a very *degenerate* People."
The community's future, in light of its various misfortunes, remained
frighteningly uncertain: "We are lately entred into a *New War,* we know the
beginning but dont know the *end* of it." New England ministers' rhetoric
evolved alongside the changing enemies of borderlands warfare. In the seventeenth and early eighteenth century, ministers like Wadsworth stressed
the urgency of patriarchal protection of home and Protestantism from
Indigenous enemies. By the late eighteenth century, the intercolonial scope
of borderlands wars meant that ministers framed New English masculinity
in anti-French, anti-Catholic, pro-British terms. Throughout the period,
however, ministers argued for fasting as a crucial means of maintaining order as war menaced communities from within and without.[29]

Fasting brought colonial communities together to seek God's favor in wartime. Properly observed, the many facets of the fast day—the proclamations and sermons, the hunger and prayer, the rules and regulations—could produce wonders. Fasting could be a spiritual weapon in the war against supposedly godless enemies; fast days meant to vanquish evil and seek God's aid. But much to the frustration of religious authorities, fasting and prayer without true repentance could neither turn God's anger away from a community nor hold external enemies at bay. The constant violence of the colonial invasion illustrated this harsh truth over and over again.

John Williams saw firsthand how fast days lacked effectiveness in the face of a community's sins, with dire consequences. In February 1704, a French and Native raiding party attacked the English town of Deerfield, Massachusetts. Williams's wife Eunice and two of their children died in the raid or soon afterwards, and John and the five remaining children became captives. Over half of Deerfield's residents died or were captured in the raid; the captives endured a long journey north. After spending years in New France, Williams and all but one of his surviving children eventually returned from captivity. The minister came home to a shattered community. It was in this spirit that he warned his readers, in the first lines of *The Redeemed Captive:* "Days of *Fasting* and *Prayer* without REFORMATION, will not avail, to turn away the Anger of God from a Professing People."[30]

For ministers like Williams, the internal lives of their charges must have often remained frustratingly out of reach, in the divide between clergy and their flock and between communal and individual life. No matter how much people fasted and prayed, if they did not change their behavior or thoughts, they might simply be acting out piety without truly embracing it. Without reformation, Williams believed that the kind of disaster that struck Deerfield would only continue. Preoccupied with other forms of sinful behavior, Williams did not see colonialism as his community's original sin. But it was this sin that continued to bring violence to colonists and Native people again and again.[31]

In 1741, twelve years after John Williams died, and thirty-seven years after the raid that upended his life and community, his nephew Solomon Williams, also a minister, had the opportunity to preach a thanksgiving sermon at the meeting house in Mansfield, Connecticut. The town had declared the feast day in response to a miraculous occurrence, which Solomon saw as the result of sustained acts of repentance and prayer that had taken place throughout New England communities for decades. Marguerite Kanenstenhawi, formerly known as Eunice Williams, John Williams's daughter, had come to visit her English relations. Taken captive at age seven in the 1704 raid, Eunice had acculturated into the Kahnawake Mohawk community, converting to Catholicism and marrying a Mohawk man named François-Xavier Arosen. Even as she refused to do as the rest of her family and return to English colonial life, she remained, in their minds, an "unredeemed captive." But she had come all the way to Connecticut with her Mohawk kin, and the English colonists there desperately hoped she would choose to stay with them permanently. With the middle-aged Kanenstenhawi sitting in the front row, Solomon Williams reminded his listeners that as a Catholic, she remained "in the Thickness of *popish* Darkness & Superstition." Yet Williams beseeched his listeners to wonder at the power of prayer: "How long she has been the *Subject of Prayer*, what *numberless* Prayers have been put up to God for her?" The community had prayed fervently for Eunice to return to what they saw as her true home.[32]

Despite the miraculous occasion of her return to an English village, despite Solomon Williams's sermon (which Kanenstenhawi would not have understood, as she had forgotten the English language), despite the power of all the prayers that had been directed at her over the decades, Kanenstenhawi went home to Kahnawake in 1741. She returned to New England to visit her relatives twice more before she died in 1785, Mohawk and Catholic, as she had been almost all her life. Solomon Williams and other New England believers would be left to wonder whether Kanenstenhawi's refusal to return, like generations of violence, was evidence of Deerfield's spiritual unworthiness.

Christian religious authorities, like the generations of Williams ministers, argued that fasting achieved miraculous results only under very specific circumstances. A "true fast" required the complete devotion of a community's bodies, minds, and spirits. It was a task in which many colonial communities and individuals saw themselves falling short. And it was a task that many colonists could not reconcile with Native practices of self-mortification.

Wabanaki and Mohawk Feasts and Fasts

In July 1757, thirty-one Native nations massed with French forces to attack the English stronghold at Fort William Henry in one of the most famous battles of the Seven Years' War. The Jesuit missionary Pierre Roubaud, accompanying the Wabanaki he had been missionizing for a year, took part in a war feast with the Nipmuc, Maliseet, and many other Algonquian-speaking nations. Roubaud described how the attendees ornamented their bodies in full ceremonial regalia, rubbing their skin with "vermilion, white, green, yellow, and black" pigments mixed with tallow, anointing themselves with earrings and nose rings, "porcelain necklaces," and "silver bracelets." The men gathered to sit in rows around kettles of cooked meat. War captains led the assembly in song, and a speaker addressed the group with "reasons that prove the legitimacy of the war, the motives of glory and of Religion" to encourage men to join the expedition.[33]

Finally, the leader of the expedition rose to his feet. He reached into the kettles and picked up the cooked head of an animal, announcing, "*Behold the head of the enemy.*" This man walked through the rows of attendees, singing a war song, "in which he exhausts himself in bravado, in defiant insults for the enemy," and describing his own glorious deeds in battle. The speaker concluded this performance by "disdainfully throwing down the head," demonstrating, as Roubaud believed, that "meat from another species is needed to satisfy his military appetite." Other leaders would make similar performances, drawing "recruitments" to the expedition, before the group feasted together, readying themselves for the exertions of war.[34]

Like colonists, Native peoples including the Wabanaki and Mohawk disciplined their bodies using rituals of eating and not-eating. As in European ceremonies, food played an important role, but it was only part of larger systems of bodily mortification, which might encompass sexual abstinence, flagellation, or other practices. Native rituals had their own appointed times, regulations, and participants, though colonists rarely grasped these nuances. Wabanaki war feasts, which used extreme eating as a means of bodily mortification and preparation for battle, confused English and French observers, who did not recognize gorging one's self as a form of bodily control. Despite colonists' misunderstandings of and attempts to dismantle traditional Wabanaki culture, Wabanaki communities continued to enact the same ceremonies for decades. The resilience of these rituals, in a time when colonists attacked many other aspects of Wabanaki life, showed the power of Native communities to protect their traditions. French missionaries were often more eager than English observers to draw parallels between Native and colonial fasting rituals, recognizing overlaps between different systems of bodily control and lauding Wabanaki observance of Catholic fasts. Nevertheless, French observers drew the line at the fasting practices of a group of late seventeenth-century Kahnawake Mohawk women, including Kateri Tekakwitha. Missionaries decried these women's devotions as dangerous, demonic, and subversive of the Catholic rituals the priests were trying to inculcate. Read differently, however, these women's merging of Mohawk and Catholic traditions of bodily mortification demonstrated how Haudenosaunee women continued to perform spiritual leadership even as colonialism destabilized their communities.

On the eve of war, Wabanaki communities held ceremonial feasts, such as the ritual that Roubaud witnessed in 1757. Roubaud's account echoed two earlier colonial descriptions: one from the English captive John Gyles in the 1690s, and one from another Jesuit missionary, Sébastien Rale, in 1722. Gyles, taken captive by the Maliseet from Pemaquid, Maine, in 1690, wrote that when the Maliseet "determine for war or are entering upon a particular expedition," they would butcher dogs for a feast and roast one dog's head whole until "the lips have shrunk from the teeth and left them bare and grinning." The leader of the expedition mounted the head on a stick, and sang that the dog's head symbolized the head of the enemy, which he would soon carry. The group passed the dog's head from man to man to select members of the expedition. Rale likewise noted in 1722 that when news arrived to his mission in Norridgewock that war had broken out between Britain and France, the Norridgewock "kill[ed] dogs to make the war-feast, and to learn which men would engage in war."[35]

European observers did not recognize the parallels between Indigenous war preparation and English fast days on the eve of war, but there were many similarities. In both colonial and Native ceremonies, the community assembled, and male leaders instructed warriors on the necessity and spiritual responsibilities of war. In Wabanaki as in Puritan and Catholic fast days, proper spiritual preparation extended beyond controlling one's consumption of food. And like the English, the Wabanaki considered war a strictly male activity. Wabanaki ceremonies were segregated by sex, status, and age: men attended the feast, widowed and postmenopausal women and captive men were permitted to sit by the door, and married women ate in their dwellings with their children. This segregation stemmed partly from the fact that Wabanaki cultures saw female fertility, especially menstrual blood, as dangerous to male hunters and warriors. The observance of the feast affirmed each part of the community's commitment to the war effort, even as it stratified the community along lines of gender, status, and age.[36]

The Wabanaki war feast made far more tactical and nutritional sense than the fasts that Puritan congregations observed on the eve of war. Raiding parties traveled quickly over long distances with limited food supplies, and soldiers frequently faced limited or spoiled rations. Stockpiling calories before such an intense physical undertaking would have been a more practical choice than fasting. Just as Protestants and Catholics balanced feast days with fast days, Native peoples who feasted before setting out to war prepared themselves for hungry times to come. When they came home from the exertions of war, they likewise marked the occasion by feasting. Returning from a successful raid, Elizabeth Hanson's Wabanaki captors celebrated in a way that Hanson saw as analogous to English thanksgivings: the raiders were "Dancing, Firing Guns, . . . shouting, drinking, and Feasting," as "a Kind of Thanks to God put up for their safe Return and good Success."[37] Wabanaki raiders ceremonially concluded a physically demanding journey with feasts that restored spent energy to their bodies.

These feasts reflected an important component of Wabanaki eating culture, which guided both ceremonial and everyday meals. Wabanaki eating culture adapted to scarcity by forcing those at meals to finish all they had been served, "even should [they] burst." A feast attendee who had reached his limits had to find someone else to finish his portion, pleading, "my brother, take pity on me; I am dead if you don't give me life," and "eat what I have left." Translating Wabanaki phrases for a dictionary, Rale documented the varied vocabulary used during these gut-busting feasts: "I take pleasure in eating, I eat willingly"; "I give to him to eat what I have been given to eat"; and "You want to finish my food? Well, I'll give you everything!"[38]

The same code of conduct at feasts extended to mundane meals, and the English colonist Quentin Stockwell, taken from Deerfield, Massachusetts, in 1677 by the Wabanaki, faced consequences for breaking this rule. After running short of food near Lake Champlain in the winter, Stockwell's captors finally caught "a company of raccoons" and "made a feast." "The manner was that we must eat all," but Stockwell became full and wanted to save some of the meal to eat later. The man sitting next to him offered to hide a piece of meat under his coat for Stockwell, then "discovered" Stockwell's deception to the rest of the group. As punishment for neither consuming the meat nor sharing it with the group, the men forced Stockwell to keep eating, then to drink raccoon fat until he vomited. Because Stockwell had insisted that "I had enough," his captors denied him food for days, goading him that "I [still] had raccoon enough."[39]

Rale called these practices "ridiculous," and Stockwell complained that he "suffered much" after violating mealtime regulations. Hanson similarly criticized what she saw as her captors' lack of self-control around food: "When they have plenty, [they] spend it as freely as they can get it . . . . They live, for the most Part, either in Excess or Gluttony and Drunkenness, or under great Straits for Want of Necessaries." But this Wabanaki system of eating when you had food, and hungering when you had none, presented a rational adaptation to extremes of scarcity and plenty. These extremes arose from normal seasonal variation but also from war, when enemies destroyed farms and food stores and cut off access to hunting and fishing territories. Like the feasts that began and ended a raid, Wabanaki feasting and fasting—whether for ritual occasions or everyday meals—were adaptations to a world of uneven access to food. As colonialism, disease, and war buffeted Wabanaki communities, food shortage became more common, and these kinds of ceremonial responses to scarcity became particularly necessary.[40]

But because Wabanaki bodily mortification took the form of ceremonial gorging, fasting-oriented European observers did not recognize feasts as a kind of bodily control—or Native bodies as disciplinable at all. Although English and French colonists did not understand it as such, the requirement "that we must eat all" represented a kind of ritualistic bodily mortification not unlike fasting, testing the limits of the body's powers to consume instead of abstain. For colonists eager to accuse Indigenous peoples of gluttony, however, Indigenous bodies were incapable of discipline, unable to endure the sacrifices that might draw God's favor to a community.

Some French commentators had a more nuanced understanding of Wabanaki feasts and fasts, such as the Jesuit missionaries who described how Wabanaki converts to Catholicism undertook feast and fast days. In the early 1640s, Barthelemy Vimont wrote that the Wabanaki he mission-ized in Sillery (present-day Quebec City) "observe Sundays and Festival days, abstain from hunting, and make longer prayers." Like many Catholics, the Wabanaki only participated in fasts when they could, and Vimont seemed impressed that "there are some, amid the great labors and fatigues of their hunt, who observe the required fasts." Of course, aside from Catholic dates for fasting, many would have been accustomed to fast-ing "amid . . . great labors and fatigues" during hunts and wartime. In 1647, the missionary Jacques Buteux similarly related that the community in Sillery observed fast days by "abstain[ing] from work, except in case of necessity, and spend[ing] more time in prayer" than on a non-sacred day. During feast and fast days at another Jesuit mission at Norridgewock, a Wabanaki elder declared to the community that a particular day was "numbered among those that we honor." Banned from work, and in-structed not to eat or drink until worship had concluded, the community gathered in their finest clothing at a dwelling carpeted with spruce boughs. After prayer, the elder warned the community to be "very careful . . . to do no evil action, or any servile work" throughout the rest of the day. In the Jesuits' telling, these Wabanaki converts expressed their belief in the effi-cacy of prayer and fasting to bring God's favor. Charles Meiaskewat, a Wabanaki convert in Sillery, explicitly linked God's grace to sustenance in his preaching: "He takes care of us in the woods; he gives us moose; . . . he nourishes us." Meiaskewat called on his community to continue to observe feast and fast days in order to have successful hunts.[41]

Native peoples involved in Jesuit missions diligently observed Catholic feasts and fasts, although, like colonists, their inner commitment to the spiritual aspects of the fast is more difficult to ascertain. Whereas English colonists could not see Wabanaki bodies as disciplinable at all, Buteux and Vimont believed that the Wabanaki adapted to the corporeal and spiritual ritual of the Catholic fast. Jesuits also expressed astonishment at the asceti-cism of other Indigenous nations, as when François de Crépieul compared the Innu he missionized to Christian pilgrims who led a "wandering, penitent, and Humiliating . . . life in the woods." Moreover, he noted, the Innu could "endure Hunger, thirst, cold, and Fatigue more bravely than us."[42] While the Jesuits wrote approvingly of some forms of Indigenous bodily devotion, they were not always comfortable with other rituals of bodily mortification that bridged Native and Catholic practices. If Native bodies could be disciplined through fasting, Mohawk people in the latter decades of the seventeenth century performed this discipline in ways that colonizers found disturbing, dangerous, and even demonic.

The Jesuit missionary Claude Chauchetière, who served as missionary to the Kahnawake Mohawk from the 1670s to 1690s, described outbreaks of religious enthusiasm at the mission. One of the mission's inhabitants would become a famous Native convert. Kateri Tekakwitha was born around 1656 to a Mohawk father and a Christian Algonquian mother in Ossenon, a Mohawk village. When Tekakwitha was a small child, her entire family died of smallpox, but she survived, pockmarked and partially blind. She moved north to Kahnawake, a Jesuit mission on the banks of the St. Lawrence River. Refusing to marry, converting to Catholicism, and taking the French name Catherine, Tekakwitha began a regime of bodily mortification that would inspire those around her to new heights of asceticism. In one practice of penance, Tekakwitha and another Mohawk woman vowed to "make each other suffer" by secretly beating each other with a whip. After impressing Jesuit missionaries with the intensity of her faith and the extremes to which she would push her body, Tekakwitha died in 1680 at age twenty-four. Centuries later she became the first Native saint, canonized in 2012.[43]

But Tekakwitha was not the only Mohawk woman to fast and take part in bodily mortification. Chauchetière felt both inspired and concerned by the religious fervor of some of the Kahnawake converts, especially women, who fasted as part of a larger program of disciplining their bodies. Men and women "covered themselves with blood by disciplining themselves with blows from iron rods, thorns, and nettles," burned themselves with hot coals, and walked "bare-legged" in the snow. Pious women "fasted rigorously," on top of a diet that the priest deemed "not sufficient to keep a man alive." Despite their reduced intake of food, the women continued their labors of farming and chopping firewood. When these women did eat, they mixed ashes into their food as a further penance. Echoing the rhetoric of English and French texts about Christian fasting, the enthusiastic converts of Kahnawake proclaimed their bodies "their greatest enemy."[44]

Chauchetière himself had introduced whips, hair shirts, and iron girdles to the Kahnawake community, seeking to replace thorns, willow branches, and other traditional Mohawk instruments of bodily mortification. But instead of interpreting the Mohawk women's asceticism as an extension of Catholic ideals, Chauchetière found it disturbing and worried that Satan inspired their zeal. Chauchetière wrote that "the demon . . . urged on the devotion of some persons who wished to imitate Catherine." The priest saw these devotions as "excess" and worried that girls and women were particularly vulnerable to dangerous acts of bodily mortification because their "prudence has never equaled that of Catherine, whom they wanted to imitate." Chauchetière concluded his narrative of these practices by noting that the Holy Ghost "regulated" the behavior of the converts "without diminishing their fervor."[45]

With this account, Chauchetière failed to recognize the ways Mohawk converts understood Christian asceticism within their own traditions of mourning and mortification. By harming their bodies, Kahnawake's women sought stability in a world colonialism had destabilized. Although it was a Christian mission, Kahnawake was populated by Mohawk people who lived within Haudenosaunee traditions. Torn away from her family and home, Tekakwitha had suffered terrible trauma and loss, and she would not have been alone in bearing these kinds of burdens as a Haudenosaunee woman in the 1680s. But Tekakwitha transformed her grief into spiritual leadership in her new community. She inhabited a role that Haudenosaunee women had played for generations in their matrilineal society, helping their communities endure suffering and using mourning to process grief into an affirmation of relationships. Haudenosaunee mourners turned to a ritual, interpreted in English as Condolence but in Mohawk meaning both "sharing" and "nourishing." Tekakwitha and her followers would have understood their fasting as a meal that sustained the community rather than the body. Chauchetière and generations of Catholics after him would instead interpret Tekakwitha's life and work as evidence of her sainthood.[46]

Native practices of bodily discipline survived the forces of colonial violence and assimilation that attempted to dismantle traditional rituals. The
Wabanaki war feast endured throughout decades of colonial invasion
even as colonists brought with them dispossession, war, disease, and famine. Mohawk rituals of fasting, self-mortification, and grief withstood the
same destabilizing forces. Both the Mohawk and the Wabanaki adapted
Catholic rituals to their own beliefs and practices, in ways that missionaries did not necessarily comprehend. Colonists' misapprehension of
Native bodily discipline reflected both the larger desire to subjugate
Indigenous peoples and a more specific fear: that Native peoples were
physically and spiritually stronger, more able to withstand fasting and
God's other holy tasks, than those who invaded Native lands. The invaders wondered: if fasting was one of the fundamental expressions of colonial religious authority, why were Native people so much better at it?

The Changing Christian Fast

Colonists and Native peoples brought different ideas about fasting and
self-mortification to their interactions with each other. Some Indigenous
people, like Tekakwitha and others at Kahnawake in the late seventeenth
century, continued traditional rituals of self-mortification that missionaries interpreted within their own Christian frameworks. The Wabanaki
carried on their rites of self-mortification largely unchanged through
years of colonial invasion while also adapting to Catholic fast days. As colonial missionaries tried to dismantle many aspects of Native culture, colonists had complex reactions to Native traditions of self-denial, in ways
that caused them to question their own understandings of fasting as a
means for enacting change in the world.

The ideas of two Great Awakening ministers about fasting and community reveal how the colonial institution of the communal fast began to
evolve by the second half of the eighteenth century. Both ministers
served as missionaries to Native peoples, but they experienced Indigenous
fasting and repentance in dramatically different ways. Jonathan Edwards,
an English minister, championed a turn away from communal fast days
to private fasting and prayer, and he interpreted his missionary posting
and the lives of Mohican and Mohawk people as opportunities for asceti-

cism. Samson Occom, a Mohegan minister, also participated in fast days and other rituals of repentance among Native Christians. But unlike Edwards, Occom used these rituals to maintain fulfilling community bonds and abundant lifeways for Indigenous peoples.

Born in 1703, Jonathan Edwards studied at Yale and was ordained as a minister in Northampton, Massachusetts, in 1727. Active in the religious revivals of the Great Awakening in the following decades, he found himself increasingly at odds with his congregation, who eventually banished him in 1751. Edwards faced banishment partly because he refused to accept the Halfway Covenant, the generations-long compromise that had allowed people to become partial members of their congregations without a public statement of conversion. The Halfway Covenant had stressed the importance of community belonging over the individual conversion experience. With the Great Awakening, Edwards and others attacked this compromise because they wanted to elevate an individual experience of God, in contrast to the communitarian world of faith that had characterized the Puritan colonies for the past century. In his own life and in his writings, Edwards's commitment to a personal experience of God often took the form of individual, as opposed to communal, prayer and fasting.[47]

Like other colonial ministers who preached to New England congregations during the many conflicts of the eighteenth century, Edwards fretted about the efficacy of the communal fast. He worried that people might keep up the appearances of "external religion" even as they engaged in "great degeneracy." In a 1734 sermon entitled *Fast Days in Dead Times*, he told his Northampton congregation that "a person may be a zealous Papist or a zealous heathen and yet be a very wicked man." Like their Catholic and Indigenous enemies, Protestants could exhibit such hypocrisy in their public religious behavior, Edwards warned. He asked, "Are we zealous of fasts and thanksgivings any otherwise than the Papists are zealous of their saints days?" Worst of all, people who engaged in public fasts by appearance alone did not shoulder their burden of the prayer and reformation that a true fast required: "They have no sort of sense of their having contributed to the guilt of the land," and as such "they have so little sense of guilt that they don't think it worth their while . . . to pray in secret." Despite Edwards's reservations, his congregations observed the same days of fasting and thanksgiving as others across New England.[48]

Still, Edwards placed much more faith in what he called "secret fasting and prayer." In Edwards's view, secret, or wholly private, observances did not present the same opportunities for insincerity as public fasting. Where people could hide their hypocrisy from their neighbors, they could not hide it from God in their private communications. Secret fasts, in Edwards's view, could thus be much more effective for spiritual transformation. Edwards did not invent the private fast, which had a longer history in reform Christianity. Lewis Bayly's Puritan text *The Practice of Piety*, initially published in the early seventeenth century and reprinted for generations, contained an extremely comprehensive definition of private fasting. Drawing on Leviticus 23:28, Bayly first declared that fasters must not work or engage in "worldly Business." Second, fasting required complete abstention from food, or at least "so far as health will permit." Fasters had to deprive themselves of *"good* and *costly Apparel"* as well as adequate sleep. In addition to these restrictions, Bayly proposed a more wide-ranging series of bodily mortifications, arguing that a true fast encompassed all the senses and the whole body. Bayly urged fasting people to keep "our eyes . . . from *beholding vanities,"* *"our Ears* from hearing *Mirth* or *Musick,"* "our *Nostrils* from pleasant *Smells,"* and "our *Tongues* from *Lying, Disembling,* and *Slandering"* (or, of course, tasting). Moreover, "the *use* of the *Marriage-bed"* was forbidden. With work, food, sleep, sex, and any sensual pleasure prohibited, the hungry, uncomfortable, tired, perhaps sexually frustrated fasting person was primed to engage in the "inward" work of the day: first *"Repentance,"* then *"Prayer."*[49]

Although penned over a century later, Edwards's procedure for private fasting and prayer much resembled Bayly's. "Set apart a day of fasting and prayer alone," Edwards instructed. He did not elaborate on what "fasting" entailed—it likely resembled the Puritan fasts in idealizing total abstention from food—but he had much to say about the contents of the prayer, which was different than "as is wont to be done in public prayer." Secret prayer demanded something far more difficult and personal: "a very particular rehearsal before God, of the sins of your past life," as well as "spreading all the abominations of your heart before him." While ministers encouraged secret prayer, Edwards lamented that they did not instruct their communities frequently enough about the importance of secret fasting.[50]

Like the Mohawk women in Kahnawake in the late seventeenth century, Edwards felt a strong pull toward asceticism, routinely depriving himself of food and sleep, in the midst of a regime of other devotional behaviors. In a diary he kept as a young man, Edwards wrote frequently of his resolve "to maintain the strictest temperance in eating and drinking" and "to inquire every night, before I go to bed, whether I have acted in the best way I possibly could, with respect to eating and drinking." Often he did not meet his own expectations, leading him to lament, "I do not seem so greatly and constantly to mortify and deny myself." Samuel Hopkins's biography of Edwards, published soon after his death, emphasized both Edwards's commitment to self-mortification and his "tender and delicate Constitution." Hopkins related that Edwards "often kept Days of Fasting and Prayer in secret." Despite his "comparative small Stock of animal Life," Edwards practiced "great Self-denial," Hopkins wrote.[51]

After his banishment from Northampton, Edwards traveled west to Stockbridge to missionize the Mohican and Mohawk communities there. Edwards came to Stockbridge in 1751 already inspired by the missionary career of David Brainerd, who had been engaged to Edwards's daughter and of whom Edwards wrote a biography. Brainerd's missionary travels through Indigenous communities in southern New England and New Jersey ended with his death from tuberculosis, at age thirty-one, in Edwards's Northampton home in 1747. Brainerd's spiritual journey resembled Edwards's in many ways, punctuated by frequent days of "secret fasting and prayer." In Edwards's biography of him, Brainerd reflected after a day of fasting, "Oh how much better is this, than one's *necessary Food!* I had at this Time no Disposition to eat . . . for earthly Food appear'd wholly Tastless." But Brainerd found his primary spiritual challenge in missionary work, as he attempted to convert Indigenous peoples over years of grueling travel throughout the northeast. In Edwards's words, Brainerd "forsook the world, with its possessions, delights, and common comforts, to dwell . . . with wild beasts in a howling wilderness." Brainerd's endless individual fasting stood in marked contrast to the "idolatrous Feast[ing] and Devil-Worship" Edwards decried among the Indigenous peoples Brainerd missionized. Much like the seventeenth-century Jesuits, Edwards and Brainerd saw Indigenous peoples' lives as "wandering, penitent, and humiliating." In this colonial interpretation, Brainerd's travel and fasting became what one scholar has termed "wilderness penitentialism," an asceticism that Brainerd and Edwards also saw as "inherently" part of Native peoples' existence.[52]

Seeing Indigenous life as fundamentally punishing and impoverished ignored the fact that Indigenous ways were sufficient, that Native peoples experienced plenty where colonists saw scarcity, and that colonization, not any innate inadequacy of Native foodways, was most likely to lead to Native hunger. When he arrived to missionize the Mohican and Mohawk in Stockbridge, Edwards was horrified by what he perceived as their material and spiritual poverty. He saw some of the problems as the result of years of war, land theft, and general colonial mistreatment at the mission. "You are kept a poor, miserable people," Edwards told the Mohican and Mohawk audiences of his sermons, the verb "kept" implying that colonial malfeasance was to blame. But he also blamed the Mohican and Mohawk for their own plight. Edwards went on to excoriate his listeners, repeating typical colonial complaints that alcohol, idleness, "want of prayer," and "wandering so much about" were at fault for their misery.[53]

While he advocated to the Massachusetts government on behalf of the Stockbridge Mohican and Mohawk, Edwards remained at a remove from the people whose lives he sought to change, refusing even to learn their languages. As a colonial project, the Stockbridge mission would continue to be a place of conflict between colonizers and Indigenous peoples, conflict that would erupt into the Seven Years' War by 1756. Edwards wrote some of his most famous prose in a palisaded house quartered with soldiers, his apocalyptic tone matching his violent colonial context. This world of colonialism and war dramatically tested fasting's efficacy, again and again. As much as Edwards's theology challenged Puritan orthodoxy, he maintained the providentialism of his ancestors. "[God] orders all the affairs of all mankind, [and determines] how they shall live. [He] gives 'em meat and drink, [but he also dispenses] all their trouble and afflictions, [and determines] when they shall die," he stated in a 1753 sermon to his Mohawk and Mohican congregation. Like the Puritans before him, Edwards perceived the successes and failures of the mission and the Seven Years' War as God's referendum upon New England.[54]

Nevertheless, Edwards's devotion to the private fast challenged one of the central tools of Protestant providentialism. Where compromises such as the Halfway Covenant had shored up communities of faith, the Great Awakening's emphasis on personal spiritual engagement threw such communal compromises into jeopardy. So, too, did Edwards's deep commitment to private fasting test the power of the communal fast, and his own health. Edwards left Stockbridge to become the president of Princeton in 1758. His constant fasting and sleep deprivation had weakened him, probably contributing to his death during the smallpox inoculation process that same year.[55]

A generation later, Samson Occom was, like Edwards, a Great Awakening minister who participated in fasting rituals. But Occom's uses of fasting would hold completely different meanings for Native communities. Occom was the most famous Native missionary of the eighteenth-century northeast. Born into a Mohegan family in 1723, he experienced a Christian religious awakening in his early twenties and was ordained as a minister in 1759. As a young man he entered the tutelage of Eleazar Wheelock, whose Moor's Indian Charity School trained many Indigenous missionaries as well as Samuel Kirkland. Like most Wheelock protégées, Occom would eventually break with his mentor in the 1760s, when Wheelock abandoned the effort to train Native missionaries and denigrated those he had already trained. While Occom's ties to the White Protestant establishment waxed and waned, his commitment to his people did not. Throughout his adult life, Occom preached and maintained ties across the Native northeast.[56]

Occom's Mohegan identity would lead him to chart a very different course than Edwards. But the men's fates intertwined in bringing Christianity to the Native communities of southern New England, as both of them became involved with the Stockbridge mission, about thirty years apart. Like Edwards, Occom was a New Light minister who moved in Christian and Native worlds. And like Edwards and many other Protestant authorities of the time, Occom worried that external signs of religion could hide a lack of true piety. In his introduction to a collection of hymns, he warned his readers "not to be contented with the outward Form of Singing," instead exhorting them to "seek after the *inward* part." Like Edwards, Occom called out the prevalence of poverty among Indigenous peoples. In 1783, he wrote, "Indians, . . . are Universally Poor, they have no Notion of Laying up much for the Future, they all live from Hand to Mouth, . . . Chiefly by Hunting Fishing and Fowling; the Women Raise little Corn, Beans, and Pompkins, and pick Wild Fruts, and do other Drudgery." Even following colonial ways did not relieve Native suffering: "those that live among or near the White People, have Learnt, Some of them, to live a little in immitation of them, but very poor Still." His critiques of Native subsistence sounded much like those of colonial observers, blaming Native peoples' improvidence rather than colonization for their struggles. Like other missionaries, Occom saw embracing Christianity, as well as colonial agriculture and gender roles, as essential to improving the lives of Native people.[57]

But Occom's use of colonial rhetoric intertwined with radical reimaginings of Native sovereignty, in which he was a key participant. Indigenous peoples across the northeast maintained intertribal connections in the face of colonial disease and land theft. Reformed Protestantism became another means of uniting members of different nations, culminating in the drive for a Christian Indigenous separatist community. By the 1780s, the Christian Mohican and Mohawk inhabitants of Stockbridge, as well as Farmington, Mohegan, Niantic, Mashantucket Pequot, Eastern Pequot, Narragansett, and Montaukket Indigenous Christians, decided to found a new community, Brothertown, on land the Oneida nation granted them in what is now New York.[58]

Native Christian communities had grown through distinctive rituals of communal confession, mourning, and reconciliation that drew on both Native and Christian traditions. Beginning among Narragansett Christians, prayer meetings small enough to be held in someone's home had spread throughout the Native Christian communities of southern New England. These gatherings encompassed spiritual work of a kind similar to that of English Protestant fast days of prayer and repentance. But there were key differences: these observances did not explicitly entail abstention from food, and they had strong ties to older Indigenous traditions. As Native Christians collectively suffered hunger, poverty, disease, loss of land, and the innumerable indignities of colonial injustice, they also recognized that many people would go through cycles of sin and redemption. Even Occom had had an embarrassing episode of public drunkenness in 1769, in the midst of a winter of poverty, hunger, and uncertainty for his family. Native Christian rituals offered healing of such wounds. Meeting to pray, grieve, and renew communal bonds welcomed wayward individuals back into embattled communities who needed them. Constantly reaffirming their ties to each other, Native Christians made their own Christian Indigenous rituals to help them withstand colonization.[59]

These same communities formally organized the Brothertown settlement on November 7, 1785, with the backing of the charismatic and powerful minister Samson Occom. Having used ceremonies of repentance to maintain their relationships for decades, the inhabitants of the new Christian settlement needed a rite of fasting and confession to bind themselves together once more. On November 8, Occom led the community in a fast day devoted to prayer "to Confess their Sins before god, . . . and to Prosper them in their New Settlement." In the morning Occom preached from Jonah 3:8, a familiar fast day message of self-mortification and lamentation before committing to life without sin: "But let man . . . be covered with sackcloth, and cry mightily unto God: yea, let them turn every one from his evil way, and from the violence that is in their hands." The afternoon's text, however, was more joyful and invoked the bonds of familial and intertribal ties in the new community: "Thy father and thy mother shall be glad, and she that bare thee shall rejoice." The community had exposed and mourned its many wounds and looked optimistically to a new beginning together. After the day of fasting, Occom spent the next few days exploring the settlement, which he called "the best land I ever did see in all my Travils." The Brothertown community grew out of the strength of intertribal bonds cemented in part by the rituals of Native Christianity, and it did so in a fertile landscape.[60]

The stories of Edwards and Occom offered two different paths for the evolution of Protestant fasting in the eighteenth century. Edwards moved away from communal fasting toward an individualized experience of mortification and prayer intertwined with his sense of his missionary journey as a penitent travail through the wilderness. Edwards both defied the communal role that fasting had played in Protestant communities and denigrated Native ways as indigent and sinful. For Occom, by contrast, days of fasting and repentance were a tool of Indigenous self-determination, as the Brothertown community used Christianity to strengthen a pan-tribal movement for sovereignty. Occom and the Brothertown inhabitants' rituals had ties to other Indigenous practices of self-mortification in the seventeenth and eighteenth centuries, even if the particulars of these different rituals were specific to their nations, places, and times. Like the Wabanaki who incorporated the Catholic calendar of fasting and feasting into their own practices, the Brothertown community used rituals of mortification to preserve their cultures across the years. In their purpose and effect, the rites of Occom and his Brothertown relations also resembled the Mohawk practices of collective mourning that Catholic converts like Kateri Tekakwitha carried on in the late seventeenth century. Across Native space, Indigenous communities appropriated Christian traditions of repentance even as they carried on those of their own, to help them maintain their communities and endure the sufferings that the invading colonists inflicted on Native people.

In the northeastern borderlands, English, French, and Native communities carried out rituals of bodily mortification through food. Across cultures, such ceremonies were a form of hunger knowledge, carefully codified practices that made meaning from food's abundance or absence. Colonial observers continually misapprehended Native ritual practices. While colonists had much to say about the Wabanaki feasts, English and French writers did not recognize these trials of eating as acts of mortification, as another way of disciplining the body. When the Kahnawake Mohawk punished their bodies through hunger, Jesuit missionaries were horrified at the lengths to which they were willing to go. In European eyes, Native bodies were simultaneously undisciplinably gluttonous and frighteningly austere. Either way, Native people never fulfilled European expectations of the body and appetite, which became yet another rationalization for colonization.[61]

For colonists, disciplining the body always remained an uphill battle in an era when communities were embattled in many other ways. The cycles of colonial violence in the borderlands, coupled with the increasing emphasis on private spiritual engagement represented by the Great Awakening, began to erode the institution of Protestant communal fasting. In spite of the many declared days of fasting and prayer, colonists watched war and violence ripple through the borderlands for decades. Religious authorities insisted that these troubles continued because sinners had failed to reform themselves and had failed to slay the lust that lived inside them, in Arthur Browne's words. Marston Cabot decried those for whom *"Repentance is only transient and temporary,"* people who were "religious, sober, and devout" on a fast day and the next day "drowned in sensual Excesses."[62] With true reformation elusive, and borderlands violence rampant, colonial religious authorities watched as fasting and prayer failed to bring an end to their communities' calamities.

For Native peoples, however, rituals of self-denial offered different possibilities for survivance. Occom, Tekakwitha, Meiaskewat, and many others enacted communal traditions of fasting, repentance, and mourning throughout the colonial invasion. Although these rituals sometimes took explicitly Christian forms or were interpreted by Christian interlocutors as such, they drew on traditions that had lasted for generations. Indigenous rites helped to maintain cultural continuity and community bonds in an era when colonial violence threatened to fragment both.

Onoonghwandekha feared the decline of Seneca feasts and offerings because he knew, like the other Native people who turned to such rituals, how carrying on traditions could keep communities together in the face of invasion. "I am in earnest," he told his listeners, "because I love my nation and revere the customs and practices of our ancestors." Although Onoonghwandekha may have disparaged Native Christians as "ruined" by their "embracing" of Christianity, Occom and those at Brothertown used Christianity much as Onoonghwandekha wanted his community to use their traditional customs: to maintain their nations and lifeways.[63]

At Brothertown, Occom fasted one day, and the next day he surveyed farmland so rich an acre could produce terrific abundance: "20 Bushels of good Corn 56 Bushels of Potatoes about 200 Heads of Cabage, and about 3 Bushels of Beans, and about 2 Bushels of [Parsnips] and Beats together; besides Cucumbers and Watermelon."[64] For Occom, fasting made community, and the fruits of the land, all the sweeter.

Throughout the northeastern borderlands, colonial and Native authorities brought unique hunger cultures and knowledges to bear as they attempted to understand and control hunger. But the failures of fasting were revealing. In spite of the prominence of Christian fasting, it remained limited in its utility as hunger knowledge, because fasting was intentional hunger. Although the Christian fasting calendar quietly attempted to map fasts onto periods of unintentional hunger—hence the observance of Lent in the late winter and early spring—fasting still could not make sense of the pain of unintentional hunger. For Indigenous communities, too, the colonial invasion created new forms of scarcity that put their established ways of dealing with hunger to the test. Survival required maintaining these established ways while turning to new means of enduring scarcity.

Hunger could be defined and regulated, but it could not be tamed. Scarcity was only one of many kinds of danger in the northeastern borderlands of the seventeenth and eighteenth centuries, where different peoples collided and created new identities, environments, and cultures. Colonizers resisted the pull of these new worlds even as these spaces irrevocably changed them. But their old definitions of food and the body would not fit anymore. Attempts to make meaning from hunger foundered in the face of its brutal realities, as people ate rotten meat and human flesh and society threatened to collapse. People on the edge of starvation could become people that they could not recognize. They might even become monsters.

CHAPTER THREE

NOTHING WHICH HUNGER WILL NOT DEVOUR

Disgust

Samuel Kirkland stared down into a bowl of rotten bear stew, the flesh riddled with "streaks and mortified parts." "I viewed the meat," he wrote, torn between "the cravings of my appetite" and the "disgusting and forbidding cast of the dish." Finally, he forced down "a *pint* or more" but almost immediately ran from the house to "unload my stomach by emiting." It was a story to "offend a delicate stomach" and even a strong one. Kirkland ate the bear stew because he had no other choice. The Seneca with whom he lived were starving. His adoptive older brother, Tekânadie, had set a "tree trap" for bear but because of illness could not check the trap for several days. When he finally returned to the trap, he found a bear which "appeared to have been dead some days" in "sultry and warm" weather. Back at the family home, Kirkland watched his sister-in-law butcher the carcass. Maggots crawled through the flesh, and with horror, Kirkland "observed some white and living animals fall on the floor" and "scamper about like *lusty fellows*." The Seneca woman filled a kettle with water, corn, and the flesh of the bear, "once *dead*," in Kirkland's words, "now almost come to *life again*." She turned to Tekânadie and whispered that she feared "their *brother whiteman* could not eat of it," but she served

Kirkland a double portion because he was a guest. The missionary could not turn away food in front of his starving Seneca family, but he could not keep his body from rejecting it all the same.[1]

Colonists and Native peoples tried to control hunger, by defining it and by collecting knowledges for surviving it. When people defined hunger, or the lack of food, they also defined food itself. These definitions varied based upon culture, gender, religious tradition, age, and social status, among other factors. But across these categories of difference, food consisted only of certain substances, prepared, served, and consumed in particular ways.[2] Substances that fell outside of these parameters produced disgust: they were disgusting.

Native peoples and colonists brought to their interactions different hunger knowledges and cultures. For Haudenosaunee and Algonquian peoples, the flexibility of eating a broad range of foods made an important form of protection against starvation. In the mixed agricultural and wild diets of Indigenous peoples of the northeast, hunger knowledge involved not just knowing *what* to eat among a wide breadth of edibles but also *how* to produce, preserve, and prepare various foods. Staples such as moose meat for Wabanaki, or the Three Sisters of corn, beans, and squash across the northeast, formed the first line of defense against hunger. But Indigenous peoples also drew on a broad range of survival foods eaten only in more exceptional circumstances. Having knowledge of these foods, and being willing to eat them, could help to reduce the strain of food shortage, even if such adaptations could not necessarily prevent famine.

Europeans, by contrast, had been consuming an increasingly restricted variety of foods more or less since the Middle Ages. Wild foods might play a role in the diets of the wealthy, in the form of venison and other valuable game, or in the foods of the poor, in foraged plants and (sometimes illicitly) trapped and hunted small game. But overall, early modern Europeans were accustomed to an agricultural, domesticated diet with only a limited number of permissible foods.[3] Ignorance about North American landscapes, about wild food provision, and about how to eat a diverse diet more generally, placed the invaders at a tremendous disadvantage to Indigenous hunger knowledges. Moreover, because so many foods were new to them, colonists were probably more likely than Indigenous peoples to experience disgust at encountering new foods.

There were times when hunger could not be avoided, or to be more specific, when hunger could not be avoided without encountering disgust. Colonists and Indigenous peoples sometimes confronted the choice of whether to eat things that they found disgusting or to starve. Those who chose the former, who consumed disgusting not-foods, reported a plethora of reactions. They felt revulsion. They vomited. But they also experienced satiety and came to accept new foods, or even to take pleasure in eating them. Not only was hunger stronger than disgust, hunger threatened to transform bodies and identities in ways that profoundly challenged colonists' narratives of their superiority over Native peoples.[4]

In much of the historical record of the northeastern borderlands, disgust operates in only one direction, with colonists expressing revulsion at Native foods and bodies. Many colonial accounts of disgust come from contexts of captivity or missionary work: Kirkland missionizing and living with a Seneca family; Sébastien Rale and another Jesuit, François de Crépieul, missionizing Wabanaki and Innu communities; and Susanna Johnson, taken captive by Wabanaki raiders. As they expressed revulsion over rotten flesh, or meat eaten like bread, or food from a bowl licked by a dog, or the meat of a horse named Scoggin, these colonists' accounts of their disgust served particular rhetorical purposes for colonialism: showing that Native peoples ate disgusting things reinforced a belief in their savagery and suitability for being colonized.[5]

With the specificity of their accounts of trials and temptations, and their catalogues of disgusting meals, colonial writers attested to their non-Nativeness, rejecting Native foods and bodies. Despite intimate contact with Native peoples, these colonists protested that they had not been lured by Native ways. Yet colonists often experienced troubling sensations of satiety or even pleasure when they consumed Native foods. In their narratives, they struggled to confine their disgusting experiences within familiar language. The violence of one's appetite, in Kirkland's words, threatened the boundaries of colonial and Native cultures.[6]

The rhetorical aims of this literature of disgust also reverberated into the archive, where British and French voices have dominated the history of disgust in the northeastern borderlands. While colonists wrote in nauseating detail about their loathing of Native foodways, their archive has recorded far fewer equivalent episodes for Native people. Indeed, colonial writers seemed to assume that Native disgust was impossible, that Native people could eat anything without feeling revulsion. This lack of revulsion was, in colonists' eyes, further proof of Native abjection.[7]

On the contrary, Native people did feel disgust when confronted with new foodways. Sometimes they rejected colonists' foods, as when the Wampanoag saunkskwa Weetamoo refused to eat a dish that Mary Rowlandson cooked. But they also expressed disgust at the food habits of other Indigenous cultures, as when a Montaukket missionary, David Fowler, decried the practices of the Oneida he missionized. Moreover, colonists also recorded instances where Indigenous people explicitly recognized colonial disgust. These Native experiences of disgust deny the colonial narrative of the absence of Native revulsion.

While colonists and Indigenous peoples might express disgust with each other, the blurry line between fermentation and decay revealed the ways that disgust was subjective and culturally constructed. Both colonial and Native cultures consumed fermented foods, but the difference between fermentation and rot remained in the eye of the beholder, proving to be one of the most divisive distinctions in cross-cultural food experiences. Kirkland's vomit and the wife of Tekânadie's worry that a White man could not stomach maggoty bear meat took place amidst social conventions of rot and fermentation.

In the northeastern borderlands, hunger forced people into "terrible eating," eating terrible things in a context of violence. Such food was "fearsome" and "beyond the limits" of what eaters can conceptualize, in the words of the philosopher of aesthetics Carolyn Korsmeyer.[8] Hunger forced people to overcome and to question their innate understandings of what was food and how it should be served. Disgust tested, transgressed, and reified cultural boundaries. Not unlike the other kinds of violent dislocation that took place in the borderlands—captivity and war, conquest and dispossession—disgust fundamentally challenged peoples' ways of understanding themselves.

The History of Disgust

Contemporary theorists have defined disgust in ways that do not align with Indigenous and early modern European notions about food and the body. The study of disgust has largely been the province of biologists, psychologists, literary theorists, and philosophers. These scholars have generally grouped disgust into two major categories: physiological disgust, or the physical rejection of substances via nausea, vomiting, grimacing and the like; and moral disgust, a negative response to the actions of other people and, more rarely, ourselves. Biologists and psychologists argue that physiological disgust evolved to protect the body from contagion and contamination—and indeed, these concepts existed long before the discovery of microbial pathogens. Further, some scholars have contended that physiological disgust laid the neural pathways for moral disgust, that the latter could not exist without the former. Humanists have rejected these purely biological theories of disgust as reductive, instead drawing attention to the ways that revulsion makes the world, "organizing and internalizing our attitudes toward the moral, social, and political domains," according to William Ian Miller. In the words of the literary theorist Sianne Ngai, disgust has long served to police "the boundaries between self and 'contaminating' others," to devastating political effect.[9]

In the early American past, people understood disgust differently. Given how heavily intertwined the body, mind, and soul were in Native and early modern European cultures, contemporary scholars' neat division between the moral and the physiological realms cannot explain disgust as it existed in the seventeenth and eighteenth centuries. The period saw considerable flux in ideas about food and disgust on both sides of the Atlantic. Europeans debated food in the context of the Reformation, adjusted to new norms of politeness, and confronted new peoples and foodways through exploration and colonization. Many resisted these changes: Gervase Markham's 1615 recipe book called for housewives to feed their families with English food, not to be seduced by the new tastes flooding Europe. "Let [a woman's cooking] be rather esteemed for the familiar acquaintance she hath with it, than for the strangeness and rarity it bringeth from other Countries," Markham wrote. Indigenous peoples, meanwhile, fought to preserve their own food traditions in the face of invading people, plants, and animals.[10] Just as Native peoples and colonists struggled to understand each other's hunger knowledges, so they navigated each other's food norms, even as these norms were in the midst of radical change. The task became particularly difficult when one culture considered a substance food and the other considered it disgusting, even to the point of violently rejecting that food, as Kirkland's stomach rejected the rotten bear.

From its inception, disgust has policed cultural, gendered, and class boundaries. It was a relatively new concept when English and French colonists began their conquest of North America. The word "disgust" entered the English language around the early seventeenth century, from the French *dégoût*, which first appeared in the previous century, although *dégoûté* or "disgusted" has been traced back to the fourteenth century. It was an adjective before it was a noun, a feeling before it was a phenomenon. Colonists also located this concept in Indigenous languages. Sébastien Rale's Abenaki dictionary translated Abenaki phrases using the French verb *dégoûter*, including such phrases as "I am disgusted . . . to eat meat." Though colonists like Rale would go on to argue that Native people did not experience disgust, they nevertheless recorded the existence of at least a similar concept in Native languages.[11]

While its etymological relationship to taste in French and English implies that disgust is primarily a response to food, a wide spectrum of substances, concepts, and behaviors can elicit disgust. Scholars have attempted to catalogue universally disgusting phenomena, but disgust triggers vary widely because culture seems to determine a large portion of what individuals find disgusting. While some disgust triggers appear to be inborn, others can vary over the course of a lifetime.[12] Indeed, many colonists and Native peoples were forced to recalibrate their expectations of disgustingness when they were thrust into new circumstances and new foodways.

It is no coincidence that Europeans began to need a word for disgust as they began to explore and colonize a world of peoples very different than themselves. Early America was a formative place and time in the history of disgust because of the forced confluence of peoples from the Americas, western Europe, and West Africa. More often than not, people on the other side of cultural, gendered, or class boundaries were seen as disgusting. Categorizing substances or people as "clean" or "unclean" served to "create unity in experience" for cultural groups, argued the anthropologist Mary Douglas. Colonists saw many, if not most, Native foods as not-foods.[13] As captives or missionaries living in Native communities, however, colonists would be forced to eat precisely these foods or risk starvation. Colonists did not fully appreciate that their disgust was maladaptive to a world of sometimes sporadic access to food. Moreover, colonial experiences of Indigenous foodways would have far-reaching consequences for the history of colonization—both as colonists rejected new foods and as they embraced them.

Colonial Disgust

"I ate all these things, for there is nothing which hunger will not devour," declared Sébastien Rale, after listing the mushrooms, lichens, and bark that he consumed on his late-winter journey with Wabanaki guides in the early 1720s. English and French colonists who lived with Native peoples as captives or missionaries found themselves exposed to new foodways, and they usually did not like what they found. Their expressions of repugnance at Native foods were so frequent and formulaic that they have been called "a trope of the genre" of captivity narratives. Like all colonial narratives, the rhetoric of disgust in these accounts served particular purposes. With florid descriptions of disgusting foods and their effects on colonial bodies, these accounts reassured readers that colonists who lived in intimate contact with Indigenous people had nevertheless not absorbed their ways.[14]

But colonists also protested their disgust to distance themselves from the fact that they were dependent on Native people for food. Such dependence had marked all early colonial ventures, with colonists seeking out food supplies from Native peoples via exchange or outright theft. In the eighteenth century, colonists became more capable of supporting themselves through agriculture, but they still relied heavily upon Native staples, such as corn, for sustenance.[15]

Narratives of individual colonists' cross-cultural experiences vividly illustrated how captives and missionaries could not feed themselves: only through reliance on Native people's hunger knowledges could colonists survive. Colonists teetered between repulsion at new foods and the need for sustenance. Susanna Johnson, a British captive of the Wabanaki and then the French; Rale, a Jesuit missionary to the Wabanaki; and François de Crépieul, a missionary to the Innu, all described their experiences of disgust in elaborate detail, enumerating varieties of revulsion with Native foods and foodways. These three accounts constitute just a handful of the array of disgust narratives produced by English and French colonists who ate Native foods in the seventeenth and eighteenth centuries.

Colonists objected to many of the ingredients of Native foods, irrespective of handling, cooking, or serving. Colonial observers found many Native sources of animal protein particularly revolting. Between the Middle Ages and the early modern period, Europeans decreased the variety of species that they ate and began to eat more domesticated than wild animals. Choice of animal proteins might reflect national identities—the English, for example, venerated beef and turned up their noses at French consumption of horsemeat. By contrast, Indigenous peoples often consumed the flesh of animals that Europeans did not consider appropriate to eat under anything but life-or-death circumstances. Eating only certain animals in specific preparations, Europeans saw themselves as civilized and removed from more animal appetites, in contrast to Native peoples, who did not discriminate about animal proteins to the same degree. Nevertheless, hungry colonists often conquered their initial hesitation to eat these "foreign" foods, though not without emphasizing the effects of unusual meats upon colonial bodies and souls.[16]

The captivity narrative of Susanna Johnson neatly illustrated British attitudes toward Native animal protein choices. When a party of eleven Wabanaki men captured Johnson and her husband from Charlestown, New Hampshire, in August 1754, she was heavily pregnant. As the party prepared to embark for Canada, another colonist's horse, "known to us as Scoggin," came along, and Johnson's husband caught the horse for her to ride. The next day, Johnson delivered her baby, and then continued to ride Scoggin for five days, crossing west over present-day Vermont. On the fifth night, the raiding party reached "the waters that run into Lake Champlain," but a hard journey still lay in front of them. With provisions exhausted and hunting unsuccessful, the Wabanaki chose to sacrifice Scoggin. The Wabanaki sliced and roasted horse flesh to eat that day, boiled broth for Johnson and her newborn, then smoked and dried the rest of the meat to preserve it. The next morning, the Wabanaki broke "the marrow bones of old Scoggin" and boiled them. On the flesh and broth of a single horse, eleven Wabanaki and eight colonists survived for several days.[17]

Johnson recorded a variety of responses among the Wabanaki and British members of the party to the butchering and eating of Scoggin the horse. The Wabanaki "satiated their craving appetites" without hesitation, which Johnson ascribed to "Native gluttony." She contrasted their hunger, which she found uncivilized, with the meal they provided their prisoners: "An epicure could not have catered nicer slices," she noted, the polite serving contrasting with her horror at consuming horsemeat. "Each [colonist] partook as much as his feelings would allow," Johnson wrote, not clarifying what these "feelings" might be. It could have been simple disgust at eating horsemeat, which the English had long outlawed and associated with paganism and the French. Or, as Johnson's repeated invocation of Scoggin's name suggested, a sentimental attachment to the animal: eating this *particular* horse may well have been uncomfortable for Johnson and other colonists. Whatever the cause, horsemeat was surely "novel" and not particularly appetizing to Johnson, even in a time of scarcity: "Appetite is said to be the best sauce; yet our abundance of it did not render savory this novel steak," she wrote. Despite her reservations, Johnson could not, in the end, "turn with disgust from a breakfast of steaks which were cut from the thigh of a horse." She assured her readers that they would do the same, too, if they were in her position, "if my feelings can be realized." She remained, however, devastated at the loss of her mount, fearing that she would not have the strength to continue the journey on foot: "By the assistance of Scoggin I had been brought so far," she lamented, "but now, alas! this conveyance was no more." Instead, Scoggin had become a different kind of conveyance, his flesh providing Johnson the sustenance she needed to carry her own toward Canada.[18]

While Johnson agonized over eating Scoggin the horse, her hungry children "ate too much" of the meat, which left them "extremely sick and weak." This eager acceptance of horsemeat as food would be only the first step in more dramatic changes for the Johnson children. Four years after their capture, Johnson's children were scattered to French and Wabanaki communities. Reunited with her son Sylvanus, who had been captured at age seven and lived for three years with the Wabanaki and one year with the French, Johnson would report that "he had entirely forgotten the English language, spoke a little broken French, but was perfect in Indian." Sylvanus barely remembered his mother. Her daughter, also named Susanna, captured at age four, "did not know [her mother] at her return" and had forgotten English in favor of French. With a French-speaking daughter and a French- and Wabanaki-speaking son, "my family was a mixture of nations," Johnson would reflect.[19]

The Johnson children's journey from new foods to complete accultura-tion illustrated how much more flexible colonial children could be than their parents. Johnson's children's "Complaints" were of hunger, not dis-gust at new foods. Unlike their parents, children did not necessarily reject unfamiliar foods; they were simply too young to stay within the boundar-ies of food and not-food that culture had drawn around adults. Johnson's children felt ill after eating horsemeat but only because they ate too much, not because they were disturbed at eating Scoggin as their mother was. Native peoples captured English children precisely because of their cultural malleability, their potential to take on new ways. Children under age ten proved particularly adaptable (and adoptable) into Native com-munities precisely because they did not share their parents' intense dis-gust at Native cultures.[20]

Colonists objected not just to individual food items, like horsemeat, but to Native foodways as a whole, from preparation to consumption. Colonists brought with them an understanding of the food preparation process that was imbued with meanings both moral and medical: Markham's 1615 rec-ipe book called for cooks to "be cleanly both in body and garments," essen-tial qualities for a person to prepare food "in good and wholesome manner." Another English cookbook author, Hannah Woolley, instructed cooks to be "cleanly about every thing," keeping a spotless kitchen with "all things scoured in due time," without leaving food residue "to spoil and stink." The actual conditions in early modern European kitchens could not be described as remotely healthful by modern standards: contaminated wa-ter and produce, spoiled food due to the lack of refrigeration, and the ne-glect of handwashing or cleaning utensils all could transmit disease.[21]

Despite the very real health risks that European cooking habits posed, the majority of colonists who described Native meals saw them as chaotic, unhealthful, and unclean. Colonists discussed Native meal preparation and serving in detail in order to highlight what they saw as its deficiencies. Rale wrote that there was "nothing more disgusting" than "sharing my meals" with the Wabanaki he missionized. His concerns related partly to the physical preparation of the food: Wabanaki cooks boiled their meat for only "three-quarters of an hour," which Rale apparently found insufficient. But what "revolted [Rale] the most" was, instead, a difference in manners: the way that Wabanaki picked up pieces of cooked meat in their hands and bit into them "as one would do with a piece of bread." When Rale refused to eat with them, the Wabanaki asked him why, and he replied that he was "not accustomed to eating meat without adding first a little bread." Both Wabanaki food preparation and dining practices repulsed Rale, who was accustomed to French habits. Yet in Rale's telling, the Wabanaki reminded him that they, too, were navigating new cultural territory by accepting a Christian missionary into their community: "We have to overcome ourselves to believe in what we cannot see," they told the priest. By comparison, the Wabanaki reasoned, eating meat without bread presented far fewer challenges than adapting to a new religion, as Rale urged them to do. It was one thing to change one's stomach; it was another to change one's soul. During his mission, Rale struggled mightily with the former.[22]

Another Jesuit, Crépieul, condemned Innu foodways and bodily habits in a brief 1697 document entitled "The Life of a Montagnaix Missionary," in which he listed his "sufferings and Miseries" while living in Innu communities around Tadoussac. Worst of all was the food: Crépieul devoted more than half of his litany of complaints to his disgust with Innu foodways. Dishes were "very seldom clean or washed," except "wiped with a greasy piece of skin" or "Licked by The dogs." While eating, the Innu wiped their hands on their clothing, shoes, or hair, or "the dogs' skins." Crépieul shared communal dishes with people who suffered from scrofula, and "the stench" from their sores "made my Gorge rise." He drank "very dirty" water from ponds, "in which I saw toads" (frogs) swimming. Visiting one village, Crépieul wrote, "I have never seen [people] dirtier than these" in matters of food handling. "An old woman, with her long nails," served up "handfuls of grease" into "very dirty" communal dishes. They ate food "covered with moose-hairs or Sand." But like Rale, Crépieul ate and drank in situations that he found utterly revolting because he had no other choice. He reported that he "suffer[ed] also from Hunger," eating "only when there is something to eat," and "in times of abundance," only twice a day. In the face of what he saw as food scarcity, Crépieul overcame his revulsion with Innu foodways, but the disgust animating his account is impossible to ignore.[23]

One example serves to illustrate some of the many ways Crépieul misunderstood his Innu hosts. The priest grumbled that he had to sleep in a dwelling with men, women, and children (the latter upon whom lice "always swarm"), as well as dogs—"when he awakes he finds himself surrounded by dogs," he related with horror. But what Crépieul ascribed to foreign Native ways would have been perfectly normal among most Europeans and colonists of the time: large households of different ages and genders sharing sleeping quarters, potentially with lice or bedbugs. The priest's eagerness to see the same personal habits as utterly reprehensible among Native people draws attention to the ugly colonial assumptions underlying Crépieul's account.[24]

Colonial narratives like Crépieul's brim with detail, and yet they begin to blur together: a vividly populated but ultimately repetitive archive of colonists' disgust with Native practices. Yet colonists' narratives also acknowledge that Native foods were all that stood between them and starvation. Colonists resented this dependence on Native hunger knowledges and food supplies, a resentment that ran so deep that colonists proved nearly incapable of recognizing that Native people felt the same kinds of disgust that they did.

Native Disgust

While the historical record overflows with colonial expressions of disgust, Native disgust appears only infrequently. On the one hand it is possible to lump disgust together with colonists' dehumanizing dismissals of Native affective lives: many European observers did not believe that Native people could feel real emotions. But on the other hand, ignoring or hiding Indigenous disgust cut particularly deeply. Viewing cleanliness as a marker of gentility, colonists argued that Native peoples' "dirty" habits justified their dispossession. Colonists' refusal to recognize Native disgust carried over into their production of the textual record. If colonists saw the experience of disgust as an assertion of personhood, then denying the possibility of Native disgust constituted archival violence.[25]

Two Indigenous expressions of disgust that were recorded in the archive challenge colonists' implicit assumptions about Native disgust. In one, Weetamoo refused to eat a dish prepared by Mary Rowlandson. In another, the Montaukket missionary David Fowler complained about the foodways of the Oneidas he missionized. Like colonists' experiences of disgust, these Native experiences show how disgust marked cultural difference. Moreover, Kirkland and Rowlandson noted moments when Indigenous people drew attention to colonists' disgust, from Tekânadie's wife worrying that Kirkland could not stomach the rotten bear to a Native man expressing surprise that Rowlandson would eat horse organs.

In her narrative of her captivity, Mary Rowlandson graphically described her own oscillations between disgust and appetite, but she also noted an instance of Native disgust and refusal to eat. One day, Rowlandson "boiled . . . peas and bear together" and invited Weetamoo and her husband Quinnapin to a meal. To her dismay, Weetamoo "would eat nothing, except one bit that he gave her upon the point of a knife." Rowlandson explained that Weetamoo refused the meal because Rowlandson had "served them both in one dish," meaning that she did not provide separate dishes to Quinnapin and Weetamoo. In the seventeenth and eighteenth centuries, European dining conventions were undergoing a shift from communal dishes to individual place settings; as a colonist removed from European trends, Rowlandson might have still served her family from communal dishes at home. While eating from a common pot was an important Indigenous metaphor for community, Wampanoag dining conventions dictated that men and women not share the same dish. Rowlandson called Weetamoo a "proud gossip" for rebuffing the meal, in keeping with Rowlandson's horror that the Wampanoag leader did not behave with the submission or humility that was expected of English women.[26]

But Weetamoo's reasons for refusal reflected deeper currents of food and hierarchy. Refusing Rowlandson's gift offered a means of demonstrating Weetamoo's power over her servant. While many aspects of captivity proved disorienting and disturbing to Rowlandson, she particularly struggled with her change of status, from being the wife of a minister who had Indigenous servants to becoming the servant of a female Wampanoag leader. Rowlandson's dish of bear and peas attempted to perform her lack of dependence on Weetamoo, in a journey largely characterized by Rowlandson begging Weetamoo and other members of her party for food. By serving a meal to Weetamoo and Quinnapin, Rowlandson tried to meet them as equals instead of as a servant reliant on the good graces of her betters. But Weetamoo rejected Rowlandson's gesture as inappropriate. Rowlandson served her meal incorrectly, violating cultural norms of division between the genders and also the hierarchical differences between a saunkskwa and her captive. Given Rowlandson's errors, it is surprising that Weetamoo ate even a bite. Weetamoo's distaste lacked the drama of Kirkland's vomit, but it, too, demonstrated differing definitions of uncleanliness: if dirt is "matter out of place," as Mary Douglas contended, then Rowlandson's out-of-place meal was definitely unclean by Wampanoag standards and therefore worthy of disgust.[27]

Disgust did not only operate between colonists and Indigenous peoples. Instead of a colonist complaining about Native food habits, David Fowler was a Montaukett missionary complaining about Oneida foodways. Educated at Moor's Indian Charity School like Kirkland and Samson Occom (he was also Occom's brother-in-law), Fowler traveled to Canajoharie to missionize the Oneida community in 1765. Reporting back to the school's founder, Eleazar Wheelock, via letter soon after his arrival, Fowler launched into a series of invectives about the foodways of his hosts. Fowler was repulsed that his hosts ate in close quarters with their domesticated animals: "I am oblig'd to eat with Dogs, I say, with Dogs," he complained. The Oneida let their dogs lick "water out off their Pales and Kettles," or steal food straight from the dish: "I have often seen Dogs eating their Victuals when they have set their Dishes down, they'll only make a little Noise to show their Displeasure to Dogs and take up the Dish" again. These scenes apparently made quite an impression on Fowler; when he wrote to Wheelock months later, he again noted that he "was oblig'd to eat with the Dogs" and that they licked the dishes.[28]

While Fowler documented the disgust he felt at the contact actual animals had with food, he went further and compared the Oneida themselves to animals. "My Cooks are nasty as Hogs," he grumbled; "their Cloaths" were "black and greasy as my Shoes," and "their Hands . . . as dirty as my Feet." Fowler expressed revulsion that these same hands touched his food: "they cleanse them by kneading Bread," he claimed. Using further animal language, he called the Oneidas the most "lazy and inhuman pack of Creatures as I ever saw in the World." In the same letter in which Fowler compared his hosts to pigs, however, *he* also identified with swine. He insisted that "I determine to live better than a Hog" and that "my Food now is not fit for any Man, that has been used to have his Victuals drest clean." He dreamed of the "clean," "nourishing" cooking of Wheelock's wife, Mary, who made "Bread & Milk, little sweet Cake and good boild Meat" for Wheelock's students. But these "civilized" foods, prepared, served, and eaten so differently than his meals among the Oneidas, produced in Fowler an animal appetite. The pig imagery returned, but now Fowler himself took the place of a hungry swine: "I could eat those things gready as a Hog that has been kept in a Pen two Days without it's Swill," he admitted.[29]

This final identification with animals illustrated the differences between Crépieul's and Fowler's lists of complaints with Native foodways. Despite critiquing Innu food as Fowler did Oneida food, Crépieul, as a European missionary, occupied a very different position than a Native one. Crépieul would never be mistaken for one of the people he missionized—no matter how long he ate their food and slept in their houses, he remained French and Christian, wholly committed to changing every facet he could about the Innu. As a Christianized and Europeanized Montaukket proselytizing the Oneida, Fowler occupied a more complicated position, knowing well that European observers might choose to describe *him* in the same ways as the Oneida whose bodily habits he so loathed. Like Crépieul, Fowler struggled to adapt to the language and culture of an alien people, the Oneida. His letters attempted to illustrate that Fowler identified more with the British culture in which he had been indoctrinated at Moor's. With his palpable disgust at Oneida foodways, and his comparisons of the Oneida to pigs and dogs, Fowler worked to distance himself from what he saw as Oneida animal appetites. Yet he confessed that he, too, experienced a swinish hunger for British food.[30]

Fowler's revulsion helped to fuel his mission to Europeanize Oneida religion and lifeways: "I am oblig'd to eat whatsoever they give me for fear they will be displeas'd with me," he wrote in his first letter, but "after this Month I shall try to clean some of them." The process would be slow, lest the Oneidas reject Fowler's efforts: "I must move along by Degrees, if they once get out with me it is all over with me." The first chance he had, with financial support from Wheelock's organization, he set up house with his wife, the Pequot Moor's alumna Hannah Garrett, and lived "like a Gentleman," with "a planty of Corn, Flour, Meat and rotten Fish."[31] But within a few years, after inadequate support for his mission from Wheelock's organization, Fowler returned home to Long Island, to more familiar people, surroundings, and foodways.

Weetamoo's and Fowler's expressions of revulsion challenged colonists' contentions that Native peoples were too dirty and disgusting themselves to experience disgust. These accounts of Native disgust also demonstrate the factors that may have rendered such revulsion less legible to colonists. Weetamoo's disgust originated in a gendered system of social relations that flummoxed Mary Rowlandson, a system in which a woman could be one of the most powerful Wampanoag leaders but could not eat from the same dish as her husband. Rowlandson violated Wampanoag social conventions, yet she dismissed Weetamoo's censure as "pride" because she did not fully understand the depths of her mistake or the system in which that mistake took place. Colonists reading Fowler's letters may have interpreted them as merely a Christianized Native man expressing disgust with Native ways, not as a member of one nation expressing discomfort with the manners of another.[32] To be sure, Fowler's disgust originated at least partly with his adaptation to British culture at Moor's, an acculturation suggested by his nostalgic descriptions of Mary Wheelock's cooking. But Fowler also confronted Oneida foodways across a large linguistic and cultural gulf from his own Montaukket upbringing, a gulf that, like those of Rale and Crépieul, left the missionary daunted about the task of changing Oneida culture "by degrees." Culture changed in the borderlands "by degrees" or violently all at once, with disgust as a crucial arbiter of identity for Native peoples and colonists alike. For Fowler, disgust was one of the factors that drove him away from missionary work with the Oneida.

Colonists may have believed that Native people were incapable of experiencing or even conceptualizing disgust, but the archive preserves a few notable instances where Native observers explicitly noted colonists' discomfort with Native foodways. The first instance has already been mentioned—the whispered conversation between Tekânadie and his wife, expressing concern that Kirkland "could not eat" bear meat infested with maggots. A second instance appears in Rowlandson's narrative, when she asked a Native man for a piece of horse liver to eat. Rowlandson described the man's response: "*What,* says he *can you eat Horse-liver?*" The man's question implied skepticism or surprise that an English woman would want to eat the liver of a horse. It seems that the man had observed the differences between the diets of the English and the Wampanoag, Nipmuc, and other peoples with whom Rowlandson traveled as a captive. The man recognized that the English did not ordinarily eat horses, and that they, like Susanna Johnson, found even the concept of eating a horse repellant. Indeed, Rowlandson expressed ambivalence about the horse liver, telling the man that she "would try" to eat it "if he would give me a piece." In the end, Rowlandson had no trouble stomaching the meat: after someone stole part of the liver while she was roasting it, she bolted it "with the blood about my mouth." These moments when Native people commented upon colonial disgust further trouble the colonial archive's efforts to categorize Indigenous people as incapable of seeing or feeling disgust. Contrary to colonists' attempts to obscure Native experiences of or ideas about disgust, the actions and words of Weetamoo, Fowler, Tekânadie's wife, and the man in Rowlandson's narrative register in an archive that is stacked against them. They are rare voices in an archive that is overwhelmingly tilted toward colonial disgust.[33]

Fermentation and Rot

Colonists' inability or refusal to recognize Indigenous food systems formed a crucial component of colonialism. When colonists dismissed Native foodways as disgusting and refused to see Native food as food, they also denied the ability of Native people to provide for themselves. Wabanaki and Haudenosaunee peoples did suffer from food scarcity at various points in the eighteenth century, as a direct result of colonial disease, violence, and other disruptions. Moreover, colonists increasingly perceived Indigenous peoples as hungry, their bodies weak and starving, their foodways and land use deficient. These perceptions were in part a backlash against the dependency on Indigenous food supplies that had marked earlier colonial ventures. Colonists argued that Indigenous people used their land inefficiently, leading to Native hunger and poverty. This belief in Indigenous poverty would be a crucial rationalization for colonization.[34] One of the means by which colonists emphasized Indigenous poverty was by misinterpreting Native fermentation as rot, claiming that starving Indigenous peoples were so desperate as to eat decayed food. As with colonial versus Native experiences of disgust, the reality was much more complex.

Like disgust, the concept of fermentation is to some degree culturally constructed. Most cultures have traditions of fermenting foods to preserve them, practices of controlled decay that arose before the advent of modern refrigeration and canning. "Rotten" is a "culturally specific adjective"—that is, one culture's rotten, "inedible" food is another's fermented, edible food, the anthropologist Sidney Mintz noted. Many agrarian peoples actively seek out the distinctive flavors and textures that fermentation produces. These characteristics of fermented foods enliven diets based on blander staple grains, adding nutrition, contrast, and variety. But these same qualities—strong flavors and bold textures—also can make other cultures' fermented foods unappetizing to outsiders. In the case of the northeastern borderlands, colonists utterly rejected Native fermented foods, believing them to be not fermented but rotten.[35]

Colonists frequently complained that Native people ate foods that Europeans considered decayed. A Jesuit missionary in Kahnawake in the 1710s, Joseph François Lafitau wrote that while the Mohawk usually preserved or cooked meat before it had "time to spoil," they still had few qualms about eating "almost spoiled" flesh that "smells bad," or consuming "rancid or infected" animal fat. When food ran low among the Seneca in 1765, Kirkland traded one of his shirts for four cornmeal cakes. So great was his hunger, "at first sight I thought I could devour them all at one meal," but he vomited up the first cake he ate "because my stomack was so debilitated." He kept the remaining cakes until they began to mold, then offered them to his adoptive nieces and nephews, "who devoured them *instantly.*" The hungry children could stomach what Kirkland could not; the fact that the cakes had begun to spoil did not deter the Seneca children from eating them. Much like the rotten bear stew, the moldy cakes were a part of Seneca foodways that remained indigestible for Kirkland.[36]

Yet rot and spoilage seemed to lie in the eye of the beholder. Other accounts suggested that Indigenous peoples fermented fish and meat and that they valued the potent flavors produced by fermentation. Joseph Johnson, a Mohegan missionary who trained at Moor's, wrote in February 1768 that the Oneida he missionized kept "rotten fish" from the previous fall "to Season their Samps" (corn soups). While Johnson seemed repulsed by this practice, the Oneida sought out the taste of fermented fish: "rottener the better they Say as it will Season more broth." This pungent condiment added variety to an otherwise repetitive late-winter diet. Where Johnson and the British saw rottenness, the Oneida saw fermentation and flavor. Even Fowler, who was otherwise critical of Oneida foodways, wrote of living abundantly with "a planty of Corn, Flour, Meat and rotten Fish."[37]

While colonists criticized Native peoples for consuming rotten meat, early modern Europeans in the days before refrigeration would have been intimately familiar with the controlled or uncontrolled decomposition of fish and flesh. Methods of preservation included pickling, such as the pickled herrings in Gervase Markham's recipe for herring pie. English recipe books abounded with hints for camouflaging flesh that had passed its prime. To counteract "Putridity" in "Hash meat," one recipe book instructed cooks to "put the tainted meat, covered with cloth, into a quantity of boiling water," for five minutes. Meat "too long kept" could be "recovered" with a stint of "being buried a foot deep in fresh earth," the cookbook also suggested. Markham's remedy for spoiled venison required the cook to boil "a strong brine" with a combination of "strong ale," "wine vinegar," and salt, to let this mixture cool, and to soak the venison in it overnight. Next, the cook would remove the meat from the brine, "press it well," then "parboil it, and season it with pepper and salt" before roasting. According to Hannah Glasse, if potted fowl smelled "so bad, that nobody could bear" the stench could be removed by boiling and seasoning "with mace, pepper, and salt." These preparations of burying, boiling, washing, and seasoning to counteract or mask spoiled meat also had their counterparts in Native cuisine: Samuel Kirkland's Seneca sister-in-law stewed rancid bear meat and served it with "half a spoonful of salt on one side."[38]

Rooted in culture, the distinction between rot and fermentation had potent political ramifications. Colonists who decried "spoiled" Native foods might have overstated food shortage in Native communities. Seeing the consumption of "rotten" meat and fish as an act of desperation, colonists would have interpreted Indigenous peoples who ate these foods as starving. But there is a clear difference between the maggoty bear stew, which Tekânadie and his family consumed in the context of food shortage and ill health interfering with hunting, and the "rottener the better" fish the Oneida used to "Season" their food, which reflected seasonal cycles of fishing and fermentation. Colonists may not have been willing to see the difference between eating rotten meat out of desperation and eating fermented fish because it tasted good, although these situations similarly arose in colonial foodways. Rather than starving, Native peoples who ate "rotten" flesh were often engaging in traditional food preservation and seeking out strong fermented flavors. Disgust, like the difference between rot and fermentation, had its origins in culture. Despite the seeming arbitrariness of the division between decay and pickling, colonists would argue that Native peoples were uncivilized because they consumed disgusting rotten food. Such dismissals joined other colonial discourses of Native savagery and lack of self-sufficiency that formed the backbone of justifications for colonization.

Leaving Disgust Behind

In the northeastern borderlands, colonists and Native peoples tried to change each other, often by force. Colonial missionaries sought to convert Native peoples to Christianity and to dismantle Native cultures and traditions. Native peoples who took captives sought to acculturate some captives into their communities. Disgust was a crucial part of this process: people might hold on to disgust in order to resist acclimatizing, or they might let go of disgust to transition to a new culture. The colonial archive reveals the complexities of captivity. While captivity was designed to break down colonists' resistance to Native cultures, sometimes it had a confounding effect, with captives gripping the cultures of their birth even more tightly. The returners who wrote captivity narratives clung to their colonial identities and worked throughout their accounts to prove to their readers that they had not been contaminated by Indigeneity. Yet even the most famous accounts of colonial disgust at Native ways could offer something much more subversive: rather than just eating Native foods out of sheer necessity to avoid starvation, colonists grew to take pleasure in Native foodways, even when this pleasure severely challenged colonists' previous identities.

Mary Rowlandson's captivity offered one such narrative of resistance to and embrace of Native foodways. At one point in her journey, when Rowlandson went into a Native dwelling to beg for food, she found two

English children eating chunks of boiled horse hoof. A woman gave Rowlandson a piece. Rowlandson, "Being very hungry," ate hers "quickly," then looked over at the younger child, struggling with the tough lump of meat. "The child could not bite it . . . but lay sucking, gnawing, chewing and slobbering of it in the mouth and hand," Rowlandson observed. She stole the hoof "and ate it myself, and savory it was to my taste." Like many English women in captivity narratives, Rowlandson emphasized her role as a mother and nurturer, and her denial of sustenance to an English child (in the name of a rubbery boiled horse hoof, no less) fell far outside of the cultural norms of motherhood. Rowlandson did not attempt to rationalize her behavior, except that hunger consumed her. The first week of her captivity, "I hardly ate any thing." By the second week, though growing hungry, she still could not stomach the "filthy trash" of Indigenous food. And in the third week, "though I could think how formerly my stomach would turn against this or that, and I could starve and die before I could eat such things, yet they were sweet and savory to my taste." By then, she savored even meat stolen from a child. The boiled horse hoof did not just satiate Rowlandson—it gave her pleasure to eat it.[39]

Such transgressions continued to haunt Rowlandson long after her return from captivity. At the end of her narrative, Rowlandson described how her spiritual journey as a captive resonated with her years later. She lay awake at night thinking "upon things past, upon the awful dispensation of the Lord toward us." While in captivity she ate a horse hoof stolen from a child, but when she returned to her home among the English, she no longer had to resort to terrible eating. She compared her family to the Prodigal Son, who in his wanderings endured scarcity, before returning home to plenty: "instead of the husk, we have the fatted calf," she wrote. Rowlandson invoked more biblical metaphors of plenty, but the plenty she described was a profusion of suffering. "The portion of some is to have their afflictions by drops, now one drop and then," she noted, but her "portion" was a flood of sorrows, "the wine of astonishment, like a sweeping rain that leaveth no food." In a journey punctuated by scarcity, it was only fitting that Rowlandson turned to scriptural metaphors of destruction, poverty, and hunger. Something had changed in Rowlandson since her captivity experience, a transformation she struggled to describe and thereby circumscribe with familiar biblical language. She tried to domesticate her hunger, and her terrible eating, and make it safe. Her sleepless nights hint that this effort remained incomplete.[40]

In his 1675 *Histoire Naturelle* of New France, the French naturalist Louis Nicolas wrote that Indigenous peoples "have an aversion to everything that we like, and prize everything that we despise." Colonial writers weaponized their dislike of Native foodways as a means of claiming their superiority over Native peoples. The captives and missionaries who wrote narratives of their cross-cultural experiences were not the colonists who were absorbed into Native communities, though they feared this possibility acutely. These authors, unlike many other colonists, failed to adapt to new and unfamiliar foods or to their tastes, textures, and preparations. Nevertheless, even the most initially recalcitrant colonists, like Rowlandson, ravenously ate new foods if hunger drove them to it. Where once Indigenous foods were disgusting, "filthy trash," they became "sweet and savory to my taste." Hunger made the unpalatable palatable, the disgusting delicious.[41]

But when colonists wrote their narratives of their experiences with terrible eating, they lingered on their disgust, as if itemizing their disgust canceled out everything else they may have felt about those foods. Their eagerness to disavow Indigenous foods betrayed their anxiety about the effect of these foods, and of Indigenous ways more generally, on their bodies and souls. The lack of disgust that colonial children showed when faced with Native foodways troubled these efforts even further, undercutting the power of disgust to enforce the boundaries between colonial and Native bodies and cultures.

The rhetoric of colonists' disgust at Native foodways served a number of purposes beyond reassuring readers of the superiority of colonial identity. Colonists' expressions of disgust endeavored to conceal the way that captives and missionaries were often wholly reliant upon Indigenous hunger knowledges and food supplies to survive. Furthermore, by arguing that Native peoples ate certain foods out of necessity, such as "rotten" fermented foods, colonists potentially overstated rates of Native food shortage. Colonists simply could not interpret many Native foods as food. The resulting tropes of the poverty of Native communities served as an important justification for dispossessing Indigenous peoples of their lands.

Native peoples experienced similar forms of disgust at the European invaders, although the colonial archive has largely elided Native revulsion.

Weetamoo's refusal to eat Mary Rowlandson's cooking and David Fowler's disgust with Oneida foodways demonstrate that Native people felt just as much disgust as did Europeans, even if colonists were unwilling to accept this fact. Indigenous peoples survived and flourished on foods that colonists did not see as food: wild plants where colonists saw weeds, fermented foods where colonists saw rot. Europeans saw this Native willingness to eat a wide variety of foods—including horse meat and "rotten" fermented fish—as an animal disregard for anything but nourishment, as a food system built on chaos. It was, in fact, resilience, with Native diets carefully calibrated to environments and seasons.

Colonists tried to use narratives of their disgust with Native foodways to assert colonial hunger cultures and demean Native ones. But reading these narratives against the grain, a different story emerges. In their narrow and inflexible diets and their theatrical disgust, colonists revealed again the paucity of their hunger knowledges. Their descriptions of their disgust at Native foodways and their insistence that starving Native people resorted to eating rotten food instead served to highlight the variety and plenty that Native hunger knowledges offered their users. In writing to deny Native abundance, colonists provided archival evidence of Native resilience. Tekânadie's family took Kirkland into their home when they had little food to spare. *"Brother whiteman"* had neither the skills nor the money to provide more, so they fed an extra mouth with what they had. That he could barely stomach it was not their fault.[42]

In the borderlands, disgusting foodstuffs did not stop at rotten bear meat. While these foods challenged individual and cultural boundaries, another food source had the power to reaffirm and to destroy communities. Hunger would drive colonists and Native peoples to acts of violence and taboo, including consuming human flesh. In the midst of the colonial invasion, hunger knowledge could take grisly forms, such as applying the skills of animal butchery to the human body. But cultural survival might also mean maintaining traditions of ritual cannibalism, from the ceremonial torture of prisoners of war to the Catholic Eucharist or Protestant communion service. Or survival might entail telling stories of cannibal beings, warning against the dangers of greed—and the peril of the colonial monsters invading Native lands.

CHAPTER FOUR

EATEN UP

Cannibalism

In the first few months of his posting to Kanadasaga in 1765, Samuel Kirkland wrote nothing about cannibalism. But around the northeastern borderlands in the seventeenth and eighteenth centuries, others had plenty to say.

"You have almost eat us up," said Teganissorens, an Onondaga diplomat, in a speech to Louis de Buade de Frontenac, governor general of New France, during a negotiation between the French and the Haudenosaunee Confederacy in Albany in 1694. He continued, "Our best men are killed in this bloody war." Teganissorens wore a scarlet coat and a beaver hat trimmed with lace, and his dignified attire suited his purpose. He was trying to end King William's War, brokering peace between the Haudenosaunee Confederacy and the French, and calling on the French and English to make peace amongst themselves. Teganissorens would take up wampum belts again and again at negotiations like the one in Albany, for this war was one of many wars in a bloody time.[1]

Thomas Brown was near death. It was 1757, and he and an English companion had escaped from being enslaved by a French family. The two men walked from Quebec toward Crown Point for twenty-two days. Having eaten only "roots, worms, and such like" for fifteen of those days, Brown's companion succumbed to starvation. In desperation, Brown resolved "to make a fire . . . and eat his Flesh, and if no Relief came, to die with him." He cut some of the flesh from his companion's corpse, buried the body, and traveled on, catching three frogs to eat along the way. The next evening, Brown "sat down," "weak and tired," but could not bring himself to consume "my Friend's Flesh."[2]

In the late seventeenth century, the English Catholic convert John Gother penned numerous devotional works trying to win Protestants to Catholicism. Gother wrote that when receiving the Eucharist, he prayed, "My Saviour Jesus Christ, I firmly believe Thou art really present in the Blessed Sacrament; I believe that it contains thy Body and Blood, accompanied with thy Soul and Divinity." Gother believed in transubstantiation, or the priest's miraculous transformation of wafers and wine into Christ's flesh and blood during the Mass. Many Protestants regarded such practices with horror. In the opinion of the Massachusetts Puritan minister Cotton Mather, Catholics like Gother were "so much worse than Canabals." One side saw themselves imbibing a miracle; the other saw a crime. A religious disagreement based on flesh and blood convulsed Europe and its colonies with war.[3]

Teganissorens, Brown, Gother, and Mather may never have met each other, but they were all part of the same conversations about cannibalism taking place across the northeastern borderlands and the Atlantic in the seventeenth and eighteenth centuries. Cannibalism held multiple meanings across Native and colonial cultures. As with hunger, fasting, and disgust, colonists and Indigenous peoples came to the topic of cannibalism with their own understandings, and they struggled to understand each other. Just as hunger cultures defined the parameters of edible food, so too did hunger cultures define acceptance or lack of acceptance of cannibalism. Cannibalism offered yet another possible form of hunger knowledge: knowing how to use the human body as a food source of last resort, knowing how to maintain ritual cannibalism even in the midst of crisis, and knowing how to protect one's family and community from cannibalistic attackers.

All of these forms of knowledge would be necessary in a hungry and violent world.

According to scholars of cannibalism, eating people takes two main forms: survival cannibalism and ritual cannibalism. Survival cannibalism, the consumption of human flesh in order to avoid starvation, is cannibalism at its most straightforward. In the early northeast, hungry people sometimes resorted to eating one another rather than starving. Using hunger knowledge to forestall hunger, people could protect themselves from the possibility of having to commit survival cannibalism. But when that hunger knowledge was not enough, survival cannibalism required its own gruesome forms of hunger knowledge. Those who partook of human flesh in desperate circumstances used butchery skills honed on nonhuman animals.[4]

Lacking the hunger knowledges that protected Native peoples from hunger, colonists were more likely to face the reality of survival cannibalism than were Indigenous peoples. Ill-prepared colonists resorted to survival cannibalism most dramatically in the early days of the colonial invasion, but it continued throughout the period. Colonial observers acknowledged that survival cannibalism often took place at what they saw as the margins of the social order, such as the borderlands, but only accepted colonial survival cannibalism under specific circumstances. When commenting on Native survival cannibalism, colonists recorded few accounts of the practice and showed confusion between survival and ritual cannibalism among Native peoples.

Ready to adapt to conditions of scarcity, Native peoples were far less likely to resort to survival cannibalism than were colonists. Nevertheless, in rare circumstances it is possible that Indigenous peoples did consume human flesh in order to survive. But Native peoples also developed hunger knowledges around the avoidance of survival cannibalism, sharing horror stories of the windigo or Chenoo monster that cautioned their listeners against the perils of insatiable hunger. As colonists invaded their lands, Indigenous storytellers incorporated the newcomers into their stories as new faces of the monsters themselves.

While survival cannibalism treated human flesh as a source of much-needed nourishment, ritual cannibalism used human flesh to fulfill another necessity: the need for social or spiritual bonds. Ritual cannibalism

is the literal or metaphorical consumption of human flesh to fulfill specific ceremonial purposes. Within ritual cannibalism, anthropologists distinguish between endocannibalism, or the consumption of people from
within a community, and exocannibalism, the consumption of outsiders.
Scholars list a variety of reasons why different societies have undertaken
ritual cannibalism, but a key reason for both colonial and Indigenous
people was maintaining community bonds in the midst of religious warfare and colonialist violence.[5]

In early modern Europe and its colonies, ritual cannibalism occurred
commonly, in the form of Protestant and Catholic communion ceremonies
and medicinal cannibalism. These uses of human flesh and blood, whether
miraculous, metaphorical, or very literal indeed, engendered enormous controversy in Europe and its colonies in the centuries of religious warfare after
the Reformation. Even as they debated cannibalism among themselves,
many colonists contended that all Indigenous peoples were cannibals. While
ritual cannibalism was not nearly as widespread as colonists alleged, certain
Indigenous peoples did practice ritual cannibalism. Anthropologists have
argued that the practice occurred among Haudenosaunee, Wendat, and
Odawa people but not among the Wabanaki or other Algonquian peoples
farther to the east. For those nations that did engage in ritual cannibalism,
ingesting the flesh of prisoners or enemies helped to strengthen ties within
their communities, a task that became particularly urgent in response to the
colonial invasion.[6]

Ritual cannibalism was a very specific kind of feast, designed to cohere
communities while dominating enemies. Where religious fasting invoked
the power of abstention, communion rituals instead relied on consumption. Ingesting sacred bodies—the transformed or metaphorical body of
Christ, or the bodies of war captives—allowed eaters to imbibe various
forms of power. Ritual cannibalism blurred the lines between spiritual
and physical warfare, as communicants participated in either symbolic or
actual violence against other communities while binding together their
own. Seeking certainty in a world in flux, participants in communion rituals were well aware that the consequences of their consumption could
be life or death.

In the northeastern borderlands, human flesh could be a food source or
a ritual substance. While participants in cannibalism sought stability and

survival in an uncertain world, accusations of cannibalism made a power-ful weapon in borderlands wars. Colonists suspected all Native peoples of being bloodthirsty cannibals and used tales of Indigenous cannibalism, however spurious, to rationalize the colonial invasion. Colonists' censure of Native ritual cannibalism, and their imaginings of such practices even where none had taken place, would have deadly consequences for Indigenous peoples. Although colonists sought to paint all Indigenous peoples with the same bloody cannibal brush, Native people fought back against these fictions with narratives of their own. Many Native communities understood Europeans as cannibals, incorporating colonial intruders into oral traditions about cannibalistic monsters. For Teganissorens and others, cannibalism served as an apt metaphor for violence, and especially for the rapacious greed of colonization. The resulting Indigenous warnings against colonial monsters have resounded through the generations.

Colonial Understandings of Cannibalism

The colonial invasion created the figure of the Indigenous cannibal in the imaginations of European people. Like "disgust," the word "cannibal" originated with European exploration and colonization, deriving from the Spanish term for one of the first Indigenous groups that Spanish invaders encountered in the Caribbean, the Carib. From this moment onward, cannibalism became a preoccupation for European and colonial commentators. These writings shared common themes. The invaders grappled with the fear that, lacking knowledge of how to survive in the so-called New World, they might have to resort to survival cannibalism—as a number of them did, particularly in the early days of colonization. From their very first encounters with Indigenous peoples, colonizers accused Native peoples of being cannibals, and particularly of consuming their enemies via ritual cannibalism. Moreover, from the beginning of the colonial invasion, colonizers used accounts of Indigenous ritual cannibalism to comment on the religious turmoil overtaking the Christian world in the form of the Reformation.[7]

Colonizers' lack of hunger knowledges left them vulnerable to having to resort to survival cannibalism. Because of the food shortages and violence that plagued early colonial efforts, cannibalism rapidly became a focal point of European food anxieties, outstripping gluttony and other prior concerns. Indeed, one French Catholic homily collapsed gluttony and cannibalism into the same sin, vividly describing the sufferings that awaited gluttons in hell: "They will be tormented by famine, . . . which compels the mother to eat her infant, and to replace in her bosom that which came out of it; which reduces the man to devour himself, and become his own sepulcher, before his death." Across the Atlantic, this gruesome scene played out over and over again—not in the afterlife but in the colonies.[8]

Hunger and survival cannibalism nearly destroyed Jamestown, England's first permanent colony in North America. Due to a combination of drought, disease, English incompetence, and resistance by the Powhatans, the Jamestown colonists in the winter of 1609 to 1610 faced the "starving times." Like other famished populations, the colonists ate anything they could: horses, dogs, cats, rats, mice, whatever they could catch in the James River, boots and other leather, snakes, and so on. Next they began to resort to cannibalism, first by "digg[ing] upp dead corpes out of graves" and "Lick[ing] up the Bloode w[hi]ch hathe fallen from their weake fellows," and then by more drastic means. A letter by George Percy, briefly president of Jamestown, described a colonist who "murdered his wyfe Ripped the Childe outt of her woambe and threwe itt into the River and after Chopped the Mother in pieces and sallted her for his foode." Authorities hanged the man by his thumbs with weights at his feet until he confessed and then executed him. The survivors abandoned Jamestown in the spring and were on the verge of sailing home when, coincidentally, new colonists arrived to reinforce the outpost. Against the odds, Jamestown would endure, but England's earliest permanent colony in the Americas nearly failed due to famine, the collapse of social order, and survival cannibalism.[9]

A century and a half after the situation in Jamestown stabilized, borderlands warfare still left colonists in danger of survival cannibalism. In 1767 and 1757, respectively, Isaac Hollister and Thomas Brown gave similar accounts of near starvation due to a lack of hunger knowledge. In both accounts, Hollister and Brown contemplated cannibalizing their traveling companions. Hollister's companion told Hollister that whichever one of them died first should eat the other. Brown and his companion do not seem to have had a similar conversation. Brown agonized over the decision as he prepared human flesh to eat. In both narratives, out-side forces forestalled the men from consuming human flesh: a Seneca party captured Hollister, and French colonial hunters captured Brown. Both men eventually made their way back into British communities and wrote narratives of their experiences. Both emphasized their courage and their willingness to sacrifice in order to survive in an unfamiliar land-scape. Despite their happy endings, these two accounts of near cannibal-ism demonstrated the deadly consequences of colonists' inability to live off the land.[10]

As these examples show, survival cannibalism encountered different de-grees of censure by European authorities at different points in history. In seventeenth-century Jamestown, survival cannibalism faced harsh penalties, in spite of the grim circumstances that drove cannibals to their crimes. Murdering someone in order to consume their flesh, like the husband who killed and salted his wife, constituted a much greater crime than eating flesh from an already deceased person. By the eighteenth century, however, Brown and Hollister both admitted to near misses with cannibalism, even going so far as to mutilate a corpse with the intent to consume human flesh, but faced no legal consequences. Both claimed that they did not actually commit cannibalism, and even if they had, they would have been eating the flesh of people who had already starved to death. But their experiences also showed colonial societies' greater willingness to accept violent behavior from colonists captured by Native peoples. Colonial captives, in the eyes of Europeans, were immersed in a dangerous landscape among "savage" Indigenous people. In this view, colonists might be driven to commit canni-balism and other crimes, but the "civilizing" power of colonization would nevertheless inevitably triumph. Regardless of the specific circumstances, colonists would remain much more accepting of survival cannibalism among fellow Europeans than of *any* cannibalism among Native peoples.[11]

Colonizers' narratives of survival cannibalism coexisted awkwardly with the other conversations about cannibalism taking place in Europe at the time. The main debate, between Protestants and Catholics in the wake of the Reformation, revolved around the interpretation of Jesus's words in 1 Corinthians 11:24–25: "This is my body . . . . This cup is the new testament in my blood." Catholics believed that, during the Mass, a priest's blessing miraculously transformed, or transubstantiated, commu-

nion wafers and wine into "the Body and Blood of JESUS CHRIST, . . . under the forms or appearances of Bread and Wine," in the words of the
Douay Catechism. The Protestant Westminster Catechism, by contrast,
asserted that communicants consumed the flesh and blood of Christ "not
after a corporal and carnal manner, but by faith." Protestants read
Christ's words as a metaphor, whereas Catholics read them more literally.
When believers consumed the Eucharist, John Gother explained, they
imbibed a miracle, firm in their faith "that it really contains the Body of
Christ . . . ; and his Blood." Christ's holy body and blood were, according
to Gother, "a Heavenly Nourishment to my Soul." Decrying transubstantiation as a "monstrous figment," Protestants like Cotton Mather called
Catholics "so much worse than cannibals." Centuries of religious warfare, in Europe and the colonies, turned these bloody words into action.[12]

Though the opposing viewpoints at first glance seemed clear—
Protestant metaphor versus Catholic miracle—many individuals fell between these extremes on the question of communion. While Protestants
may have decried Catholics as bloodthirsty, *both* Protestant and Catholic
believers hungered for the body of Christ. Mather praised the life-sustain-
ing qualities of bread and wine, declaring that Christ's love similarly fed
the soul: "The Effects of *Bread* and *Wine,* most Elegantly answer'd the
Effects of our Approaches to the Lord Jesus in the *Sacrament,*" he wrote. "If
Bread nourish & strengthen the Body, much more will the Lord Jesus do so,
to the *Souls* of them, who draw near unto Him." Though Protestants were
not consuming actual flesh and blood, a true believer would be able to
"*Discern the Lords Body in the Lords Supper,*" Mather argued. But the importance of the Lord's Supper went beyond discerning the holy in the seemingly mundane. Communion satisfied a particular kind of spiritual hunger.
Mather encouraged communicants to "bring *Hungry* and *Thirsty* souls with
us, to this Feast of our God." The English Puritan minister Thomas
Doolittle asked of communicants, "Do you love him, would you not desire
to eat and drink at his Table, yea, to feast upon him? . . . Did you hunger
after him, and thirst for him, would you not desire to be there, where you
may be filled and satisfied?" Mather and Doolittle may have been describing a spiritual hunger and thirst for Christ, but when they compared these
sensations to actual eating and drinking, they nudged Protestant metaphors closer to Catholic literalism.[13]

The life of the Massachusetts Puritan minister, poet, and physician Edward Taylor embodied many of the complexities facing Protestants in the age of the transubstantiation debates. Although they had much to say about hunger, neither Doolittle nor Mather discussed the taste of the Lord's Supper, beyond Mather stating that those with "a *sense* of Truth" would be able to "*Tast* and *See*, that, *The Lord is Good*." But to some believers, like Taylor, the Lord's Supper tasted very good indeed. A prolific writer of devotional poetry, he composed several poems inspired by John 6:53, "Except you eat the flesh of the Son of Man, and drink his blood, ye have no Life in you." Unlike Mather and Doolittle, Taylor did not belabor the distinction between wine and blood. He described the Lord's Supper in visceral terms: "Thou, Lord, Envit'st me thus to eat thy Flesh / And drinke thy blood more Spiritfull than wine." In Taylor's poems, the Lord's Supper tasted *delicious*. The consecrating words of the minister transformed plain bread and wine into "rich fare": "My Souls Plumb Cake"; "Sweet junkets," or sweetmeats; and "Fruites . . . (more sweet than wine)." The Lord's Supper, then, tasted like a whole fantasy world of sweets. It also provided a special kind of nourishment that secular food could not, nourishment without which believers would starve: "I must eate or be a witherd stem," Taylor declared. While most Puritans protested that they conceived only metaphorically of their consumption of the body of Christ, Taylor's gustatory metaphors were particularly vivid and sensual, similar to those of Catholic devotional texts. Much like Taylor's sweet words about the Lord's Supper, Gother wrote of ingesting the host, "all that is within me might be delighted with the taste of thy Sweetness."[14]

Taylor's writings on the Lord's Supper would have presented a conundrum to Protestants eager to distinguish themselves from Catholic "cannibals," and the challenges did not stop there. In addition to being a minister, Taylor was a practicing physician, who belonged to the Paracelsian school of medical thought. In contrast to the more mainstream Galenists, who believed the way to health lay in balancing the humors, Paracelsians sought to heal the sick by more spiritual means, using their remedies to attract what they called the World Soul to the afflicted body part. For this purpose, Paracelsians turned to corpse medicine. Human blood took its place among an array of potent remedies made from semen, feces, urine, breast milk, bone (especially powdered skull), and preserved flesh known as "mummy." The term might refer to ancient Egyptian mummies, to travelers who had perished in Arabian sandstorms, to a thick pitch-like substance called bitumen, or to the preserved flesh of ordinary criminals. The ideal medicinal blood or flesh for mummy came from a young, hearty, red-haired man of ruddy complexion who had died suddenly. Red hair and the blood visible beneath his flushed skin meant that he had strong blood, and a sudden demise ensured that the life essence in his blood did not have time to escape during a protracted death. Public executions of criminals created a steady supply of fresh blood; epileptics crowded at the edge of the gallows to drink the blood that dripped down from executed prisoners. Marshalling these human-derived remedies, Paracelsians sought to harness the healing powers of the human soul. Taylor read deeply in Paracelsian thought and used mummy and other human-derived remedies in his own medical practice. The rhetoric of Paracelsian corpse medicine—that consuming one body could heal another—rhymed with Catholic arguments that ingesting transubstantiated flesh and blood could remedy spiritual and bodily ills. As Gother wrote, "I come to the Sacrament . . . as one sick to the Physician of Life." Ingesting the sacred made the holy body part of one's own.[15]

Protestants like Taylor hungered for the flesh and blood of Christ, and they made use of human flesh in medical rites that were tinged with spiritual significance. They did so even as they decried transubstantiation and called Catholics cannibals. The Lord's Supper was the supreme corpse medicine, but neither corpse medicine nor the Lord's Supper had anything to do with cannibalism in the eyes of both Protestants and Catholics. Nevertheless, corpse medicine peaked in popularity in the same era when Catholics and Protestants most heatedly debated transubstantiation. This was no accident. Indeed, the enthusiasm of Taylor and other Protestants for corpse medicine seems to have stemmed in part from a hunger for the bloody, fleshly experience of the Catholic Mass that they had foresworn. Consuming actual human flesh provided an embodied experience that the cerebral metaphor of the Protestant Lord's Supper simply could not deliver. From this desire came Taylor's visceral descriptions of communion with Jesus, of living bread that spoke as it crossed the communicant's lips: "This Bread of Life dropt in my mouth, doth Cry. / Eate, Eate me, Soul, and thou shalt never dy."[16]

Taylor recognized the precarious balance he had to strike between venerating the body of Christ and being a metaphorically minded Puritan. One of his poetic meditations posed these very questions about cannibalism and communion: "What feed on Humane Flesh and Blood? Strang mess! / Nature exclaims. What Barbarousness is here?" Like a good Protestant, Taylor answered himself with the argument that Christ's words were only symbolic: "This Sense of this blesst Phrase is nonsense thus. / Some other Sense makes this a metaphor."[17] Protestants like Taylor had a vexed relationship to the embodiedness of communion. Nevertheless, the powers of miracle and metaphor convinced both Catholics and Protestants that they themselves were not cannibals, even as they consumed human and holy bodies. They were unafraid, however, to condemn their enemies for hungering for human flesh.

Native Understandings of Cannibalism

Native peoples in what is now northeastern North America inhabited their own world of understandings of cannibalism. The complexities of this world are difficult to parse because of the colonial nature of the archive, where Europeans' fevered imaginings of Native cannibalism have occupied far more pages than Native explanations of their own traditions and worldviews. European writers usually flattened or obscured the multiplicity of Native experiences of cannibalism. Colonial observers tended to address Native ritual cannibalism in only the most sensational terms, and without considering the ways that just as in colonial cultures, ritual cannibalism fulfilled specific needs for the Native communities who practiced it. Moreover, colonists often confused situations of ritual and survival cannibalism among Native peoples.

Like Europeans, Indigenous peoples had diverse ideas about survival and ritual cannibalism. The conventional historical record of how Native peoples interpreted each other's cannibalism is very thin, but engaging with contemporary Native and Indigenous Studies scholarship, as well as oral traditions, offers a more holistic view of Indigenous understandings of cannibalism. Algonquian-speaking peoples navigated both colonialism and survival cannibalism through oral traditions. The Haudenosaunee and Wendat people practiced ritual cannibalism of outsiders, ceremonies designed to imbibe the power of their enemies and strengthen their communities. All faced vicious colonial stereotypes.

Like Europeans, Native peoples confronted the bleak necessity of survival cannibalism. Despite their powerful hunger knowledges, northeastern Indigenous peoples sometimes resorted to survival cannibalism, or at least feared this possibility acutely. Such fears were particularly prominent among nations of the far north that relied more heavily upon wild food provision than extensive agriculture. These peoples lived close to the margins of survival in the winter season, but war and disease—especially the disruptions brought by colonial invasion—could tip the balance into starvation and the possibility of cannibalism. While actual incidents of survival cannibalism may have been a rare occurrence, the potential for cannibalism occupied an important space in these cultures. Before and after colonization, Native peoples wrestled with the problems of sustaining families and communities in the face of the possibility of consuming human flesh.

French accounts from the mid-seventeenth century recorded the effects of wars which, though fought between Native nations, had been exacerbated by colonialism. Seventeenth-century French missionaries described how a series of conflicts called the Beaver Wars led to sensational episodes of survival cannibalism. In 1635, Paul le Jeune described Haudenosaunee raiders destroying Innu farms: "The Iroquois . . . have burned everything," the priest explained. "One can still see the ends of the blackened stubble" of corn in the fields. With corn supplies running low, winter brought famine to the Innu. Hunting parties "have been found frozen stiff in the snow, killed by cold and hunger." The priest reported that Indigenous peoples in the area resorted to survival cannibalism, both of colonists and of members of their communities and families. "Near Gaspé" some people "killed and ate a young man who the Basques had left with them to learn their language. Those in Tadoussac . . . have eaten each other in some places," he wrote. With the exception of the Basque colonist, the cannibalism le Jeune described involved the eating of community members and was taking place among nations that did not practice ritual cannibalism in other times. It seems clear, therefore, that le Jeune described survival cannibalism, born out of desperation, famine, and war, rather than ritual practices.[18]

EATEN UP

Although the Wendat did have traditions of ritual cannibalism, some colonial accounts pointed to Wendat survival cannibalism in times of duress.
In 1650, another Catholic missionary, Paul Ragueneau, described Wendat
refugees fleeing Haudenosaunee raids and living under desperate circumstances on an island in Lake Huron. He depicted survival cannibalism
breaking down social boundaries, with starving people digging up the
corpses of their relatives: "The people have repeatedly offered, as food,
those who were lately the dear pledges of love,—not only brothers to brothers, but even children to their mothers, and the parents to their own children." Recounting these events, Ragueneau was quick to assure his readers
that colonists would have behaved no differently in the same circumstances.
"It is no less unusual among our savages than among the Europeans, who
abhor eating flesh of their own kind," he wrote. "Doubtless the teeth of the
starving man . . . do not recognize in the dead body him who a little before
was called, until he died, father, son, or brother." In his telling, Ragueneau
showed no confusion between Wendat ritual and survival cannibalism, recognizing that the eating of relatives occurred only under extreme circumstances, in contrast to ritual cannibalism's consumption of outsiders. While
Ragueneau drew parallels between Wendat and European survival cannibalism, showing an unusual degree of empathy for a colonial observer, he
still referred to the Wendat as "savages."[19]

However Europeans interpreted Indigenous survival cannibalism,
the possibility left a powerful mark on the traditions of northeastern
Indigenous peoples. Many Algonquian-speaking nations told stories of a
cannibalistic monster, most commonly called the windigo in English.
Living in seasonal cycles of plenty and scarcity, the Wabanaki were familiar
with the potential for hunger and feared what starvation could do to its sufferers. They called their version of the monster the Chenoo. M'ikmaq and
Passamaquoddy stories collected by colonizers in the nineteenth century
described the Chenoo as a monster that attacked family bands traveling
north on their winter hunts. Sometimes the Chenoo appeared fully
formed, while other times the members of a hunting party were vulnerable
to being transformed into the Chenoo themselves.[20]

The first kind of Chenoo, who met hunting bands as an outsider,
appeared as a thin old man with "shoulders and lips . . . gnawed away, as
if, when mad with hunger, he had eaten his own flesh." He hunted hu-

124

mans for food and carried with him a bundle containing "a pair of human legs and feet." In one version of the story, as told to a White
ethnographer in the nineteenth century, a family welcomed the Chenoo
into their home in the hopes that kind treatment would keep the monster
from killing them. Under their hospitality, the Chenoo underwent a reformation after drinking hot tallow, violently expelling "all the horrors and
abominations of earth" from his body. When a female Chenoo attacked
the family, the male Chenoo cut out her heart and ate part of it. Every
trace of the enemy Chenoo's body had to be destroyed, and so the human man and the Chenoo cut up the corpse and melted down the rest of
the heart, which was colder than ice. Although he had shown a great capacity for transforming himself to live in a human community, the
Chenoo could survive only in the colder northern regions of the winter
hunts. When the family brought him southward to their summer village,
he converted to Christianity at the behest of a White missionary and died
peacefully.[21]

While the Chenoo of the previous story appeared fully formed, other
Passamaquoddy and M'ikmaq traditions described how desire or witchcraft could transform people into cannibalistic monsters. Part of the horror of these stories hinged on the fact that Wabanaki hunting bands were
composed of families, so that the violence of the Chenoo imperiled the
family unit from within. In one M'ikmaq story, when a young woman re-
buffed a young man's invitation to marry, he bewitched her by drugging
her with an intoxicating plant and then placing a lump of snow on her
throat to chill her heart. The woman's "whole nature . . . changed" into
something monstrous. She began to have strange cravings for eating snow,
and then for committing violence, warning her family that "unless they
killed her she would certainly be their death." The woman instructed her
family to shoot her seven times, but it took forty-nine shots to the heart for
the woman to die. The family burned the woman's body, including her icy
heart. Recognizing that she was transforming into a Chenoo, the woman
had begged her family to kill her in order to save themselves.[22]

The story of the Chenoo or windigo cast a long shadow over the winter
traditions of northeastern Native peoples, speaking to anxieties about the
potential for survival cannibalism and the ways that hunger could endanger relationships. While Indigenous fears about hunger remain much

more elusive in the archive than European accounts of scarcity, the Chenoo was an avatar for the terrible transformations hunger wrought in its sufferers. The Chenoo's insatiable appetite, greed, and violence represented the breakdown of families and communities in a world where people had to work together and share resources to survive the long winter. It is no coincidence that most Chenoo stories began with hunting bands departing their summer lands and heading north. Carrying only limited food with them, relying almost entirely on the availability of game in the depths of winter, hunting bands operated under risks of privation. The Chenoo took possession of hungry people and turned them into monsters who threatened their families and communities. The Chenoo tradition offered northern Indigenous peoples another form of hunger knowledge—a means of illustrating the dangers of hunger and cannibalism and of passing this knowledge down through generations through stories told in winter hunting camps.

Despite the power of the Chenoo stories, it is important not to overstate the extent of food shortage the Wabanaki experienced on these winter hunts, particularly in the times before the colonial invasion. The Wabanaki were skilled at surviving in winter. They voyaged long distances through difficult weather and terrain and thrived on plentiful game. In addition to the work of subsistence, winter offered a time to maintain political and familial ties and to pass on traditional knowledge, from the technologies of snowshoe production to the stories of the Chenoo and other legendary figures. Family bands who did not have successful hunts often relied on redistributed food from other families. The cautionary tales of the Chenoo stories helped guide Wabanaki winter subsistence: mutuality, not greed, would help people survive in the cold season, as the Wabanaki thrived in their traditional ways well into the eighteenth century.[23]

The colonial invaders would appropriate Wabanaki winter knowledges as they tried to survive the cold season. It took over a generation for colonists to begin to recognize the strategic importance of Wabanaki winter ways. Once colonists formed their own raiding parties on snowshoes, they began to chip away at Wabanaki winter resources, killing Wabanaki men who hunted for their families and introducing diseases that ravaged Wabanaki communities. The resultant suffering made its way into Indigenous storytelling and also into colonial narratives. The windigo tradition intersected with monsters from European folklore; one Algonquian-French dictionary translated "windigo" as *loups garoux,* or werewolf. The intertwining of these monster traditions gave colonists a language with which to articulate their own experiences of starvation and fear in the unfamiliar landscapes of the northern borderlands.[24]

But the colonizers did not realize that they had earned themselves a starring role in Chenoo stories. The White ethnographer who collected the M'ikmaq and Passamaquoddy Chenoo stories in the nineteenth century noted that the woman who was transforming into a Chenoo told her family to shoot at her with guns. The ethnographer, however, changed this detail to arrows, noting in the footnotes his assumption that these stories were "evidently very ancient, and refer[red] to terrors of the olden time." Yet such colonial clues crop up repeatedly in the stories that the ethnographer collected, from the guns the family used to kill the young woman to the White missionary who baptized the dying Chenoo. Such details suggest that, at the very least, tradition-bearers adapted their traditions to the specifics of colonial incursion. But these stories also presented a way of grappling with colonialism itself, leading to an explosion of windigo tales in the wake of the colonial invasion.[25]

The windigo tradition was not confined to Indigenous cultures; accounts of Native people exhibiting windigo behavior also surfaced in colonial records. Jesuits in Quebec in 1661 heard a disturbing story from a party of French and Indigenous men traveling through Tadoussac. On their journey, several of the Indigenous men developed a "disease" that gave them "a more than canine hunger" for human flesh. They were "unable to appease or glut their appetite" and "forever searching for fresh prey." Eventually, the party executed those suffering from the disease. Although the account does not mention the windigo or Chenoo, the behavior that the Indigenous men exhibited matches descriptions of people transformed into windigos in Indigenous storytelling.[26]

While the windigo tradition has been associated most strongly with Algonquian-speaking peoples across the northeast and upper Midwest, the fear of becoming a cannibal haunted non-Algonquian-speaking peoples, as well. The Jesuit missionaries Joseph Chaumont and Claude Dablon reported in the 1650s that an Onondaga man had a dream of hosting a cannibalistic feast. Because many Indigenous peoples believed that dreams could be predictive, the man feared the implications of his dream. He called a meeting of community leaders and informed them "he had had a dream that could not be executed." Beyond fearing for himself, the man feared the terrible social and even global implications of his desires: "his ruination would cause that of the whole Nation; and . . . the destruction of the earth." Community leaders devised a ceremonial solution for the man's dream. The group arranged for a human sacrifice, choosing a female victim. The man who had the dream made a move to strike the woman down, but instead he declared, "I am satisfied, my dream does not want more." Ritual had reined in the man's abnormal desire for human flesh. A community solution to the dream preserved "the whole Nation" and "the earth" from upheaval.[27]

The feast of human flesh in the Onondaga man's dream would not have been out of place in other Native nations that practiced ritual cannibalism of war captives. The Jesuit Jean de Brebeuf described in a 1636 account how the Wendat community he missionized ritually processed Haudenosaunee prisoners. A male prisoner of war faced days of slow torture with fire and knives. To prove his bravery, the captive would sing throughout his torments. Upon the death of the prisoner, Wendat men would cut out his heart, "grill it on the coals, and distribute it in pieces to the youths"; others would "make an incision at the top of the [captive's] neck, and make the blood run" and drink it. The rest of the body would be cut into pieces, cooked in a kettle, and shared with the community. The Wendat men who participated argued that this ceremony allowed them to absorb the prisoner's bravery into themselves, and that "since they have mingled his blood with theirs, they can never be surprised by the enemy, and will always be aware of his approaches."[28]

Other Jesuit missionaries reported similar rituals among Haudenosaunee peoples. In 1642, Barthélemy Vimont wrote of a Haudenosaunee surprise attack on an Algonquian village, culminating in the butchering and cooking of corpses: "The wolves devoured their prey; one seized a thigh, another a breast. Some sucked out the marrow from the bones, others opened the heads to draw out the brains." The men ate this meal "with as much joy, as hunters who eat a wild boar or a stag." Vimont's description, which compared the Haudenosaunee to hunters but referred to them as not just "wolves" but "werewolves" and "half Demons," struggled to define

Haudenosaunee who participated in this ritual, mixing words for humans, animals, and other-than-human beings. Vimont continued on to relate the experiences of an Algonquian woman named Kicheuigoukwe, who was captured alongside her two-month-old infant. Collecting babies from their prisoners, the raiders "took our little children, tied them to a branch, presented them to the fire, and roasted them before our eyes." When the children died, the raiders boiled them in a kettle and ate them in front of their mothers. While this story is sensational, it was quite rare for Jesuit chroniclers to record the experiences of named Native women like Kicheuigoukwe in the first person, which raises the possibility that Kicheuigoukwe was a real person describing real events.[29]

Despite centuries of colonial condemnation, some Indigenous ritual cannibalism of prisoners of war persisted into the eighteenth century according to sensationalized colonial accounts. After the fall of Fort William Henry in 1757, during the Seven Years' War, the English soldier Jonathan Carver wrote of seeing Indigenous combatants drinking "the blood of their victims, as it flowed warm from the fatal wound." At this same battle, the Jesuit missionary Pierre Roubaud claimed he witnessed Odawa warriors washing down the flesh of British prisoners with "skullfuls of human blood." Roubaud asked one of the Odawa men why they were eating their prisoner, and the man replied, *"You have the French taste; me Savage, this meat good for me,"* before offering Roubaud a piece of the "English roast." The Jesuit rejected the gift of meat and called the Odawa man's argument "worthy of a barbarian," depicting him as a cannibal who defended his appetite in broken French.[30]

While colonists like Roubaud and Carver certainly exaggerated their descriptions of Indigenous ritual cannibalism, their accounts echoed those of earlier times. The consistency across colonial descriptions of ritual cannibalism among Wendat and Haudenosaunee peoples hints that they were based to some degree on actual practices. Such continuity across the centuries suggests that some communities maintained traditions of ritual cannibalism in spite of colonial censure. Given the centrality of cannibalism to anti-Native rhetoric, European observers rarely understood cannibalism's place in larger social systems. But, for the people who participated in it, ritual cannibalism could help to make sense of a world riven by colonialism. Like other kinds of ceremonial behavior, cannibalism performed a social function, reinforcing roles and hierarchies within and across communities. Like adoption or enslavement, ritual cannibalism offered a way for communities to absorb outsiders, such as prisoners of war; these efforts became especially necessary in response to colonial genocide.[31]

Ritual cannibalism derived its power from what the literary scholar Kyla Tompkins has termed "eating culture," recognizing that eaters have power over the eaten and that the consumed can exert their own forms of power over consumers. Wendat traditions told of the goddess Ata-entsic who "sucked the blood of men, causing them to die of illness and weakness," in the words of the French missionary Joseph François Lafitau. In a world where gods ate people, cannibalizing a captive taken in war dramatically demonstrated power over one's foes. Such ceremonies also demarcated a community's boundaries: a community member could not be eaten, but an outsider or enemy could. At the same time, consuming the flesh of another incorporated whatever advantage the enemy might have over the consumer. Describing how the Wendat consumed prisoners of war, Brebeuf wrote that the Wendat believed that consuming a captive meant that they could "never be surprised by the enemy." An individual's body mapped their community, their territory, their secrets. Ritual cannibalism harnessed the body's unique power.[32]

The Wendat might have had particular reason to demonstrate ritual cannibalism of a prisoner for Brebeuf in 1636, as the violence of colonization rocked their nation. Through a ceremony of torture and cannibalism, the Wendat sought to shore up their own social order, while demonstrating to a European outsider the power relations within their culture. A decade and a half after Brebeuf wrote his account of this ritual, as war with the Haudenosaunee uprooted and scattered Wendat communities, Haudenosaunee raiders captured, tortured, and executed him, drank his blood, and ate his heart.[33]

Experiencing Cannibalism in the Borderlands

If ritual cannibalism sought to bring people together, rhetoric about cannibalism served to drive them apart. As much as some aspects of colonists' and Native peoples' cannibalism traditions resembled each other,

Europeans could not find common ground with Native people over the consumption of human flesh because the colonial project relied upon stereotypes of ravenous Native cannibals. Colonial observers used accounts of Wendat and Haudenosaunee ritual cannibalism for shock value, stoking colonial beliefs that *all* Native people were cannibals. Deploying the figure of the Native cannibal over and over again, colonists laid the foundations for dispossession. Nevertheless, Indigenous peoples resisted these narratives, both by mocking colonial fears and by developing their own narratives of colonial invaders as cannibalistic monsters.

Cannibalism occupied a crucial space in the imagination of colonialism, far outpacing incidences of actual cannibalism. Both colonists and Native peoples used cannibalism metaphors to describe borderlands violence. Preaching on a public fast day in Boston in the midst of King George's War in 1745, the Massachusetts minister Samuel Checkley invoked Jeremiah 30:16, warning soldiers not to "delight in War, nor love to shed Blood, and *prey upon* and *devour* our Fellow-Creatures." Similarly, Teganissorens pronounced that the French had "almost eat us up" after years of war in the 1690s. In the Wabanaki prewar feast, Roubaud claimed, the captain of a raiding party held up a roasted dog's head and declared, *"Behold the head of the enemy."* The captain's statement linked the consumption of an animal to the defeat of an opponent, but only metaphorically, given that the Wabanaki did not practice ritual cannibalism of captive enemies. Roubaud wrote that the leader would then toss the dog's head on the ground, demonstrating that "meat from another species is needed to satisfy his military appetite," the missionary drawing out the cannibalism comparison even further. Another missionary described Wabanaki raiding parties dividing up enemy territory with the statement, "To you is given this village to eat." These instances of rhetorical cannibalism far outnumbered actual incidences of the ritualized consumption of human flesh.[34]

Nevertheless, the fear of cannibalism pervaded French and British colonists' imaginings of Native peoples, creating cannibalism even where it had not taken place. Colonists consistently invoked cannibalism in descriptions of Indigenous people eating, describing Native hunger in almost identical language whether they were ceremonially executing and cannibalizing a prisoner or consuming mundane foods. Roubaud wrote that the

Odawas who ate British prisoners wanted to "satiate" a "more than canine hunger" "with ... starving greed." In Susanna Johnson's account, her Wabanaki captors "satiated their craving appetites" for horsemeat with "Native gluttony." In Roubaud's depiction, the Odawa were eating the flesh of British prisoners after a battle. In Johnson's telling, the Wabanaki dined on horse meat. The nearly identical language in these descriptions suggests that Roubaud and Johnson were disgusted not merely with what Native people ate—horsemeat and human flesh, two kinds of flesh that were taboo to Europeans—but also with the fact that it was Native people doing the eating. For colonists obsessed with cannibalism, all Native hunger became suspect.[35]

Even colonists who did not witness incidents of Native cannibalism still ascribed cannibalistic behavior to Native people. Scenes of Indigenous individuals threatening to eat English children recurred over and over in colonial women's captivity narratives, with both Mary Rowlandson and Elizabeth Hanson maintaining that Native men had threatened to eat their children. One Native man told Rowlandson that he "did eat a piece of" her son "and that he was very good meat." Hanson's Wabanaki captor announced that "*when* [her baby] *was fat enough, it should be killed, and he would eat it.*" Hanson's account hinted at the possibility of survival cannibalism, with Hanson's captor's threat arriving during a time of food shortage; the man's mother-in-law explained to Hanson that "the Want of Victuals urged him" to threaten her child. Rowlandson's narrative did not offer an explanation for the man's purported cannibalism. In both cases, no children came to cannibalistic harm. Instead, the Native men who made these statements were probably poking fun at English women's fears of Native cannibals, showing an awareness of and commenting on colonial ideas about Native peoples.[36]

Moreover, the figure of the Indigenous cannibal caused colonial narrators to imagine cannibalism when it had not even taken place. When her Native captors informed Jemima Howe that her young children had died, she visualized "the naked carcasses of my deceased children hanging upon the limbs of the trees." Grieving and frightened, Howe envisioned her captors treating her children like game, displaying their corpses like "the raw hides of those beasts which they take in hunting." But the children were alive after all, and Howe reunited with them weeks later.

Howe's closest encounter with cannibalism came at this reunion, when her hungry baby "bit me with such violence that it seemed as if I must have parted with a piece of my cheek." This trope of threatened children and cannibalistic Indians pointed to a presumption of cannibalism that gnawed at the colonial imagination. For colonial women such as Johnson, Rowlandson, Hanson, and Howe, the threat of cannibalism permeated even innocuous Native actions.[37]

Cannibalism proved powerful in the colonial imagination because it offered the ultimate means for dehumanizing one's enemies. And while the rhetoric of cannibalism far outpaced documented incidences, actual cannibalism did play a role in borderlands violence. The British called all their enemies cannibals, describing cannibalism as part of French and Indigenous rituals of torture and execution. Dudley Bradstreet, a lieutenant at the siege of Louisbourg in 1745, related how Native men allied to the French tortured and killed a British soldier, then "Obligd one of our men to eat a part of him." John Norton, a British minister taken captive by French and Indigenous soldiers at the fall of Fort Massachusetts in the Berkshires in 1746, told of how a group of Indigenous men killed the fort's watchman and mutilated his corpse. Next, "a young Frenchman took one of the Arms and flay'd it, roasted the Flesh, and offer'd some of it to . . . one of the Prisoners, to eat; but he refused it." Neither Bradstreet nor Norton accused the Indigenous or French men of actually *being* cannibals themselves; rather, the Indigenous men of Bradstreet's story and the "young Frenchman" of Norton's tried to make other people *become* cannibals. British commentators saw these actions as part of a larger program of French cannibalism, in which British captives had to resist the seduction of French Catholicism and the "cannibalistic" Mass. Imbibing such rhetoric about French and Indigenous threats of cannibalism, the British feared that they might be transformed into the cannibals they perceived their enemies to be.[38]

Colonial invaders weaponized their own fears of cannibalism in order to justify the dispossession of Native peoples and the destruction of Native cultures. The Jesuits who described the Onondaga man's attempts to keep his cannibalistic dream from coming true concluded their account with, "Is it not a great charity to open the eyes of a people so grossly abused?" Upon witnessing Wendat ritual cannibalism, Brebeuf wrote, "We hope . . . , that the knowledge of the true God will banish this barbarity entirely from this country." Missionaries used Native ritual cannibalism to rationalize the spread of Christianity and the suppression of Native ritual practices. Accusing one's enemies of cannibalism dehumanized them, simultaneously rationalizing religious war between empires and the colonial conquest of the Americas. But in colonists' eagerness to call Native peoples cannibals lurked some invaders' fear that their violence against Native peoples could not be justified after all.[39]

Because the colonial invasion has privileged the invaders' voices, the myth of the bloodthirsty Native cannibal has cast a long shadow. But Indigenous peoples, too, could use cannibal rhetoric against their enemies. Seventeenth- and eighteenth-century Native peoples adapted their windigo traditions to the colonial threat, incorporating guns and missionaries into older stories. They recognized—as do their descendants—that colonialism sweeps across the earth as contagious cannibalistic violence. Colonizers' greed for land, for resources, for human bodies is the same greed that causes the windigo to stalk the frozen woods. Unlike the Native cannibals of the colonizers' imaginations, who menaced the colonial enterprise, the windigo's ravenous hunger threatens the entire world.[40]

In the midst of colonial invasion and Indigenous resistance, cannibalism formed part of hunger cultures and knowledges in the northeast. Knowing how to resort to survival cannibalism or how to maintain ritual cannibalism enabled people to survive both physically and culturally. By participating in cannibalism, or responding to other peoples' cannibalism, people in the northeastern borderlands defined themselves. Often, but not always, they wanted to define themselves as anything but cannibals. But the reality tended to be much more complicated.

Colonial and metropolitan Europeans inhabited a fractured world of ideas and practices about cannibalism. Whereas European and colonial individuals faced varying levels of punishment for committing survival cannibalism over time, Isaac Hollister and Thomas Brown could openly write about eating human flesh in the mid-eighteenth century and face no public censure or legal trouble. Although Protestants accused Catholics of being cannibals for believing in the miracle of transubstantiation, Christians of many denominations wrote about hungering for the flesh of Christ and engaged in medicinal cannibalism in the early modern period. For Europeans, survival cannibalism could be excused in times of need, and ritual cannibalism, in the form of communion or corpse medicine, was not necessarily recognized as cannibalism at all.

While Europeans saw a fairly clear dividing line between survival cannibalism and ritual cannibalism and the rationalizations for both, colonists had much more simplistic ideas about Indigenous cannibalism. Colonial observers of Native people tended to blur the two types of cannibalism together, when the invaders did not elide the possibility of Native survival cannibalism altogether. Very few accounts of Native survival cannibalism survive relative to the number of European narratives. The relative paucity of Native survival cannibalism in the archives poses two interpretative questions. Did Europeans leave instances of Native survival cannibalism out of the written archive, as they obscured much of Indigenous hunger, hunger knowledge, systems of bodily control, and disgust? Or did Native people resort to survival cannibalism less often than European people, simply because they had more effective systems of hunger knowledge that kept them from having to eat each other to survive? It was probably a combination of both of these factors: Europeans wrote Native survival cannibalism out of the record in favor of the more sensationalized (and taboo) ritual cannibalism, and superior hunger knowledge usually protected Native peoples from the extremity of eating human flesh.[41]

In the end, even more so than disgust, the hungers that drove different kinds of cannibalism fundamentally divided Native peoples and colonists. Colonists argued that cannibalism was permissible only under circumstances of dire necessity, while engaging in ritual cannibalism themselves for a variety of spiritual and medical reasons. But for those Indigenous communities that practiced it, ritual cannibalism did fulfill a need—it offered a stabilizing force of cultural cohesion in the face of colonial destruction. While Indigenous Studies scholars have described colonialism as a form of cannibalism, colonialism also *created* cannibalism, from the conditions of starvation that caused survival cannibalism among embattled Native communities, to the completely imaginary cannibalism that percolated in Jemima Howe's mind during her captivity, to the word "cannibal" itself.

Whether or not people witnessed cannibalism in the flesh, it had a hold on their minds. Priests describing an outbreak of windigo-like violence in 1661 wrote of it as a sickness that "injures their imagination." So, too, did colonialism injure the imaginations of colonists, causing them to be incapable of understanding Native cannibalism where it did occur, or to see any similarities to their own practices and, moreover, to invent Indigenous cannibalism where it did not even exist. In European eyes, all Native ritual cannibalism was horrifying, barbaric, and justification for genocide and dispossession. In debates about cannibalism, hunger violently turned French and British, Algonquian and Haudenosaunee and Wendat peoples against each other.[42]

European communion rituals offered a bloody metaphor for community in a time of great bloodshed. Brown's account of his near cannibalism bolstered colonial ideals of masculinity in the face of "savagery." Confronting colonists' ravenous hunger for Native lands, Teganissorens could not broker a permanent peace. The windigo of colonialism stalked the northern borderlands. As Samuel Kirkland realized, violent appetites threatened to consume all.

But there were ways of keeping the cannibals at bay. Indigenous traditions of cannibal monsters offered warnings against trusting colonial invaders and their insatiable greed. These stories also offered instructions for how to resist the invaders. In the version of the Chenoo story where the Chenoo appeared to a family at a hunting camp, the family's generosity and hospitality to the Chenoo initiated the monster's transformation into a human being. Wabanaki norms of hospitality and reciprocity could defang monsters.[43] Taking care of others so that all would survive—this, too, was a form of hunger knowledge.

Native hunger cultures emphasized reciprocity, arguing that members of families and communities owed each other sustenance. Colonizers, too, came from worlds with reciprocal hierarchies of status and power. Food made these relationships tangible, as people shared meals, withheld food supplies, or demanded rations based upon changing balances of power. For British imperial officials, food offered a way to demonstrate authority over both their fellow colonists and Indigenous peoples. But Indigenous leaders and ordinary colonists demanded reciprocity from British imperial authorities. As the British discovered in the eighteenth century, these kinds of resistance—and these kinds of hungers—could threaten empires from within and without.

CHAPTER FIVE

GIVE US SOME PROVISION

Resistance

When Samuel Kirkland arrived to the British Fort Brewerton in the spring of 1765, he left his family on the shores of Oneida Lake and walked up to the garrison. A soldier pointed the missionary toward the barracks of the commanding officer. Kirkland carried a "passport and recommendation" from General Thomas Gage, the commander in chief of the British army in North America, which guaranteed a warm greeting from the officer, who "received me with every mark of civility," Kirkland reported. The officer "asked me to partake of the remains of [his] dinner," which the hungry missionary did, with embarrassing voracity, and with nothing to offer in return.[1] But up until that point, Kirkland's description of his arrival to the fort had emphasized the orderliness of the British military and the norms of hospitality that welcomed the missionary to the officer's table. Kirkland's rude table manners and ruder speech to the officer violated both the officer's hospitality and the hierarchical colonial networks that had earned the missionary a recommendation from Gage. In its breakdown of hierarchy and reciprocity, Kirkland's disagreeable meal resembled many other negotiations over food taking place around the northeastern borderlands.

November 3, 1758, was a "very cold day" at the British Fort William Henry, at the southern tip of what the British called Lake George, New York. For the soldiers in the midst of the Seven Years' War, the frigid weather "so much affected" them that they "could not forgit rum." An anonymous soldier's diary reported that the men spent the day in a "Continual Caling out," shouting, "rawrum, not rum, Strong rum, home, home home." The hollering soldiers longed for "Strong rum," the sensation of warmth it provided, and for home.[2]

This "hollowing" faced a harsh punishment. The next day, one man "rec[eive]d About 20 Lashes for being so unhapy as to be Detectd in Yesterdays Frolicks" of yelling. One year later and about fifteen miles south, Luke Knowlton reported from Fort Edward that George Shaw had been court martialed for "Stealing Liquor" and received fifteen lashes "with a Cat of nine Tails." The disobedience of shouting out of turn, or of stealing liquor, faced similar penalties in the British army in the late eighteenth century.[3]

British military authorities, like colonial religious and political leaders, sought to control appetites, bodies, and minds. A properly fed and disciplined army, they hoped, could defeat the French and their Indigenous allies, furthering the cause of British colonialism in North America. Officers tried to maintain discipline, for one kind of disobedience might lead to another. One minute the men were yelling for rum; the next they yelled for home, a threat of desertion. The desire for rum, British authorities feared, was only one of many dangerous hungers for food, drink, and freedom, hungers that could only be contained through force—if they could be contained at all.

Twenty years earlier in 1738, in the chambers of the Massachusetts General Council in Boston, the governor, Jonathan Belcher, asked a delegation of Penobscot and Norridgewock negotiators from the Wabanaki Confederacy whether they were satisfied with their lodgings and meals. Such an inquiry was a formality, a host demonstrating care for the comfort of his guests. Yet in the context of intense negotiations between colonial statesmen and Wabanaki officials, the question took on immense political significance. When Belcher told the representatives that he "hope[d] you are kindly treated," the veteran Penobscot diplomat Loron disagreed: "Not so well treated as formerly," he informed Belcher. Loron continued, "We have Victuals enough at dinner but nothing but broth morning & night." Belcher drank a toast to the health of King George II, then assented: "If you ha'nt Provision enough, I'll take care that you have enough."[4]

In this moment, a colonial official capitulated to a Native diplomat's food demands—a dynamic that both reinforced and challenged colonial aspirations in the northeastern borderlands. Far from being submissive, the leaders of the Wabanaki Confederacy mandated that they receive treatment on an equal footing with English gentlemen when they came to negotiate in Boston. For the British, by contrast, feeding Wabanaki leaders offered a chance to tell the Wabanaki that they were dependent on British benevolence—a dependence that Loron and other Wabanaki denied at every turn. In Wabanaki and British diplomacy, the politics of the dinner table became the politics of the negotiating table.

Loron's assertion to Belcher that the Wabanaki negotiators were "not so well treated" was a protest against British assertions of colonial hierarchy, a demand for reciprocity, and an act of Wabanaki resistance. In the outbreak of rum-based disobedience at Fort William Henry, colonial soldiers likewise battled British authorities' attempts to control their appetites. These moments of resistance, centered around food and alcohol and based in a politics of reciprocity, challenged imperial hierarchies in the deeply hierarchical eighteenth century.[5]

Negotiations between Indigenous and colonial leaders, and interactions between soldiers and officers at colonial military installations, might at first not seem to have much in common. The forts were places of war, the treaty sites (at least ostensibly) places of peace. But all of these negotiations took place in spaces that had distinctive meanings for their participants. During treaty conferences, Massachusetts colonial representatives traveled from Boston to the Dawnland, or Wabanaki diplomats from their territories to the colonial city. One of the parties at a negotiation, then, was always far from home, a guest. In British military outposts, soldiers were always far from home, though the vastness of that distance depended on whether they were provincial soldiers or regulars shipped across the Atlantic. The forts were destinations and departure points for a variety of

GIVE US SOME PROVISION

people, locals and visitors, who lived, labored, traveled, traded, or were imprisoned in these British spaces. For the British, military or diplomatic actions often took place on the very edges of the empire, places that were difficult for colonists to access, survive in, or understand. For Wabanaki negotiators, by contrast, their homelands were the center of their world and the source of their power.

Struggles for power shaped meals in the transitional spaces of forts and negotiating tables. Visitors—people far from home—needed to be provided for. Provisioning was a gesture of hospitality—sometimes equals acknowledging equality, but more often a symbol of beneficence to dependents. But in the offering of food—the provisioning of a visitor—there was also usually an expectation of reciprocity; givers expected something from recipients. In the minds of Massachusetts colonial officials, the Wabanaki owed their fealty to the colonial government. As part of this effort, Massachusetts leaders wove a narrative of lawful, benevolent colonial authorities taking charge of naïve, helpless Native peoples and spread this narrative through published accounts of negotiations with Wabanaki representatives. In order to forcibly extend their empire in North America, the British needed soldiers to follow orders. The British government invested in a vision of orderly imperial authority that could be imposed anywhere in the world, starting with a disciplined, healthy, well-fed army. Military authorities issued rations to soldiers and camp followers on the expectation that those who received provisions would perform their duty to their employers, their nation, and their empire.[6]

Provisioning provided a means for British colonial and military authorities to assert power hierarchies over Indigenous people and British and provincial soldiers. But the targets of such provisioning often had other ideas. Savvy, eloquent Wabanaki diplomats demanded equality at the negotiating table and leveraged their own authority against colonial usurpers. By insisting that Massachusetts negotiators follow Wabanaki reciprocal diplomatic norms in the allocation of food, Wabanaki leaders resisted colonial authorities' attempts at colonial takeover. So, too, did British and colonial soldiers push back against the food politics of the British military. By refusing to follow the British army's regulations around provisioning, and revolting when provisions were too few, provin-

GIVE US SOME PROVISION

cial soldiers resisted British imperial authorities, laying the groundwork for rebellions to come.[7]

If reciprocity formed the foundations of British attempts at imposing a colonial hierarchy, reciprocity also destabilized these foundations. Wabanaki and colonial hunger cultures understood hunger as a failure of reciprocity within hierarchical relations. In early modern British society, peasants produced food, but authorities owed sustenance to the poor, who would rebel if leaders failed in their responsibilities. In Wabanaki society, while hierarchical based on gender and age, family bands provided for themselves and for each other and understood acts of selfishness as wholly monstrous; political relationships, too, relied upon mutual exchanges of food and power. For both British and Wabanaki people, failures of reciprocal relations could lead people to divest from these relationships. Hunger knowledge could take the form of knowing how to demand food and knowing what kinds of power lay in those demands.

To compare Wabanaki leaders and colonial soldiers as they resisted British authority is not to imply any form of solidarity between these two groups. Even as they fought against the day-to-day hierarchies of the British military, colonial soldiers took up arms in support of a regime bent on the destruction of Indigenous sovereignty. The Wabanaki fought, with weapons and words, to preserve their lands, cultures, and lives against these very same invaders. Common colonists had much to gain from dispossessing Native peoples of their lands, and they identified with Indigenous peoples only to assert their own form of colonial "indigeneity" against British metropolitan officials.[8]

Nevertheless, these two groups can be viewed as similarly disrupting the British colonial project, from inside and outside the empire. Both Wabanaki leaders and colonial soldiers used the language of hunger—whether for food in general or for specific foodstuffs or rights associated with food—as a rallying cry for resistance to British authority. Such resistance jeopardized the illusions of colonial hierarchies and exposed the precariousness of British colonization. Historians have tended to associate colonial fragility with the beginnings of the colonial invasion, but the actions of Indigenous diplomats and provincial soldiers demonstrated that colonial leaders continued to struggle to assert their authority well into the eighteenth century.

Wabanaki Food and Resistance, 1700–1750

In the early eighteenth century, the colonial government of Massachusetts attempted to erode Wabanaki sovereignty through numerous treaty negotiations. Massachusetts authorities legalized the seizure of Wabanaki land, cultivated dependence on English trade goods, refused commensality, and outright misled Wabanaki representatives. In turn, Wabanaki negotiators defended their sovereignty. They enacted Indigenous food rituals during diplomatic negotiations, criticized British trade policy that tried to create Wabanaki dependence, decried British violations of Wabanaki land rights, and vociferously denounced colonial officials' efforts to paint the Wabanaki as drunken, impoverished, starving wards of the British empire. Where the British thought they could outmaneuver Wabanaki diplomats, leaders like Loron called British officials to account, giving the lie to colonists' expansionist ambitions. In yet another form of hunger knowledge, the Wabanaki leveraged the political power of hunger against the British, both by performing the food rituals of the conferences themselves, and by addressing the broader issues of food sovereignty that these negotiations raised. Wabanaki demands for provisions, rather than signaling dependency on British colonial authority, instead forced British officials to adhere to Wabanaki systems of reciprocity and hierarchy.

Well into the eighteenth century, the Wabanaki held the majority of land and power in the colonial northeast. British colonization maintained only the most precarious hold in what is now northern New England, eastern Quebec, and the Maritimes. Mobilizing superior tactics and technologies such as snowshoes, the Wabanaki could conduct dramatic raids on English outposts across the region. Their many strategic advantages meant that when they confronted British colonists, the Wabanaki negotiated not from a position of weakness but from a position of strength.[9]

The key to Wabanaki power lay in the vastness of their territory and the diffuse nature of their political and social organization. Wabanaki society was organized around extended families, or bands. Several of these bands could form a village, and multiple villages could group into nations, which eventually allied together into the Wabanaki Confederacy, composed at various points in its history of Abenaki, Norridgewock, Penobscot, Kennebec, Maliseet, Passamaquoddy, and M'ikmaq peoples.

But for winter hunts, and in times of danger, bands would scatter to live independently. This political and social organization predated colonization, but proved distinctively resilient to it. United when they needed to, dispersed when they needed to, Wabanaki made themselves elusive to colonial invasion, surveillance, and control. Wabanaki the knowledge of how to sustain themselves on the abundant food resources of their territory—from the fish, shellfish, and waterfowl of the coasts, to the moose, other game, and wild plants of the forests, to the produce of the farmlands Wabanaki women cultivated—lay at the foundations of Wabanaki food sovereignty.[10] Precisely because it was never as centralized or populous as the Haudenosaunee Confederacy to the west, the Wabanaki alliance served as a commanding barrier to colonial incursion throughout the seventeenth and early eighteenth centuries. As the British attempted to invade Wabanaki lands in order to cut off the French colonizers to the north, Massachusetts negotiated with the Wabanaki Confederacy over and over again in the early eighteenth century.

Wabanaki power and resilience at first glance appear incompatible with their frequent demands for food from colonial negotiators. For example, at a conference in 1727, Loron told Massachusetts translator (and former captive of the Maliseet) John Gyles, "give us sum provision to make a fe[a]st for we have nothing to Eat." Loron would make similar requests for provisions or complaints about their quantity throughout negotiations. The British, meanwhile, argued that "The Indians here are a poor mean people, . . . constantly begging . . . for the necessities of nature," as Belcher told a Scottish correspondent in 1733.[11]

But Belcher, like many other colonial observers, fundamentally misunderstood Wabanaki food politics. The Wabanaki were perfectly capable of sustaining themselves in the absence of colonial interference. Rather than indicating actual hardship, Wabanaki leaders asked Massachusetts officials for food in order to show ties of reciprocal obligation between polities. They claimed hunger in order "to bargain for better prices, to justify low returns in the fur trade, to solicit supplies like guns and powder, to threaten a change in loyalty, and to defend their freedom to travel," in the words of one historian. The Wabanaki recognized that by using the language of starvation, even though they were not actually starving, they could gain concessions from colonial authorities at conferences, a strategy that proved particularly effective and confusing to colonists.[12] The British, meanwhile, tried to deny their own vulnerability to Wabanaki power through performances of British benefaction and Wabanaki dependence, especially in the written proceedings of treaty conferences.

Like other colonial sources, treaty conference proceedings presented a colonial narrative to their readers. They were designed to mislead, obscure, and dispossess Native people. Moreover, even in the absence of outright deception, accurate transcription of treaty conferences would have been difficult. Wabanaki and English languages did not provide neat one-to-one translations of words, much less of concepts. Worse, British translators often had a limited grasp of Wabanaki languages; at one conference, for instance, Wabanaki leaders asked the British to use one particular translator "because we understand him plainest," implying that other interpreters were difficult to understand. The necessity of translating long speeches in real time at treaty conferences rendered this task even more difficult. Differences in rhetorical and negotiating style could also lead to miscommunications: the Wabanaki had a tendency to remain silent or change the subject when they disagreed, strategies which the British misinterpreted as assent. Moreover, Wabanaki and British representatives interpreted the function of treaties differently. The British saw them as binding legal documents, while the Wabanaki more often pointed out where these writings did not match the actual state of affairs.[13]

In addition, treaty conference proceedings, reflecting the patriarchal nature of colonial society, ignored the crucial participation of women and larger communities in Wabanaki diplomacy. While Wabanaki women did not have formal political roles, they asserted authority through their labor. Although Wabanaki men were the leaders of family bands, villages, and nations, their demonstrations of authority, in the form of hosting feasts, depended upon women's agricultural and culinary labor. As in other Indigenous nations throughout the northeast, women's critical roles in growing, foraging, and preparing food offered them forms of political influence. The women who accompanied Wabanaki negotiators to treaty conferences would have carried on these forms of labor and their tacit political engagement at the conferences. Laboring to sustain their communities, Wabanaki women were fundamental to Wabanaki food sovereignty and therefore to sovereignty as a whole. Nevertheless, the English saw themselves as treating solely with male Wabanaki leaders, a bias that similarly informed the records of the negotiations.[14]

Despite the heavy mediating influence of colonial translators and scribes who misinterpreted Wabanaki speakers both intentionally and unintentionally, treaty conference proceedings nevertheless offer a powerful glimpse of the voices of important male Wabanaki leaders. The formal, repetitive, deliberative nature of these documents is exactly why someone like Loron leaps off the page.[15] A Penobscot diplomat, Loron served as spokesperson for his tribe and, often, for the entire Wabanaki Confederacy between the 1720s and 1750s. With formidable intellect, eloquence, and wit, he defended his tribe's food sovereignty in negotiation after negotiation with the English. The brilliance of his speech cut through the multiple veils of translation and transcription. Loron refused to follow the scripts that British authorities such as Belcher tried to force onto the proceedings, most notably scripted interactions about the distribution of food.

The conferences between the Wabanaki Confederacy and the Massachusetts Bay Colony, like those conducted throughout the colonial northeast, were elaborate performances. Following ceremonies to open the conference, the negotiating parties would begin to offer propositions, each of them sealed with a gift of wampum. Each party said its piece while the rest of the conference listened. After the presentation of propositions, the negotiating parties would disperse to discuss proposals with other delegates and community members. Large community delegations accompanied Wabanaki diplomats and participated in communal decision-making. The practice of presenting propositions and then adjourning to discuss them enabled Wabanaki negotiators to deliberate with their communities about how to proceed. For Wabanaki diplomats, forcing colonial representatives to adhere to the deliberative unfolding of negotiation also offered a means of showing Wabanaki power over the proceedings. Once all the proposals had been made and answered, the English would draw up a treaty for themselves and Native representatives to sign. The conference then concluded with a meal and the distribution of gifts like food, alcohol, and other trade goods; hosts also provided meals to the other negotiating parties throughout the conference.[16]

"Treating" could refer to making a treaty, but it could also refer to hosting, and treaty conferences entailed both. A day's negotiations often began with the host ceremonially asking visiting negotiators whether they had been well entertained. A 1722 journal by the Massachusetts commissioners at a negotiation with the Wabanaki Confederacy repeatedly stressed the Wabanaki satisfaction with their "entertainment": "they added their hearty thanks for the hearty entertainment"; "they were . . . pleased with their good Treatment"; "[they] have been well entertained." At the 1735 Deerfield negotiation Belcher addressed the Indigenous representatives daily with some variation of "I hope you have been well entertained." In each case, the Mohawk, Abenaki, and Schaghticoke replied that they had. With these accounts, British chroniclers stressed the generosity of British hospitality.[17]

But unlike other negotiators, Loron declined to follow these scripts, instead frequently criticizing British hospitality. At the 1738 conference in Boston referenced at the beginning of this chapter, the ceremonial greetings took on a different tone. When Belcher told the Penobscot and Norridgewock representatives that he "hope[d] you are kindly treated," Loron replied, "Not so well treated as formerly, we have Victuals enough at dinner but nothing but broth morning & night." Belcher promised to provide more substantial food to the delegates but warned, "I'll take Care that you have not too much rum." On another day of the negotiations, Belcher declared, "It is my Order that you be well provided for at your Lodgings & that you have not too much rum." In the transcript of the proceedings, the "Indians" drew attention to the vagueness of Belcher's pronouncement: "Y[our] Exc[ellenc]y don't tell us how much Provisions shall be allowed." In response to a request for *food*, Belcher replied with yet another admonishment about *alcohol:* "You must take Care of one another & see that you don't get drunk for the English despise you w[he]n you are drunk." The negotiators asked for "2 quarts of wine & some Cyder at every Meal & 3 drams a day." The next time Belcher asked whether the delegates had been well entertained, Loron answered, "Very well." Loron similarly pointed out shortcomings in Massachusetts representatives' hospitality at a conference in 1742. When governor William Shirley asked the Wabanaki negotiators whether they "were taken good Care of," Loron replied, "As your Excellency desires we may mention Things freely; We say, the Pork and Bread fell short last Night." Shirley promised to increase portions at subsequent meals. Later in the same conference, Loron dictated the times and contents of meals, asking for

food to be delivered in the evening instead of the morning, and requesting "a Dish of Peas for a change of Diet."[18]

Loron deliberately drew attention to errors in British hospitality, because food exchanges between colonists and Native peoples had long been
an arena for illustrating power differentials. The Wabanaki understood
ceremonial meals and gifts of food as the foundation of the reciprocal relationships that were negotiated in treaty conferences. In Wabanaki eyes,
meals were meant to encompass not just the leaders at the conferences but
also their communities, who were important participants in the decision-
making process. The common pot meant sharing food resources alongside
other resources. Reciprocity did not necessarily mean equality, and there
was a long history of Indigenous gifts of food meant to illustrate colonial
dependency.[19]

By contrast, British representatives saw these exchanges of food as a way
to emphasize Wabanaki dependency on benevolent colonial officials, and to
highlight British ideals of gentility justifying political authority. A list of provisions for the Governor and other commissioners to the Indians during a
1749 conference with the Wabanaki Confederacy showed stark differences
between the hospitality they provided to Wabanaki representatives and the
foods British authorities saw as necessary for their *own* "entertainment." The
"Sundry Necessarys" for the five "Gentl[emen] Commissioners," their servants, and guards included such staples as pork, bread, molasses, cider, and
rum. But the list also contained many luxury items befitting the tables of styl-
ish gentlemen, including sugar, coffee, chocolate, capers, mustard, and both
black and green tea, along with an extensive list of kitchenware and table-
ware. The Massachusetts House of Representatives allotted 350 pounds to
this expense. By comparison, for the "Suppering" of 293 Wabanaki "Men
Women & Children" during the four-day conference, the commissioners
provided a grand total of four oxen, one hogshead of cider, one hogshead of
rum, and four hogsheads of bread, paid for out of the 450 pounds the House
allotted to "presents for the Indians." The disparity between the lavish meals
of the handful of commissioners, and the cheaper and simpler fare they gave
to the hundreds of the Wabanaki delegation, says a great deal. British and
Wabanaki negotiators may have drunk toasts together, but they did not break
bread together or even eat the same foods. British negotiators refused to eat
out of the common pot with Wabanaki communities.[20]

Much as the British wanted to establish a relationship in which Native diplomats were not even fit to eat at their table, Wabanaki negotiators fought these colonial ideas. Food was not only the subtext, but the text, of treaty conferences. While there were important differences between the food and alcohol disbursed at conferences, and the trade in food and alcohol more generally, these issues often overlapped. Wabanaki leaders asserted their food sovereignty in the face of British incursion, not just through attaching meaning to food at conferences, but in their diplomatic defenses of Wabanaki foodways. Food animated several contested issues at negotiations, including intrusive British livestock, trading post locations and supplies, and the alcohol trade.

British incursions onto Wabanaki lands spurred debates about domesticated and wild animals. When the British accused the Wabanaki of killing British animals, colonists demanded payment or threatened war. While the Wabanaki could similarly point to British violence against Wabanaki animals, they did not demand the same kind of retribution. At a 1732 negotiation, Belcher raised the complaint of a colonist who claimed that a group of Norridgewock men had killed and eaten five horses, and called on a man named Packahumbanoit who had been present at the incident. Packahumbanoit replied that "I had some of the Meat, but I did not kill the Horses." Belcher pointed to another earlier incident in which Wabanaki men had killed two British cattle. The governor chastised Packahumbanoit and the other "Young Men" for "smil[ing]" at what the British considered a matter so explosive that it could "endanger a War." Loron responded by pointing out similar wrongs that Wabanaki animals had suffered at the hands of the British: "Two of our dogs were kill'd . . . . for nothing but barking at a *Cow*," he noted. While the British were dismissive of Wabanaki dogs, they served as transportation, livestock, and a food source for the Wabanaki in much the same way as other animals did for the British. Loron told Belcher, "We should not have spake of [the dogs], if your Excellency had not mentioned the cattle." The Penobscot diplomat simultaneously denied Wabanaki responsibility for the deaths of British animals, and drew parallels between Wabanaki and English livestock sovereignty.[21]

Although Loron indicated a willingness to disregard the deaths of Wabanaki animals in the name of peace in 1732, he warned the British in stronger terms about their intrusive livestock at a conference a decade later.

In 1742, Loron invoked a 1727 treaty he had negotiated with then-governor William Dummer, recalling that, "it was said, none of your young Men, should go into our Woods to Hunt." Colonists had violated these provisions in the intervening years. The Penobscot diplomat reminded his listeners that while the British had more domesticated animals, the Wabanaki relied upon "our hunting Game," aside from dogs. British inroads into Wabanaki hunting territories threatened to "destroy our Livelihood," Loron admonished his listeners. The governor William Shirley in turn blamed the Wabanaki for the death of British livestock, drawing a similar equivalence between Wabanaki and British subsistence: "Your killing our Cattle does our Inhabitants as much Injury as our taking away your Bever and Guns." He argued that the Wabanaki should "make Reparation" for British animals. Loron countered by noting that the Wabanaki and their dogs were not the only ones eating British livestock: "I know of my certain Knowledge, that Bears and Wolves have killed a great many." He voiced concern that the Wabanaki would be wrongfully blamed for the deaths of colonial animals, saying, "We pray, that when the Cattle stray away, . . . your young Men may not charge us with killing of them." As mobile food sources that did not respect colonial or Wabanaki boundaries, animals raised particular tensions during negotiations.[22]

The location of trading posts, the terms of trade agreements, and the availability of trade goods, especially food, formed another site of contention between Wabanaki and British negotiators. Loron argued forcefully on behalf of the Wabanaki Confederacy in trade matters, while the Massachusetts government tried to use the trade to cultivate Wabanaki dependence on British goods. The Wabanaki agreed to host official Massachusetts trading posts or truck houses on their lands, and often welcomed access to trade goods such as corn, cloth, and guns. Yet the specifics of these arrangements could turn contentious. During the 1732 negotiation, Belcher argued that the Massachusetts government could guarantee a fair trade at its official trading posts, but could not make such promises about other traders: "The Price of Goods at the Truck-Houses is state[d] by the Government . . . but the Government can't restrain the private Traders as to their Price."[23]

Contrary to Belcher's assertion, the Wabanaki did not always find a fair trade at official posts. In a 1738 conference, Loron accused British traders of cheating in fur transactions, asserting, "We can't trust the Truckmaster." When Loron reminded his British listeners that the Penobscots could trade with the French for money as opposed to goods, Belcher claimed that the British traded in goods for the benefit of the Wabanaki. "You can't read nor write & are much more exposed to be cheated by mony than Goods," he told Loron, and warned that the French traded only in paper money, not silver. "Paper mony is good as any," Loron replied, and would ensure that "we can tell better if we are cheated." Loron's threat to trade with the French stoked British fears about Wabanaki allegiances. Moreover, the Wabanaki were savvy enough consumers to know that they were not necessarily receiving the best deal from the British.[24]

While British authorities wanted to regulate trade, Wabanaki negotiators often desired more and better options for trade. In 1740, Loron argued for increased Wabanaki flexibility to trade beyond official British channels, stating, "We desire that over & above the Trade with the Truck Masters, we may be allowed to trade with the Soldiers for Small Things." The Wabanaki desired to trade more widely due to the limited selection and quantity of trade goods at official truck houses. Loron criticized the insufficiency of a shipment of corn to a truck house, noting, "Two Hundred Bushels is really nothing when we come to Trade," when divided among hundreds of people. As much as Massachusetts representatives tried to convince the Wabanaki that the terms of the trade were meant to protect naïve Indigenous people, leaders like Loron instead pushed for a Wabanaki agenda of fair access to trade goods. Loron acknowledged that stable trade relationships could help maintain a balance of power in northern New England: "I desire great care may be taken of the Trade, it is the great means of keeping the Peace." He also negotiated about food supplies in a time of increased hunger for the Wabanaki, when access to British corn might mean the difference between scarcity and sufficiency.[25]

But some specific aspects of the trade caused more friction. Massachusetts officials' admonitions to Wabanaki negotiators about rum point to alcohol's controversial role in treaty conferences and in Wabanaki-British relations in general. There can be no doubt that alcohol, and liquor in particular, played a difficult and complicated role in Indigenous communities in the seventeenth and eighteenth centuries. Colonial and Native leaders alike expressed concern about excessive Native drinking, and these fears were not always unfounded. Some Indigenous individuals turned to alcohol to try to numb the trauma of colonization with its attendant violence, disease, upheaval, and death. Colonial and Wabanaki officials recognized that both Native people and colonists who used alcohol excessively were prone to violence and mayhem, and were more likely to start cross-cultural conflicts. Speculators and traders used alcohol to deceive Native peoples in commodity exchange, land sales, and other transactions. Native leaders often pleaded with colonial authorities to stop the liquor trade in their communities.[26]

But alcohol could also support existing Native rituals and create cultural and cross-cultural ties. Like food, weapons, cloth, and other trade goods, alcohol played a role in ceremonies of gift-giving and hospitality, including presentations of gifts and drinking toasts at treaty conferences. Independent of the larger liquor trade, these gifts of alcohol did not constitute a significant proportion of the liquor flowing from colonial to Native hands. Within their communities, Native peoples harnessed the altered state that alcohol induced for medicinal and ceremonial purposes, adapting alcohol into traditions that already included intoxicants such as tobacco. Many Indigenous peoples had rituals of smoking tobacco to seal diplomatic agreements; adapting from one intoxicant to another, Wabanaki negotiators adopted the British ceremony of toasting with alcoholic beverages. Alcohol also played a role in mourning rituals, which became increasingly important in the face of colonization's death toll. Rather than solely destroying Native communities, the various ritual uses of alcohol could help to maintain cultural continuity.[27]

These complexities formed the backdrop of negotiations over alcohol between the Wabanaki and the British in the early eighteenth century. While it is important to distinguish between ceremonial toasts and gifts of alcohol, and the larger alcohol trade, in practice the negotiations over the trade contrasted the ceremonial drinking in dissonant ways. Colonial officials often warned the Wabanaki against overindulging, whether or not this occurred during the conference itself. During a negotiation in 1714, the governor Joseph Dudley instructed his interpreter to tell Wabanaki representatives "not [to] drink nor be quarrelsome." At a 1727 conference, Loron asked the interpreter Gyles for a "Little Refreshment" to tide the Penobscot over during their "Gret Council." Gyles responded that he was not permitted to give rum to the Wabanaki except on "Sum Extrordenary occasion," and deferred to another Massachusetts representative, who offered "not a bove 2 or 3 quarts." A Jesuit missionary who had accompanied the Penobscots chimed in that "a quart is a nough," but Gyles finally relented: "let them have it for they are a bout 50 or 60 in number it cant do them any harm." At the 1738 conference, Belcher lectured the Kennebec leader Wiwurna for requesting that the rum trade continue, saying, "It is best to live temperately, & that is the way to live healthy . . . . I have liv'd almost Sixty years & don't drink Rum." In even stronger language at a 1732 conference, Belcher berated Wabanaki representatives that drinking reduced them to animals: "When the Rhum prevailes, you are like *Bevers, Bears* and *Otters.*" Moreover, he blamed the Wabanaki for allowing alcohol to make them victims: "Ill Men cheat you when you are Drunk." British eagerness to call the Wabanaki animals or blame them for ill treatment from colonists again revealed the desire of Massachusetts officials to render the Wabanaki subordinate during treaty negotiations.[28]

While the British officials seemed to regard Wabanaki alcohol consumption negatively, except where ceremonial toasts were concerned, Wabanaki negotiators appear to have held more complicated opinions. Wabanaki leaders sometimes asked for gifts of rum from the British as ceremonial offerings to seal the deal at treaty conferences; at other times they demanded that the colonists halt the rum trade with their people. These two categories of alcohol distribution, for treaties or trade, served very different purposes within Wabanaki culture, but the way that conferences brought them together illustrated the complexity of the role of alcohol for Wabanaki leaders. At the same conference where Belcher called drunk Wabanaki beasts, Loron lobbied for an end to public or private rum trading with the Wabanaki: "It is much to our Advantage to have all other Goods but Rhum brought near us, but it is hurtful to us to bring Rhum among us." When the issue dropped during the negotiation, Loron returned it to Belcher's attention, saying, "Brother, you have not given us any answer as to the Rhum that is given out at *George's* Truck-House." At other times, Loron argued for limited rum distribution: "It was agreed that the Indians should have moderate Quantities of Rum, but they have had so much that Mischief has been done, & for the time to come we desire no more than one quart a man," he asserted at the 1738 conference; later in the same negotiation, he suggested that rum sales to women be banned entirely. At a 1753 conference, Norridgewock and Penobscot representatives accused the British of using alcohol to lure the Wabanaki into deceptive land sales: "We apprehend you got the Indians drunk, and so took the Advantage of them, when you bought the lands." Wabanaki negotiators recognized that alcohol could have destructive effects on their communities.[29]

Nevertheless, Indigenous negotiators' desire to halt the destructive liquor trade did not preclude them from indulging in ceremonial drinking during conferences. Bills to the Massachusetts government for lodging and feeding Mohawk, Pigwacket, and other Native negotiators in Boston "by His Excellencys order with the best of Provisions and Liquour" recorded the quantities of wine, rum, and cider that diplomats consumed. Meanwhile, colonial negotiators' actions often directly contradicted their spoken demands that the Wabanaki cease drinking liquor. Colonists gave alcohol to Native representatives attending conferences, both as presents and in the form of ceremonial toasts. At the close of the 1714 conference, Massachusetts disbursed "five Caggs of Rum" or "eleven Gallons, & one Quart" to Wabanaki attendees. At the same 1738 meeting in which Belcher, Loron, and Wiwurna sparred about rum consumption, the transcript records Belcher repeatedly toasting to the health of various Wabanaki delegates and nations, one after another:

The Govr. drank to the Penobscots first.
The Govr. drinks to the Norridgwalks.
The Indians return thanks & drink all the Sagamores with the Gov & Council's Health.

Similarly, at the 1742 conference, Shirley and the negotiators toasted to each other's health, then Shirley disbursed wine to all of the Wabanaki women and children in attendance, and "a Glass of Rum" apiece to 120 young Wabanaki men.[30]

Ceremonial toasts were an important part of cementing agreements in British culture, and they introduced this practice to the Wabanaki, who already had some equivalent in the act of ceremonial tobacco smoking. Nevertheless, it is impossible to completely separate the symbolic purposes of toasting from the painful effects of alcohol on Native autonomy. Speculators and officials used alcohol to ply Native representatives into signing away their land across the northeast. Observing Massachusetts officials decrying Native drinking in one breath and raising a glass in many toasts in the next, it is hard to not see colonial representatives acting in bad faith.

All of this politicking about matters of food and drink at the treaty conferences directly related to the contents of the negotiations themselves, in which Wabanaki diplomats like Loron articulated their rights to their hunting and agricultural lands, while calling for fair trading policies from the British. Land rights and food production were synonymous for a culture that relied heavily upon wild foods in addition to agriculture. Loron's defense of Wabanaki food sovereignty lay at the heart of his mission of defending Wabanaki political sovereignty. Loron clearly recognized that the performances of the treaty conferences indicated the power balance, or imbalance, at the negotiations, and he carefully restructured these ceremonial exchanges to serve his own rhetorical purposes. He knew that the ultimate goal of the British would be to take away Penobscot land and sovereignty, and so he acted to defend his nation at every turn. When in 1727 Dummer pushed Loron to acknowledge obedience to the king of England, Loron rejected it outright: "God hath willed that I have no King, and that I be master of my lands in common."[31]

Fighting the British invasion with the weapons of diplomacy, Loron served as a tireless advocate for his people for decades. He did so during a time when the Wabanaki faced food scarcity due to colonial incursion, and the British tried to situate the Wabanaki as helpless dependents of the British empire. Within this context, Loron's unwillingness to adhere to British food scripts in treaty negotiations also reveals the depths of Wabanaki resistance to colonialism. When Loron declared, "give us sum provision to make a fe[a]st for we have nothing to Eat," it was not an admission of vulnerability or dependence. It was, instead, a demand for an equal seat at the negotiating table and a call for the British to recognize the importance of reciprocity to political relations with the Wabanaki. The Wabanaki needed food to conduct their communal negotiations in their traditional ways. If the British wanted to treat with the Wabanaki, they had to participate in diplomacy on Wabanaki terms.[32]

The Wabanaki used their own hunger knowledges and cultures to set the terms of diplomacy, thereby exposing the fictive nature of British narratives of Wabanaki dependence in the first half of the eighteenth century. The military and diplomatic might of the Wabanaki rendered British colonization of northern New England vulnerable, even as the colonial invasion exposed the Wabanaki to violence, unfair trade, and alien legal systems. While the Massachusetts government tried to use food and the threat of hunger to assert colonial authority over Wabanaki people and lands, the Wabanaki charted their own paths to subsistence and resisted threats to their food sovereignty. The coming of the Seven Years' War would destabilize the power that the Wabanaki held in the northeast, but the fight for Wabanaki lands and food sovereignty continues to this day.[33]

British Military Food and Resistance, 1744–1763

Wabanaki diplomats used food and hunger to resist the colonial invasion of their lands, but the British found that hunger bred resistance from within colonial hierarchies as well. Soldiers consistently rebelled against military policies concerning food during King George's War and the Seven Years' War. These two wars joined the litany of conflicts between Native powers and British and French invaders that stretched from the late seventeenth through the late eighteenth centuries. The Seven Years' War has been called the first world war because of its global scale, which presented particular logistical challenges, but the British army had struggled to keep ahead of soldiers' bodily needs even during smaller-scale conflicts like King George's War.

Disciplining and provisioning borderlands armies, British military authorities confronted a variety of difficulties related to food and hunger. They worried that short or insufficient rations might lead soldiers to eat the wrong things, that soldiers would resist anti-scurvy efforts, that alcohol would lead to unruly behavior, or worst of all, that hunger would lead soldiers to steal or desert from the army. In fact, these worries were well-founded. Military authorities failed in their vision of a well-fed army, leading to hunger and disease but also low morale, discipline problems, and desertion. The latter issue became so pervasive during the Seven Years' War that one scholar has described attempts to recapture deserters as "a war within a war."[34] The saying about an army marching on its stomach turned out to be true.

As military officials learned, if the army could not provision its soldiers, they would not fight to defend the colonies. Given that the military ideology of the time equated logistical efficiency with moral imperatives, authorities were forced to confront the question: if soldiers went hungry, how could the cause of colonial war be just? Soldiers, meanwhile, fought back against military authorities' policing of their bodies, in their demands for food and alcohol and their uses of hunger knowledge to find sustenance no matter what. Their demands for reciprocity and resistance against military hierarchy would help to disrupt the British empire's ambitions in North America.

The borderlands forts that became so strategically important in the conflicts of the mid-eighteenth century signified a major evolution in British military tactics. After decades of devastating Indigenous and French raids on British towns like Deerfield, Massachusetts, British officials realized that building forts, accompanied by roads, in strategic sites along waterways could draw the attacks away from civilians. The result was a line of forts stretching along Lake Champlain, Lake George, and the Hudson River. The British military also set their sights on coastal French forts and fortified towns, such as the Nova Scotia fortress of Louisbourg, which they besieged during both King George's War and the Seven Years' War. For the British, the locations of these forts, at the very edges of the imperial imagination, in an unfamiliar climate, proved tactically successful, but at a cost. For Indigenous peoples, of course, these places were part of Native space, the homelands of Wabanaki and Haudenosaunee peoples among others, familiar territories for seasonal subsistence. But for British military authorities, borderlands forts presented the vexing challenge of how to keep soldiers provisioned on the peripheries of empire.[35]

At the idealistic level, the British military believed that meeting the physical needs of soldiers would lead to victory in battle. During the Seven Years' War, John Campbell, 4th Earl of Loudon, as commander in chief of the British army in North America, leveraged Britain's logistical bureaucracy against Indigenous and French enemies. Under Loudon's system, British military contractors stocked warehouses around the northeast with a six-month supply of rations for twelve thousand soldiers.

From these warehouses, boatmen and wagoners transported provisions along rivers, lakes, and roads to the forts. In spite of Loudon's innovations, these supply chains were as fragile as they were extensive. Ensuring adequate food, water, shelter, medicine, and clothing for thousands of bodies presented enormous difficulties to British military authorities.[36]

The challenges in supplying British outposts manifested growing challenges to political and social hierarchies within the British empire. During borderlands conflicts, British authorities tried to meet the needs and control the bodies of not just British regulars, but colonial soldiers. Although mainland British and colonial soldiers were part of the same empire, tensions between them grew. At the outset of the Seven Years' war, British authorities assumed that provincial forces would carry out the bulk of military operations. After a series of embarrassing losses early in the war, metropolitan officials adopted a new strategy. Loudon wanted to combine the provincial forces with the regulars and to rank provincial officers below regular officers, among many other unpopular measures. When Loudon's authoritarian approach did not translate into military victories, the British government recalled him and rolled back many of the controversial policies. Nevertheless, doubts about colonial military capacity remained. British authorities viewed the colonies, in the words of the military historian P. J. Marshall, "not as allies . . . , but as dependents." These assumptions of colonial inferiority informed British military policy, and colonists chafed at what they saw as disrespect.[37]

Between fighting Indigenous and French enemies and navigating pressures within the empire, the stakes of the British military's logistical challenges were nothing less than the colonial project itself. In the eyes of British authorities, a disciplined and well-fed army with a clean, orderly camp would be not just physically stronger than their enemies but also capable of representing the British empire as an ideal. Leaders hoped that the healthy bodies of British soldiers would affirm the so-called natural hierarchies, logistical might, and moral superiority of British rule.[38] But the conditions on the ground in the borderlands, where drunkenness, disease, and desertion ran rampant, bore little resemblance to these hopes.

Early modern European manuals on military discipline usually concerned themselves more with the particularities of fortification and maneuvering than with managing discipline problems. Often these writers seemed not to acknowledge the problem of disobedient soldiers at all. Captain Thomas Venn dedicated *Military and Maritime Discipline* "TO ALL MY FELLOW-OFFICERS SOULDIERS AND LOVING COUNTRY-MEN to whom the Exercise of ARMES Is Delightful," leaving out those soldiers who did not find military service a delight. Or, writers who did admit the possibility of disobedience described it only in the starkest terms. One French manual advised that according to the articles of war, soldiers owed "Absolute Obedience" to their superiors. Lieutenant-General Richard Lambart Cavan's *A New System of Military Discipline* declared that "no authority can exist, where there is not a proper submission" and that "obedience suffers no reflection." The writers of these military treatises did not seem to consider what other kinds of motivations soldiers might have beyond pure obedience. John Darker's 1692 manual *A Breviary of Military Discipline,* aimed at English militia, optimistically stated that for a soldier, "Honour must be his greatest Wages," rather than the monetary wages on which so many ordinary soldiers relied. These maxims existed in tension with the actual bodies and needs of colonial soldiers, whose requirements for specific kinds and quantities of food and alcohol led them to acts of resistance large and small.[39]

The potential for disorder necessitated the heavy apparatus of regulation found in orderly books and military manuals. British forts in North America were crowded and poorly planned. In 1755, Fort William Henry was nine times more densely populated than Boston, one of the biggest cities in North America at the time. Such a fort was a far cry from the neat rows of tents and wagons depicted in the 1688 volume *Fortification and Military Discipline.* For the vast majority of colonial soldiers who hailed from rural areas, their time in the military would have been their first taste of urban life, full of dizzying new regulations, even for bodily functions.[40]

European experts on military discipline and health described the ideal camps as clean and efficient. Camps needed to be laid out with "what space of Ground will suffice to encamp [an army] with all their Provision," proclaimed J. S. in *Fortification and Military Discipline.* A reliable, regulated food supply was one of the most important parts of any campaign. Writing in 1752, the British army physician John Pringle advised that soldiers be "oblige[d] . . . to eat in messes," because left to their own devices they were unlikely to choose "wholesome food." Stocking the messes required its own logistical apparatus, Pringle noted: "markets" needed to be "so regulated that the traders have encouragement to come to the camp" to sell the messes "good provisions at a moderate price." If soldiers could not be fed with a mess system, quartermasters issued rations, often with instructions on how and when soldiers were to cook and eat them. September 1760 orders at St. John, New Brunswick, declared "five days pork and flour to be issued"; July 1758 orders at Lake George instructed "that all the provisions in the Regiment Be Cookd this Day." For military authorities, the proper nutrition and health of soldiers required the regulation of provisioning, cooking, eating, and the disposal of waste.[41]

Although officers could exert some control over soldiers' diets, soldiers were not the only inhabitants of military installations—many others worked to maintain the army. All sorts of suppliers—"Bakers merchants, shop Kepers & Victulers" and sutlers (merchants who sold supplies to soldiers)—thronged to camps and garrisons, in the words of Captain David Holmes. Sutlers were officially attached to regiments and subject to military regulation, while other types of vendors might operate more extra-legally. Holmes wrote that merchants at Fort Edward were ordered to report to the "Waggon Master Giving an acct of them Selves & By whose authority they Carry on that Business." Sutlers who did not have official approval would be "told, if they are found in Camp they shall be hanged," warned one military manual. Officers frequently regulated sutlers' sales of alcohol: "Sutlers are only to sell Rum to the men of their Regiment" and only "by an Order from the Capt[ain]," according to one set of orders; another limited the sales to commissioned officers between 11 a.m. and 3 p.m.; others completely forbade the sale of liquor to Indigenous peoples. Sutlers also could attract trouble in the form of unscrupulous clients; at Crown Point in August 1759, a man named John Lewis "was found Guilty of Counterfitting Orders upon the Sutler."[42]

At least some of those who provisioned soldiers would have been women, though they were rarely discussed in official documents. For much of the early modern period, the British army relied on the labor of military families, and in return, the army offered financial support to soldiers' dependents. However, over the course of the eighteenth century, the British army absorbed many of these support services, meaning that fewer women lived and worked in military settings. In the Seven Years' War, army regulations permitted only six women per regiment of British regulars, probably owing to the difficulty of transporting camp followers across the Atlantic. Citing concerns about sexual morality, New England militias did not allow women to follow soldiers and resented the presence of the women accompanying the regulars. In spite of these limits, women following the army served as some combination of wives and mothers, sex workers, servants, nurses, laundresses, money changers, gardeners, shepherds, sutlers, and cooks. Often these labors received little written attention from military authorities, with some exceptions: for example, when the British forces in Quebec under General James Murray were under siege in 1760, orders commanded women to cook for the army. Women in army encampments cooked for regiments, officers, and their families; they also tended gardens and herded livestock and probably foraged for wild foods. Of the gendered labors that women tended to perform in military camps, cooking was perhaps the most likely to cross over into being a male activity.[43]

In addition to feeding the army, camp-following women needed to eat, and their provisioning proved a source of particular frustration for military authorities. In garrisons, military leaders usually expected women to work for pay, but rarely could they earn enough to afford to support themselves and their families. During the Seven Years' War, military wives received rations alongside soldiers but often in smaller quantities, and some leaders banned rations for women. Despite the necessary labor that women performed for the army, leaders sometimes refused to repay that labor with provisions. Like soldiers, then, the women of military encampments were likely to face food shortage. Like soldiers, military women were likely to violate orders in efforts to assuage their hunger, for which they might face punishments ranging from whipping to loss of rations to being drummed out of camp. Like soldiers, the women of military encampments experienced hunger in line with their social status, with the wives of enlisted men facing more hardship than officers' wives.[44]

Of all the challenges facing the British military in North America, provisioning was one of the hardest. Through extensive supply chains of wagons, ships, and river bateaux, forts routinely received rations of preserved foods and dry goods: salt meat, cornmeal or wheat flour, dried peas or beans, and alcohol, often rum. The army struggled to transport fresh food to forts, instead relying on soldiers (or women) foraging or growing fruits and vegetables and raising livestock themselves. This was a departure from the policy laid out in General Richard Kane's *A System of Camp-Discipline*, which strictly regulated soldiers' gathering and hunting. "No Game to be killed," the manual proclaimed. Moreover, "None of the Troops . . . shall forage out of Camp; but when it shall be specified in the public Orders of the Day." Military authorities feared—not without reason—that foraging could easily spiral into looting, marauding, or plundering.[45]

In the northeastern borderlands, soldiers supplemented their rations with foraging wild foods and gardening. Sometimes their efforts paid off: during the 1745 siege of Louisbourg, Lieutenant Dudley Bradstreet found straw-berries "ful in the Bloom," and two weeks later "went a Strawberrying." In other instances, however, soldiers lacked hunger knowledge about foraging and could not tell edible from toxic wild plants, with unpleasant results. An anonymous orderly book from the 1759 siege of Louisbourg reported that "several of ye men are flux'd by Eating unwholesome herbs," leading the company surgeon to order that "no greens are made use of . . . but such as are known to be inoffensive." At other times, authorities struggled to regu-late gardens and livestock: "the Gardens are hurt by the Hogs and Small Swine," reported Captain Josiah Perry from Nova Scotia in 1759. Moreover, many northern forts had short growing seasons that made agriculture chal-lenging for soldiers used to farming in more southerly latitudes. The combi-nation of vulnerable supply chains and often ill-fated attempts at foraging or farming did not always equal balanced diets for soldiers.[46]

As much as military leaders tried to regulate what soldiers consumed, medical authorities feared that soldiers would eat the wrong foods if given the opportunity. Kane's *A System of Camp Discipline* mandated "All green Fruit, brought to Camp, to be destroyed," reflecting concerns that underripe fruit could cause digestive distress. Raymund Minderer wrote of the frequency of "Stomack-fevers" in the army. "Bloody and other Fluxes are very frequent," he explained, blaming these ailments on sol-diers' tendency to eat contaminated food and on the close quarters of army camps. Pringle argued that the only solution to this problem was to require soldiers to eat in mess halls and encourage them "to eat moder-ately." Still, dysentery and other digestive illness were a common feature of military life. Bradstreet recorded his own bout of the "Bloody Flux" in his diary.[47]

One of the greatest sources of worry for military medical authorities was scurvy, a common ailment among soldiers subsisting on dry goods and preserved foods. In the eighteenth century, European physicians disagreed about what exactly caused scurvy or how to treat it. To fight scurvy, British military officials often relied upon alternative forms of knowledge—from the Indigenous knowledge that introduced Europeans to spruce beer, to the foraging knowledge that provided fresh foods—in order to adapt to the landscapes of the northeastern borderlands. In northern forts, scurvy cases began to appear every January and February, and many sufferers died or were hospitalized by late spring. Following the medical protocols of the time, military authorities prescribed vinegar, wine, cider, ginger, and a drink called spruce beer as antiscorbutics, or anti-scurvy treatments. It was this latter beverage that caused particular controversy among officers and common soldiers in the Seven Years' War.[48]

The military tonic of spruce beer dated back to early interactions between French colonizers and Native peoples. The early French invader Jacques Cartier wrote that Indigenous guides taught his expedition to drink an infusion of tree leaves and bark to cure scurvy. In the hands of colonizers, the drink evolved into a fermented mix of molasses, yeast, hops, water, and the new growth of black spruce (*Picea mariana*). The molasses would have come all the way from the sugar plantations of the Caribbean, but British soldiers foraged spruce themselves (and, perhaps, relied on Indigenous women foragers as well) in the forests around the forts. Orderly books laid out instructions for the brewing and distribution of spruce beer among British troops. Each barrel of spruce beer was required to contain "five quarters of meloses," Major John Hawks recorded at Fort Edward in May 1759; "All setlars [sutlers] are att liberty to brue as much as they will." Military authorities preferred spruce beer as a drink for men performing manual labor. "Four Barrils of Spruce Beere Shall be Cept Constantly at Different Places with in the fort that the men at work may be Constantly Supplyed," wrote Holmes from Crown Point in August 1759.[49]

But common soldiers did not express the same enthusiasm for spruce beer as did officers, instead preferring to use its ingredients for their own purposes. Ordered to consume spruce beer, Massachusetts soldiers faced the choice of paying sutlers to brew it for them or brewing their own. But some soldiers chose an alternative path after requesting their molasses rations directly. Perry lamented that contrary to "the way Which the government Designd," the soldiers simply ate their molasses with their food instead of brewing it into beer. Eating molasses, Perry fretted, "I have found by Long Experience Is Very Projuditial to their Helth." Perry did not specify what kind of "Dammage" he feared the soldiers would cause to themselves—it couldn't have been particularly good for their teeth—but given spruce beer's reputation as an antiscorbutic, the dangers of scurvy would have probably been foremost in Perry's mind.[50]

Eating the molasses on its own, rather than brewing it into beer, might have had several attractions to the soldiers. The sweetness of molasses would have offered an appetizing contrast to the salty, bland army rations. The simple sugars in molasses would have provided a quick burst of energy to hard-working bodies. Eating a calorie-dense food such as molasses would have been a more efficient way to take in energy than fermenting it, a process that would have converted many of the simple sugars into alcohol. Moreover, calories consumed in solid food are more satiating than those consumed by drinking. Finally, the difficulty of delaying gratification may have also come into play for soldiers who might have intended to brew the molasses into beer but were too tempted to wait for its sweetness. At any rate, rather than drinking spruce beer, Perry's enlisted men ate their molasses, sating their appetites in violation of their orders.[51]

Beyond its purported antiscorbutic properties, military authorities encouraged the consumption of spruce beer because it offered a lower-alcohol alternative to rum. Rum and other hard liquors had become both hugely popular and objects of concern in the mid-eighteenth-century British Atlantic. In England, the problematic spirit was gin. In London between 1700 and 1743, the average adult's annual consumption of liquor, mostly in the form of gin, increased sevenfold to 2.2 gallons per year, driving hysterical media coverage of gin's effects on the populace. In New England, the rum that began flowing from the Caribbean (and from Massachusetts distilleries) by the late seventeenth century stoked much the same fears. Potent, cheap, accessible spirits offered a much more intoxicating beverage landscape than the lower-alcohol wines and beers consumed throughout previous centuries.[52]

Medical, religious, and political authorities responded to this surge in the availability of alcohol with varying levels of concern. Medical writers held a plethora of opinions on alcohol consumption, often arguing for its medicinal uses while generally agreeing on the dangers of drunkenness as a form of "intemperance" alongside gluttony. Although modern notions of alcoholism had not yet developed, many recognized that certain people drank to excess with dangerous effects. The Reformation, meanwhile, rendered sensual pleasure suspect and encouraged authorities to see social regulation as essential to creating a godly society. Few reformers called for banning alcohol outright, given that beer was more or less a staple food. Yet many authorities called for expanded policing of alcohol consumption, by regulating taverns, alehouses, and other establishments that served alcohol and by controlling who could purchase or consume it. In 1712, Massachusetts officials went so far as to try to ban the sale of rum in taverns. Such measures proved largely ineffectual and would only stoke the antiauthoritarian strains of political thought on the rise in the colony's tavern cultures.[53]

In spite of the many perceived dangers of spirits in British society, rum was a common component of soldiers' rations. Given rum's risks, military leaders generally considered rum optional compared to food rations and often imposed heavy regulations on its distribution. Cornelius Stowel, a lieutenant at Crown Point in 1759, wrote that "The Men shall have Rum given to them as the Service may Require and Circumstances will permit." Hawks recorded that soldiers on fatigue duty, or manual labor, should not receive rum in their rations "unless . . . the weather be wet and bad," emphasizing the warming qualities of liquor in much the same way as the disobedient men at Fort Edward. Men on fatigue duty would instead receive spruce beer because "rum will be of more disservice than good to them"; intoxication dulled the work ethic and made manual labor more dangerous. Nathaniel Bangs recorded orders for Massachusetts Bay troops sailing to Nova Scotia forbidding the transportation or sale of "Rum or any other Kind of Spiritously Liquor" because existing rum rations were "Quite Sufficient for the Health of the Troop." Officers were required to ensure that rum rations "be Mixed with a Propper Quantity of Water" rather than enjoyed undiluted. Men and women both vended liquor to soldiers, but military authorities expressed particular concern about the participation of soldiers' wives in the alcohol trade.[54]

All of these precautions reflected authorities' views that while a certain amount of rum might support "the Health of the Troop," liquor could easily disrupt military discipline. "No Soldier is to Sell or Give any Rum to any man which is known to abuse himself with Liquor," declared Bangs's orders. Such soldiers certainly existed. A man named William Thomas appeared four times in Bradstreet's diary: twice generically "drunk," once court-martialed for threatening a woman that "he would knock her Down if she would not give him Liq[uo]r," and once dead. But beyond intoxicated individuals, liquor might also drive broader disorder among the troops, such as the rum-based yelling at Fort William Henry or the actions of Massachusetts soldiers under Perry, which went beyond improper use of molasses rations. Perry wrote in his orderly book that some soldiers had taken articles of clothing issued by the Massachusetts government and sold them in exchange for "Spiritos Liquors." This act violated the articles of war, "which Exposes such offenders to Corporal Punnishment," Perry's orders decreed. But a lack of clothing also exposed the liquor buyers to other discomforts: "Most Certainly Rum will not Defend [the soldiers] from the Inclemency of the Weather nor the Stinging of the Insects with which this Country very Plentifully abounds," Perry observed. Those who sold their clothes in the summer would certainly miss them when the weather turned cold. And like other military authorities, Perry emphasized that liquor sapped the labor potential of soldiers, making them "unfit for millitary Duty or any thing Else."[55]

Just as the appetite for alcohol might wreak havoc on military discipline, so too might the appetite for food. Soldiers divided their time between guard duty around the fort and fatigue duty, which was the manual labor of building roads and fortifications, clearing trees, and similar tasks. Fatigue duty required incredible amounts of energy, but soldiers on fatigue duty in the Seven Years' War received only somewhere between 2300 and 3000 calories in rations per day. The modern US army recommends up to 4500 calories per day for soldiers engaged in this kind of work. While it is always risky to read twenty-first-century bodies onto eighteenth-century ones, it is safe to say that the underfed soldiers of the Seven Years' War would have been very hungry, and food would have been on their minds all the time. Adding insult to injury, officers could draw up to six times the rations of enlisted men. In response to food shortage, soldiers used hunger knowledge to supplement their rations—by foraging and gardening, but also via plunder and theft.[56]

Soldiers frequently stole food from allies, enemies, and civilians. Captain Silas Brown's orders forbade British soldiers from plundering French stores on pain of hanging, explaining that generous treatment of French colonists "will prevent their men from Joyning the French Army." Three weeks later orders reiterated, "No person on any accompt whatever to touch or Distroy any of the Indian corn pees or Oats." In *A System of Camp-Discipline*, Kane explained that plundering the enemy put food supplies at risk, noting that civilians would "secrete or destroy" provisions "rather than be plundered; quit the country, and leave you a Desart." Military authorities also expressed concern that soldiers' wives would participate in marauding, although only isolated incidents survive in the archive.[57]

Regardless of the potential penalties, soldiers were wont to pillage. An anonymous diary from Captain Richardson's company in the siege of Louisbourg in 1745 described British soldiers looting French colonists' livestock and alcohol: "we Plonderd there Camps of all Their Goods." While this kind of plunder might be a normal part of campaigns, it could also be the result of military authorities' logistical failures. Obadiah Harris, a private assigned to a crew building roads from Albany to Fort Edward, reported in 1758 that their rations "for a week [were] not sufficient for four days." Hunger made the soldiers "so cross and touchy they can't speak to one another," and then they began to take food forcibly from civilians, including one farmer's entire crop of apples. If the soldiers had been in camp and authorities discovered the thievery, they would have faced harsh military discipline. Kane threatened "severe or capital punishment" for those caught plundering. Nevertheless, for soldiers like Harris, hunger was stronger than the fear of punishment. He and his companions flouted military discipline in order to supplement their meager diets.[58]

When authorities failed in their responsibility to keep soldiers fed, soldiers rebelled against military hierarchy. The smaller rebellions of hungry bellies could lead soldiers to even bigger acts of disobedience, no matter the penalties. Desertion proved to be one of the most troubling worries for military authorities during the Seven Years' War. Provincial soldiers were more resistant to military discipline, and they knew the geography and landscape of the northeast much better than their British regular counterparts. When these issues collided with a British military that struggled to provision their troops adequately in borderlands forts, a number of provincial soldiers took matters into their own hands and deserted.

The diary of Luke Knowlton, a Massachusetts soldier, demonstrated both the power of soldiers' resistance and the dangerous situations that disobedient soldiers could face. Knowlton's ordeal in the autumn of 1759 is particularly striking given the larger British narrative of the war. British commentators on both sides of the Atlantic called 1759 the "annus mirabilis," the "wonderful year," in which British forces finally began to win battles after losing for much of the war to date.[59] These successes, and the rise in British morale they supposedly brought, were nowhere to be found in Knowlton's journal. Instead, Knowlton recorded hunger and rebellion, before he deserted alongside hundreds of other colonial soldiers. Knowlton's experiences illustrated the challenges facing both British military authorities and the soldiers that they tried to discipline in the northeastern borderlands—even at a time when British military affairs were ostensibly going very well.

Knowlton's diary revealed multiple instances of soldiers' dissatisfaction with the conditions of military service. He wrote of George Shaw's punishment—fifteen lashes for stealing liquor. He recorded a miserable boat trip from Fort Ticonderoga to Crown Point when the soldiers "had Nothing to Eat" except raw pork and parsnips looted from a French colonist's garden. A little over a week after Knowlton arrived in Crown Point, the situation deteriorated further. On October 28, the colonel at the fort read the soldiers an act from the Massachusetts General Court and subsequent orders from the general, both requiring them to continue to serve after their enlistments expired on November 1. "The men in general seem to Decline it," Knowlton observed, and by that date, two hundred of them had signed a petition refusing to stay on. On November 2, another order came from the general: the soldiers were "not [to] Presume to go home Before we have a Regular Discharg tho [the general] Confesses that our time is Expir'd." Unyielding, the soldiers met on the parade ground "with our Packs Swung in order to March." Two hundred men deserted en masse. As they left camp, officers confronted them "with orders to Fire upon us if we would not return but Did not though we refus'd to Obey them." While individual deserters could be punished harshly, military authorities proceeded with caution in the face of a mass desertion. More officers brought a letter from the colonel promising not to punish anyone who went back to camp, but only "Very few return'd," Knowlton reported. The rest marched on.[60]

Having successfully deserted from service, the soldiers faced an arduous and illegal journey of hundreds of miles on foot in late autumn with limited supplies. From an account of rebellion against military authority, Knowlton's diary quickly turned into something even more desperate. The men marched south into an autumn storm, and "Over Some of the Worst Mountains that Ever I Crost I think in my Life," Knowlton wrote. The storm continued for three days as the group marched through eastern New York. By November 6, the group's food ran "exceeding short," relieved only when they caught two turkeys. Two days later, the men reached Saratoga, boarded a small boat, and "Eat Some Bread and Meat." The crew of the boat encouraged the deserters to rest by the river until the following day, when they would return with more food, but on November 9 the deserters waited to no avail: the boat "Durst not come Ashoar to us and the Reason why I cannot Tell," Knowlton remarked. Perhaps the crew had reconsidered the dangers of bartering with the surely intimidating dozens of hungry deserters.[61]

The group continued on, ravenous. On November 10, a rainy day, they used up all their food. Fortunately, some of the party knew how to forage. They "Dug up some Ground Nuts And Eat," Knowlton wrote, the syntax suggesting that the men scarcely finished digging the tubers before they ate them. They ate as fast as they could find food. When one of the men caught an owl, Knowlton reported, "we Eat Very Suddenly," with no mention of cooking. The next day, the group probably euphemistically "found a horse," perhaps stealing it, and "Eat very hearty," without soul-searching about consuming horsemeat. The full meal left them "quite Encourag'd," until they spent the greater part of November 12 completely lost. On November 13, "we got to a Dutchman house where we got Some Provision to Eat," Knowlton wrote, again vague on how the group "got" this food and whether the Dutch colonist gave it freely or by force. For the next four days, Knowlton's diary did not mention food. This absence suggests that the group no longer suffered from food scarcity and that Knowlton no longer fixated on food because of hunger. On November 18, after sixteen days of walking through the hills of eastern New York and western Massachusetts, Knowlton arrived home to central Massachusetts and "found my honor'd Parents well."[62]

The group of deserters had survived their journey through hunting and foraging, but also theft and intimidation. Their hunger had run wild. They had taken their diets and their lives into their own hands, rebelling against British military authority. But they had done so at the risk of severe privation and peril. Even as they resisted military discipline, Knowlton and other deserters navigated a dangerous situation. They found themselves vulnerable to recapture and execution or to starving to death on their poorly provisioned escape journey. The year 1759 might have been a year of triumph in battle for the British military, but the hungry bodies and disobedient minds of provincial soldiers told an altogether different story.

Knowlton's flight from military service offered but one particularly glaring example of soldiers resisting the British colonial project. The British army could not sufficiently provision its soldiers, and soldiers responded by fighting military hierarchy. Throughout King George's War and the Seven Years' War, soldiers stole food and alcohol, overindulged in both, ate poisonous plants and molasses, swapped their clothes for rum, refused antiscorbutic medicine, and otherwise asserted their bodily autonomy in the face of regulations of their diet. These forms of corporeal disobedience quickly crossed over into even more flagrant flouting of military authority, including desertion from service.

Soldiers like Knowlton probably did not oppose the British military's broader mission of expanding the empire in North America. Nevertheless, their rebellions against military discipline had the effect of challenging the colonial project, both by encumbering the war effort and by exposing the holes in the empire's aspirations to rational benevolence. In the following decades, many scholars have argued, provincial soldiers' negative experiences in imperial wars would come to color their perceptions of the empire overall, leading to the crisis of imperial authority that would become the American Revolution. Despite the military successes the British achieved in mid-eighteenth-century North America, soldiers' revolts showed the precarity of the colonial project. Hunger could even undermine the empire from within.

Hunger like that of Knowlton and his deserter brethren fundamentally challenged not just military discipline but the rule of law and, indeed, the possibility of social order. Loron's diplomatic uses of hunger fundamentally threatened British dreams of control over Wabanaki peoples. As much as British authorities wished to present themselves as the generous overseers of submissive Indigenous peoples, or the rational overlords of obedient colonial soldiers, the borderlands challenged these fantasies. While British authorities tried to impose imperial hierarchies on Native and colonial people, Wabanaki leaders and provincial soldiers fought back using languages of hunger and reciprocity.

These moments of resistance showed the limited grasp of British authorities in the northeastern borderlands. As much as British political and military officials tried to use food or the threat of hunger to force submission in Wabanaki diplomats or colonial soldiers, the possibility of food scarcity instead challenged the very basis of colonial authorities' power. Resistance jeopardized British leaders' dreams of a placid colonial hierarchy in which everyone knew their place. Hunger not only showed the limits of imperial power and the colonial project; it threatened to overthrow these European ideals entirely. Far from the steady spread of colonial "settlement" that colonial boosters envisioned, European colonization of the northeast remained vulnerable deep into the eighteenth century.

While they may have similarly imperiled British colonial ambitions, colonial and Wabanaki resistance did not share a common cause. Colonists, with their desires for more and more land, diametrically opposed Wabanaki defenses of their sovereignty. The Seven Years' War would erode Wabanaki power relations in the northeast. After the war, British imperial authorities would issue the Proclamation of 1763, seeking to limit further colonial trespasses into Indigenous lands, and hoping to forestall further wars. The discontentment that many provincial soldiers felt with British military leadership would merge with protests of the Proclamation, protests that would begin to blossom into revolutionary fervor. Colonists' greed for Native land would help to drive the British colonies toward greater resistance to imperial rule, and toward revolution.

In spite of the unruliness of provincial soldiers, British authorities would learn from their victory in the Seven Years' War that feeding people was a primary means of controlling them. Policymakers began to believe that managing hunger throughout the empire would enable them to exploit the lives and lands of colonized peoples in the most efficient manner. But Native peoples used hunger cultures and knowledges to resist, even as colonial threats to their food sovereignty became increasingly dire. They had already survived this much. They would continue to endure.

CONCLUSION

Plenty amid Scarcity

When Samuel Kirkland set off for Kanadasaga, he brought with him "as much ham, bread & hard biscuit . . . as I could carry." Kirkland departed from the home of the British empire's superintendent for Indian affairs, William Johnson, who warned the missionary that he might have to share provisions with his Seneca guides. On the second night of Kirkland's two-hundred-mile journey, he and his two guides shared a meal. The Seneca men gathered firewood and built a fire, perfuming the January air with "exceedingly agreeable & pleasant" spruce boughs. Kirkland provided tea and ham for the meal while the guides offered bread. The guides showed Kirkland how to broil slices of ham on sticks thrust into the ground around the fire—"new scenes to me, but highly gratifying," Kirkland observed—and the missionary made a "handsome boiling" of tea. Finally, Kirkland wrote, "we sat round our dish & ate like Brethren." "A better supper I have seldom made," he concluded, although because Kirkland had not yet learned the Seneca language, he could not converse with his dinner companions.[1]

It was a scene of plenty and possibility, Kirkland and his guides eating "like Brethren" from a common pot. Though a seemingly auspicious beginning to

Kirkland's mission, this peaceful vision would not last long. Over the next four months, Kirkland's presence would help to bring danger and scarcity to Kanadasaga. The missionary's first foray into the Seneca community saw a man's mysterious death, a famine, a rotten bear stew, a disastrous meal with an English military officer, multiple episodes of vomit and shame, and the death of Kirkland's adoptive sister from disease and starvation. Kirkland would become intimately familiar with the hunger that faced the Seneca caught in the shifting winds of the British empire. Though he was adopted into a Seneca family and showed admiration for their hunger knowledges, Kirkland would never doubt his colonizing mission—or be able to repay his Seneca family's generosity to him. The distance implied in he and his Seneca guides' inability to speak to each other would endure throughout Kirkland's decades-long borderlands career.[2]

In the northeast, colonizers met hunger either as a foe they did not recognize, like the British, or as a foe of the poor, like the French. Rather than learn from Indigenous ways of managing hunger, colonizers categorized scarcity—and those who experienced it—as aberrant, dependent, and in need of rescue. As the eighteenth century came to a close and the balance of power in the northeast shifted toward British and then American colonizers, the invaders would only further defamiliarize hunger and discount Indigenous hunger knowledges.

In the end, hunger led colonists not only to eat terrible things but to *do* terrible things. It led them to eat and, indeed, enjoy substances they had previously found disgusting. Colonists' borderlands experiences of Indigenous foods challenged colonial ways of categorizing hunger and the body. But hunger also made colonists like Kirkland snarl at a gracious host and forget all about starving Native relations; hunger made Mary Rowlandson steal food from a child. The invaders typically felt more shame about the things that they ate than about the Indigenous peoples that they harmed.

Whether they tightened their belts or told Chenoo tales, the Indigenous peoples of the northeast in the seventeenth and eighteenth centuries had a home for hunger in their cultures. They kept scarcity at bay by foraging, fermenting, and feasting, and they passed down the knowledge of how to do so throughout the generations. They fought hunger with ethics of reciprocity that extended beyond their communities and with systems of knowledge that made plenty out of sufficiency.

Colonial and Indigenous hunger knowledges would only continue to diverge in the coming years. Colonizers might have chosen to adapt to Indigenous hunger cultures, but only very few of them did. The rest participated in regimes that aspired to greater and greater control of food and the body, in the service of colonialism, imperialism, and authoritarianism. Such regimes would weaponize the rhetoric of hunger prevention, as well as hunger itself, against marginalized peoples around the world. The Indigenous targets of such efforts, in the northeast and beyond, would continue to adapt and maintain their traditional knowledges against centuries of colonial oppression.

Seventeenth- and eighteenth-century colonialism provided the template for the imperial and global approaches to hunger that would follow in the centuries to come. Colonizers approached hunger as abnormal, a problem to be solved—or exploited it in the service of genocide. Emphasizing the unnaturalness of hunger would serve to devalue the hunger knowledges of peoples across the globe.

By the late eighteenth century, with the first colonial efforts behind them, imperial authorities shifted their attention away from simply sustaining colonies toward optimizing colonial populations. While England and other European states had commenced colonization in part as a way of removing undesirable people—not solely the criminal but the landless and discontented—from the metropole, the need for soldiers in the global wars of the eighteenth century kicked off a new imperial obsession with demography. The British empire would point to their victory over the French in the Seven Years' War as proof that imperial management of soldiers' food and bodies had worked—and would work on a larger scale. Imperial leaders realized that the colonial invasion demanded more European bodies to colonize it, to displace Indigenous nations, to exploit the land and labor of people of Native and African descent. Politicians, physicians, and other authorities began to believe that more rigorous management would be necessary to ensure stable populations of colonizers and colonized labor. Public health authorities refined new technologies and policies, such as smallpox vaccination, on the bodies of the most vulnerable members of society.[3]

An abundant food supply would be key to this effort to maintain and control populations. As Enlightenment capitalism blossomed, European authorities began to turn from traditional systems of preventing food shortage, such as elites distributing food aid to peasants, to market-based solutions, which would supposedly discourage peasants' dependency. In the colonies, food assistance took its place among an array of increasingly authoritarian mechanisms of bodily control that would come to define imperial regimes throughout the world.[4]

Hunger, and its prevention, would play a central role in imperialist thought and policy throughout the heyday of imperialism. Thomas Malthus, whose *Essay on the Principle of Population* theorized that people's inability to contain their procreative urges would doom the world to overpopulation and famine, set the modern terms of debate over world hunger in 1798. Examining British colonial contexts around the globe, Malthus blamed the hungry for their misery, as had many before him and many would after him. By the time of Malthus's influential text, eighteenth-century imperial reformers had already begun experimenting with nutrition in colonial settings, with the bodies of the enslaved, the Indigenous, and the poor as their test subjects. These authorities drew their inspiration from the very latest in livestock science, believing that hungry people, especially enslaved people and the poor, were akin to animals.[5]

This Enlightenment equation of hunger with irrationality and dependence would shape humanitarian policy for the next two centuries. Imperial authorities continued to spread antihunger policies through the world in the nineteenth and twentieth centuries, arguing for imperialism as a way to relieve the hunger of colonized peoples and ignoring the fact that imperialism was often to blame for that hunger in the first place. At the turn of the twentieth century, nutritional science would create a mechanized, medicalized understanding of the body, fueled by calories and nutrients. A complementary technocratic vision of agriculture would soon follow. Driven by imperial science, governments and nongovernmental organizations implemented policies to try to address scarcity on national, imperial, and global scales. These policies included rationing during war, food assistance at home, and food aid abroad. The Green Revolution sought to replace longstanding Indigenous agricultural knowledges with Western industrial agriculture in the developing world. While these efforts in many ways have been successful at reducing food scarcity, they have often had the effect of demonizing the poor, and they have failed to address the root causes of hunger, especially poverty and inequality. The clumsiest humanitarian policy continues to equate poverty with ignorance while ignoring the environmental and political causes of famine. By dismissing local knowledges and contexts, international aid has risked worsening the lives of the people it intends to help.[6]

Since Malthus, generations of observers have expressed concern about the global food supply, often predicting dire famine in the near future. These concerns might take the form of calls for sustainability and food justice, movements that have become deeply rooted in communities of color in recent years. But concerns over famine have also taken more sinister forms, scapegoating marginalized peoples for resource scarcity. Historically, fears of food shortage have spiked in response to increasing food prices, rising birthrates, and environmental problems, but also in times of broader anxiety about cultural differences, immigration, sexuality, and race. Capitalizing on these fears of marginalized peoples, authoritarian regimes have used hunger as a slow genocidal weapon. Such brutality, and the inadequacy of international responses, shows the dangers of technocratic definitions of hunger that do not recognize the power relations of its origins. Where Malthus assumed that hunger was an unavoidable consequence of poor people's insatiable sexual appetites, critics have argued that injustice, not a shortfall of food, is to blame for most hunger. In the words of the economist Amartya Sen, "There is, indeed, no such thing as an apolitical food problem."[7]

Food is an essential part of settler colonial regimes in North America. Since the colonial invasion began, British and then American and Canadian colonial authorities have worked to deny Native peoples the ability to provide for themselves. Attacks on Native food sovereignty have included destroying food stores, forcing Native people off of their homelands, damming rivers and polluting waterways, and distributing government rations of colonial foods such as flour, beef, and sugar. In addition to these physical attacks on food sovereignty, cultural genocide has disrupted the transmission of hunger knowledges between the generations. The result has been an epidemic of food insecurity, malnutrition, metabolic disorders, and health disparities in Indigenous communities. As in

175

other parts of the world, colonial authorities have used hunger as a slow genocidal weapon. Today, Native Americans and Alaska Natives are 20 percent more likely to experience food insecurity than White Americans.[8]

But Indigenous peoples have not been the only victims of the United States' colonial approaches to hunger. The United States is home to a "paradox of plenty": a place where unprecedented affluence obscures brutal inequality. Across American history, the racialization of poverty and hunger has stigmatized government assistance to the poor. The result is that millions of Americans—disproportionately people who live in rural places, elderly people, children, or Black, Indigenous, and/or Latinx people—go hungry every day. Using their own forms of hunger knowledges, families across America struggle with what one historian has called "the hard work of being poor." "This has been the cruel irony of America to me," writes Melissa Chadburn in a 2018 essay about her food-insecure childhood in an impoverished Filipino immigrant family: "It is the place of dreams, yet to long for anything in this country is to be an object of shame and repulsion." Chadburn's family deployed their own hunger knowledges "to get in front of the hunger" by filling their stomachs with fatty, sugary processed foods: "casseroles, greasy noodle dishes, and white bread covered in that sweetened condensed milk." In the words of Raphael Richmond, a Black mother of six relying on food assistance in Washington, D.C., surviving from month to month on shrinking benefits is "Mama's version of the hunger games," games that are impossible to win.[9]

For Native people, as for non-Native people, the fight for food justice is simultaneously a fight for political justice. For centuries, Indigenous peoples have fought to protect their food sovereignty from the forces of colonial destruction. Food sovereignty is also foundational to broader fights for Indigenous self-determination, land rights, and sustainability. These efforts overlap with movements to revitalize Indigenous languages and cultures: "food sovereignty is not just a goal in and of itself, but a tool to achieve other aspects of cultural restoration," writes the food studies scholar Elizabeth Hoover, who is of Mohawk and M'ikmaq descent. Indigenous food sovereignty efforts today take the form of maintaining and revitalizing traditional agricultural methods, including saving heritage seeds; foraging, hunting, fishing, preserving, and cooking traditional foods; redistributing these foods to communities; and educating younger generations about heritage foodways. These movements are hyperlocal, rooted in the lands and communities that are so critical to Indigenous peoples, but they also form part of larger pan-tribal movements for Indigenous rights.[10]

At the time of the completion of this book, in early 2021, the United States finds itself in the grip of interlocking crises: a pandemic which has taken hundreds of thousands of lives, disproportionately of people of color; a White supremacist insurrection, which in addition to threatening American democracy has once again laid bare the racism and colonialism that date back to America's origins; runaway climate change, which has produced horrifyingly destructive wildfires, hurricanes, and extreme heat and cold; and inadequate economic policy that has left millions staring into the abyss of poverty and hunger. In response to these crises have come protests for racial justice, unprecedented in scale: in the United Sates, the Black Lives Matter movement, and, in Canada, the Land Back movement for Indigenous sovereignty. There is a feeling that we are on the brink either of a new world or of a brutal retrenchment of the old order.

The interconnected nature of these present-day disasters would have come as no surprise to either the colonial invaders or the Indigenous peoples of the early northeast. Early modern Europeans, living through their own age of violence, disease, and famine, recognized that crises create further crises. The English minister John Norden wrote in 1615 that "warres follow securitie, famine war, and the pestilence followes famine." Even one of these disasters, Norden observed, had the "force to confound kingdoms." Indigenous commentators have noted the echoes of early America in the present moment. As Jamie Azure, the tribal chairman of the Turtle Mountain Band of Chippewa, observed about living through the COVID-19 pandemic, "It is kind of a Catch-22 to be so well-adjusted to react to threats . . . . You're forced to stay in a specific area, you're told to trust the government, you're told food will be scarce— welcome to 1700s Native nation."[11]

In these times, the resilience of Native peoples remains an inspiration and a warning. In response to the pandemic and the food scarcity it has brought, Native communities are turning to the same hunger knowledges that have helped them to survive for generations. In the Seneca Nation, the pandemic has spurred new growth at Gakwi:yo:h Farms, where farmers are expanding maple sap collection, establishing a new bison herd, and selling and distributing food throughout the reservation. While rates of the virus have been comparatively low in the Seneca Nation due to public health measures, the pandemic has imperiled cherished knowledges in Indigenous communities across the continent. The virus has killed Native Americans at approaching twice the rate as White Americans, and it is particularly deadly for the elders who pass along language and cultural traditions.[12]

As in the seventeenth- and eighteenth-century Indigenous cultures of the northeast, today's Indigenous scholars continue to see reciprocity as a fundamental aspect of Indigenous food systems. The philosopher Kyle Whyte, an enrolled member of the Citizen Potawatomi Nation, writes of the importance of "collective food relations" as part of Indigenous food sovereignty and emphasizes "moral relationships" with human and non-human entities as essential to resilience. The Native nations of the northeast have survived centuries of colonization by maintaining these principles. Indigenous paradigms, long discounted by colonial authorities, offer alternative knowledge systems for sustenance and survival in the twenty-first century.[13]

Non-Native people have a great deal to learn from Indigenous hunger knowledges. Colonial narratives of hunger as aberrant, as the product of poverty, as symptomatic of undesirable dependence, ignore the other roles that hunger, hunger culture, and hunger knowledges have played in Indigenous communities for many generations. Traditional understandings of hunger and ways of surviving it have persisted within Indigenous cultures even as colonialism attempted to destroy them. While non-Native people have much to learn from Indigenous knowledges, such learning must be bounded by what Indigenous peoples want to teach. Otherwise, the colonial appropriation of Indigenous knowledges will continue to have brutal consequences for Native people. Hoover notes that during the grocery shortages at the beginning of the pandemic, non-Native consumers bought up Diné survival foods, leaving inadequate supplies for tribal elders—an example of colonizers learning all the wrong lessons from Indigenous strategies of resilience.[14]

By contrast, living in reciprocity with each other, and with the land, generates its own form of abundance. In her 2006 poem "Algonkian Paradise," the Abenaki poet Cheryl Savageau declares, "It would be hard to starve here." Listing the bounty of her home landscape as it was before the colonial invasion, she writes, "Every place you turn, there is food." She quotes the seventeenth-century French missionary Pierre Biard's claim that Wabanaki people had "a lavish living, all without work": "A condition, he felt, that should only be found in Paradise." Then Savageau questions whether Biard himself had ever performed the intensive labor of seeking sustenance in these traditional ways: "Had he ever gone fishing for the elusive food? Gathered nuts, or berries deep in thorns and mosquitoes?" The poem closes on twin notes of loss and survivance. "If we could have the land back the way it was, it would be Paradise, for sure," Savageau concludes. Paradise with the pleasures of working hard for one's food—an Indigenous world a colonial missionary could not understand.[15]

But, according to Robin Wall Kimmerer, a botanist and enrolled member of the Citizen Potawatomi Nation, Indigenous ideas are not limited to Native people. "Each of us comes from people who were once [I]ndigenous," she reminds her readers. Invoking the dangers of the windigo's greed, Kimmerer calls for "cultures of gratitude" as "a powerful antidote to Windigo psychosis."[16] Like the peoples of the early northeast, humans in the twenty-first century confront an uncertain future. Listening to Indigenous knowledges will be vital and necessary in a world where the greed of the windigos threatens to devour everyone.

NOTES

Introduction

1. Likely Lieutenant Henry Congalton. Samuel Kirkland, "A Journal of the Reverend Samuel Kirkland, November 1764–June 1765," in *The Journals of Samuel Kirkland*, ed. Walter Pilkington (Clinton, N.Y.: Hamilton College Press, 1980), n54.

2. Kirkland, "Journal," 31. Emphasis in the original.

3. Kirkland, "Journal," 32. Emphasis in the original.

4. On Kirkland's first mission, see Alan Taylor, *The Divided Ground: Indians, Settlers, and the Northern Borderland of the American Revolution* (New York: Vintage Books, 2006), 52–54.

5. *Violent Appetites* theorizes the history of hunger in and beyond early America. It is a cultural history of scarcity that focuses on knowledge-making while keeping the physiological experience of hunger at the forefront. Although in this book I consider the political ramifications of different cultures' definitions and uses of hunger in early America, the political dimensions of hunger are not the main focus of analysis here. For a work devoted to the politics of hunger in the larger Atlantic World in the late eighteenth and early nineteenth centuries, see Rachel B. Herrmann, *No Useless Mouth: Waging War and Fighting Hunger in the American Revolution* (Ithaca: Cornell University Press, 2019).

6. Ann Little pointed to the importance of cultural rationalizations for colonization in *Abraham in Arms: War and Gender in Colonial New England* (Philadelphia: University of Pennsylvania Press, 2007), 5.

7. The literary critic Rob Nixon has argued that environmental catastrophe unfolds in a "slow violence" against marginalized peoples. Rob Nixon, *Slow Violence and the Environmentalism of the Poor* (Cambridge: Harvard University Press, 2013).

8. Some literary readings of hunger in early America have viewed it solely as metaphorical. For one example, see Jordan Alexander Stein, "Mary Rowlandson's Hunger and the Historiography of Sexuality," *American Literature* 81, no. 3 (September 2009): 469–95. A foundational work on colonial mythology is Richard Slotkin, *Regeneration through Violence: The Mythology of the American Frontier, 1600–1860* (Norman: University of Oklahoma Press, 1973).

9. I use the term "northeastern borderlands" following the example of Little, *Abraham in Arms,* and other scholars of the region. Rather than linear frontiers, borderlands are "ambiguous and often-unstable realms where boundaries are also crossroads, peripheries are also central places, homelands are also passing-through places, and the end points of empire are also forks in the road." Pekka Hämäläinen and Samuel Truett, "On Borderlands," *Journal of American History* 98, no. 2 (September 2011): 338. On Indigenous place names in the northeast, see Lisa Brooks, *The Common Pot: The Recovery of Native Space in the Northeast* (Minneapolis: University of Minnesota Press, 2008), introduction; Lisa Brooks, "Awikhigawôgan ta Pildowi Ôjmowôgan: Mapping a New History," *William and Mary Quarterly* 75, no. 2 (April 2018): 259–94.

10. There has been much debate in the field of early American studies about the use of the term "settler," which faces some scrutiny for the implication that Indigenous peoples were somehow "unsettled," but it has been embraced by such fields as Native American and Indigenous Studies. I employ the term "settler" sparingly, only in discussions of the field of settler colonial studies. I am drawing my definition of settler colonialism from Patrick Wolfe, "Settler Colonialism and the Elimination of the Native," *Journal of Genocide Research* 8, no. 4 (December 2006): 387–409; see also "Forum: Settler Colonialism in Early American History," *William and Mary Quarterly* 76, no. 3 (July 2019): 361–443. Questions about the best language to describe interactions between Indigenous peoples and colonists have been extensively discussed in early American studies. See "Forum: Colonial Historians and American Indians," *William and Mary Quarterly* 69, no. 3 (July 2012): 451–540. On terminology and style within Native and Indigenous Studies, see Gregory Younging, *Elements of Indigenous Style: A Guide for Writing by and about Indigenous Peoples* (Edmonton: Brush Education, 2018).

11. My thanks to Cristobal Silva for helping me to think through these definitions. John Harris, *The Divine Physician* (Norwich: T. Goddard and L. Reeve, 1709), 18.

12. Sébastian Rale, *A Dictionary of the Abnaki Language, In North America* (Cambridge, Mass.: Charles Folsom, 1833), 452, 480. My translations from the French. On this source and the challenges of Abenaki-French-English translation more generally, see Brooks, "Awikhigawôgan ta Pildowi Ôjmowôgan," 262–67. *The Jesuit Relations and Allied Documents: Travels and Explorations of the Jesuit Missionaries in New France, 1610–1791,* ed. Reuben Gold Thwaites (Cleveland: Burrows Brothers, 1900), 54 (hereafter JR). My translation. For more

on Wabanaki uses of words related to hunger, see Mary Black-Rogers, "Varieties of 'Starving': Semantics and Survival in the Subarctic Fur Trade, 1750–1850," *Ethnohistory* 33, no. 4 (Fall 1986): 353–83.

13. Iroquois translation manual for the missionaries at Lac de Deux Montagnes, Quebec, 1754, John Carter Brown Library, Providence, R.I., leaves 32 recto–33 recto, Archive.org, https://archive.org/details/iroquoistranslatooguic. Pierre Joseph Marie Chaumonot, French-Huron dictionary and vocabulary, c. 1640, John Carter Brown Library, Archive.org, https://archive.org/details/frenchhurondictioochau/page/n115/mode/2up. My translation from the French.

14. On the assumptions embedded in the calorie, see Nick Cullather, "The Foreign Policy of the Calorie," *American Historical Review* 112, no. 2 (April 2007): 337–64. On the cultural definition of hunger, see Martin Bruegel, "From the Crisis of Food to Food in Crisis," *Gastronomica: The Journal of Food and Culture* 11, no. 3 (Fall 2011): 42.

15. These are my terms and not the words that my historical actors would have used. The interdisciplinarity of these terms, however, is very much in line with the densely intertwined ways people in the seventeenth and eighteenth centuries would have viewed nature, the body, religion, culture, and politics, rather than the ways that these forms of knowledge have been segmented in the academy since the late nineteenth century. I am using William Sewell's definition of culture as "a system of symbols and meanings" and "practice." William Sewell, "The Concepts of Culture," in *Logics of History: Social Theory and Social Transformation* (Chicago: University of Chicago Press, 2005), 164. Elaine Scarry famously stated that the physical experience of pain is fundamentally "inexpressible"; however, a number of scholars have argued for distinctive cultural ideas about pain in early modern Europe. Elaine Scarry, *The Body in Pain: The Making and Unmaking of the World* (New York: Oxford University Press, 1985), 3–11; Jan Frans van Dijkhuizen and Karl A. E. Enenkel, eds., *The Sense of Suffering: Constructions of Physical Pain in Early Modern Culture* (Leiden: Brill, 2009); Tomas Macsotay, Cornelius van der Haven, and Karen Vanhaesebrouch, eds., *The Hurtful Body: Performing and Beholding Pain, 1600–1800* (Manchester: Manchester University Press, 2017); Lisa Silverman, *Tortured Subjects: Pain, Truth, and the Body in Early Modern France* (Chicago: University of Chicago Press, 2001).

16. Cameron B. Strang, *Frontiers of Science: Imperialism and Natural Knowledge in the Gulf South Borderlands, 1500–1850* (Chapel Hill: Omohundro Institute of Early American History and Culture and University of North Carolina Press, 2018); Kelly Wisecup, *Medical Encounters: Knowledge and Identity in Early American Literatures* (Amherst: University of Massachusetts Press, 2013); Christopher M. Parsons, *A Not-So-New World: Empire and Environment in Colonial North America* (Philadelphia: University of Pennsylvania Press, 2018); Anya Zilberstein, *A Temperate Empire: Making Climate Change in Early America* (New York: Oxford University Press, 2016); Thomas M. Wickman, *Snowshoe Country: An Environmental and Cultural History of Winter in the Early American Northeast* (New York: Cambridge University Press, 2018); Marcy Norton, "Subaltern Technologies and Early Modernity in the Atlantic World," *Colonial Latin American Review* 26, no. 1 (2017): 18–13. On "tacit

knowledge," see Michael Polyani, *The Tacit Dimension* (Gloucester: Peter Smith, 1983); and Whitney Barlow Robles, "Flatness," in *The Philosophy Chamber: Art and Science in Harvard's Teaching Cabinet, 1766–1820,* ed. Ethan W. Lasser (Cambridge: Harvard Art Museums, 2017). On marginalized peoples' roles in the production of natural history knowledge in early America, see Susan Scott Parrish, *American Curiosity: Cultures of Natural History in the Colonial British Atlantic World* (Chapel Hill: Omohundro Institute of Early American History and Culture and University of North Carolina Press, 2006), 174–258; Strang, *Frontiers of Science*; Andrew Lewis, *A Democracy of Facts: Natural History in the Early Republic* (Philadelphia: University of Pennsylvania Press, 2011). On the "culturally-induced igno-rances" that keep knowledge from being transmitted, see Londa Schiebinger, *Plants and Empire: Colonial Bioprospecting in the Atlanta World* (Cambridge: Harvard University Press, 2004), 3; see also *Agnotology: The Making and Unmaking of Ignorance,* ed. Robert N. Proctor and Londa Schiebinger (Stanford: Stanford University Press, 2008); Paul Mapp, *The Elusive West and the Contest for Empire, 1713–1763* (Chapel Hill: Omohundro Institute of Early American History and Culture and University of North Carolina Press, 2011).

17. On the challenges of estimating Indigenous populations in North America before colonization, see George R. Milner and George Chaplin, "Eastern North American Population at CA. A.D. 1500," *American Antiquity* 75, no. 4 (October 2010): 707–26.

18. Zachary McLeod Hutchins, *Inventing Eden: Primitivism, Millennialism, and the Making of New England* (New York: Oxford University Press, 2014). John Demos, *Circles and Lines: The Shape of Life in Early America* (Cambridge: Harvard University Press, 2004), 32. Kathleen Donegan, *Seasons of Misery: Catastrophe and Colonial Settlement in Early America* (Philadelphia: University of Pennsylvania Press, 2014), 2–3.

19. For an overview and critique of the New England town social history genre, see Robert C. Twombly, "What Was Important and What Was Not: Review of *The Minutemen and Their World* by Robert A. Gross," *Reviews in American History* 4, no. 4 (December 1976), 526–32. Important scholarship on New England from the last two decades includes: Lisa Brooks, *Our Beloved Kin: A New History of King Philip's War* (New Haven: Yale University Press, 2018); Cristobal Silva, *Miraculous Plagues: An Epidemiology of Early New England Narrative* (New York: Oxford University Press, 2011); Katherine Grandjean, *American Passage: The Communications Frontier in Early New England* (Cambridge: Harvard University Press, 2015); Wendy Warren, *New England Bound: Slavery and Colonization in Early America* (New York: Liveright, 2016); Ann M. Little, *The Many Captivities of Esther Wheelwright* (New Haven: Yale University Press, 2016); Gina M. Martino, *Women at War in the Borderlands of the Early American Northeast* (Chapel Hill: University of North Carolina Press, 2018).

20. The statistics on population in New France come from Joseph Bouchette, *A Topographical Description of the Provinces of Lower Canada* (London, 1815), 8; on population in New England, see Robert V. Wells, *Population of the British Colonies in America before 1776: A Survey of Census Data* (Princeton: Princeton University Press, 1975), 69, 79, 89, 97. On French policies of assimilation, see Sara E. Melzer, *Colonizer or Colonized: The Hidden Stories of Early Modern French Culture* (Philadelphia: University of Pennsylvania Press, 2012), chap.

4. On the demographics of Montreal and the surrounding colonial areas, see Louise Dechêne, *Habitants and Merchants in Seventeenth-Century Montreal,* trans. Liani Vardi (Montreal: McGill–Queen's University Press, 1993), chaps. 2–3.

21. On changing French understandings and uses of landscapes, see Colin M. Coates, *Metamorphoses of Landscape and Community in Early Quebec* (Montreal: McGill–Queen's University Press, 2000), 10–12; Parsons, *Not-So-New World.* On the fur trade and French assimilation with Indigenous peoples, see Melzer, *Colonizer or Colonized,* 112–13; Dechêne, *Habitants and Merchants,* 5–15; Guillaume Aubert, " 'The Blood of France': Race and Purity of Blood in the French Atlantic World," *William and Mary Quarterly* 61, no. 3 (July 2004): 439–78. On slavery in New France, see Brett Rushforth, *Bonds of Alliance: Indigenous and Atlantic Slaveries in New France* (Chapel Hill: Omohundro Institute of Early American History and Culture and University of North Carolina Press, 2012). The faulty assertion that Indigenous peoples "receded into the shadows" appears in Coates, *Metamorphoses of Landscape and Community,* 8.

22. On the myth of the "disappearing Indian" as crafted by colonial historians, see Jean O'Brien, *Firsting and Lasting: Writing Indians Out of Existence in New England* (Minneapolis: University of Minnesota Press, 2010). On Indigenous dominance in early America, see Emerson W. Baker and John G. Reid, "Amerindian Power in the Early Modern Northeast: A Reappraisal," *William and Mary Quarterly* 61, no. 1 (January 2004): 77–106; Michael Witgen, *An Infinity of Nations: How the Native New World Shaped Early America* (Philadelphia: University of Pennsylvania Press, 2013). On the ways Indigenous peoples balanced rival empires in the eighteenth century, see Taylor, *Divided Ground;* Richard White, *The Middle Ground: Indians, Empires, and Republics in the Great Lakes Region, 1650–1815* (Cambridge: Cambridge University Press, 1991).

23. Quotation is from Martino, *Women at War in the Borderlands of the Early American Northeast,* 4. Important scholarship on King Philip's War includes: Brooks, *Our Beloved Kin;* Christine DeLucia, *Memory Lands: King Philip's War and the Place of Violence in the Northeast* (New Haven: Yale University Press, 2018); Jill Lepore, *The Name of War: King Phillip's War and the Origins of American Identity* (New York: Knopf, 1998). Important scholarship on the global intercolonial conflicts includes: Christian Ayne Crouch, *Nobility Lost: French and Canadian Martial Cultures, Indians and The End of New France* (Ithaca: Cornell University Press, 2014); Erica Charters, *Disease, War, and the Imperial State: The Welfare of the British Armed Forces during the Seven Years' War* (Chicago: University of Chicago Press, 2014); John Grenier, *The First Way of War: American War Making on the Frontier, 1607–1814* (New York: Cambridge University Press, 2005); Fred Anderson, *Crucible of War: The Seven Years' War and the Fate of Empire in British North America, 1754–1766* (New York: Knopf, 2000); Guy Chet, *Conquering the American Wilderness: The Triumph of European Warfare in the Colonial Northeast* (Amherst: University of Massachusetts Press, 2003); Wayne E. Lee, *Barbarians and Brothers: Anglo-American Warfare, 1500–1865* (Oxford University Press, 2011).

24. My discussion of resistance is informed by scholarship on race, Indigeneity, and class. Important works include: Gerald Vizenor, *Manifest Manners: Narratives on Postindian*

Survivance (Lincoln: University of Nebraska Press, 1994); Gerald Vizenor, ed., *Survivance: Narratives of Native Presence* (Lincoln: University of Nebraska Press, 2008); Robin D. G. Kelley, *Race Rebels: Culture, Politics, and the Black Working Class* (New York: Free Press, 1994); James C. Scott, *Weapons of the Weak: Everyday Forms of Peasant Resistance* (New Haven: Yale University Press, 1985); James C. Scott, *Domination and the Arts of Resistance: Hidden Transcripts* (New Haven: Yale University Press, 1992); Leanne Betasamosake Simpson, *As We Have Always Done: Indigenous Freedom through Radical Resistance* (Minneapolis: University of Minnesota Press, 2017). Scholars have traced Indigenous survival and resistance in New England; for example, see Brooks, *Our Beloved Kin;* Colin G. Calloway, *The Western Abenakis of Vermont, 1600–1800: War, Migration, and the Survival of an Indian People* (Norman: University of Oklahoma Press, 1994).

25. On Haudenosaunee and Algonquian foodways, see Jane Mt. Pleasant, "A New Paradigm for Pre-Columbian Agriculture in North America," *Early American Studies* 13, no. 2 (Spring 2015): 374–412; William Cronon, *Changes in the Land: Indians, Colonists, and the Ecology of New England* (New York: Hill and Wang, 1984); Michael A. LaCombe, *Political Gastronomy: Food and Authority in the English Atlantic World* (Philadelphia: University of Pennsylvania Press, 2012), 12–15; Howard S. Russell, *Indian New England before the Mayflower* (Hanover: University Press of New England, 1980), 76–91; Alison Norman, " 'Fit for the Table of the Most Fastidious Epicure': Culinary Colonialism in the Upper Canadian Contact Zone," in *Edible Histories, Cultural Politics: Towards a Canadian Food History,* ed. Franca Iacovetta, Valerie J. Korinek, Marlene Epp (Toronto: University of Toronto Press, 2012), 33–35; Coates, *Metamorphoses of Landscape and Community,* 7; Carolyn Raine, *A Woodland Feast: Native American Foodways of the 17th and 18th Centuries* (Stonington, Me.: Penobscot Press, 2000), 1.

26. JR 67:213–19. Frederick Matthew Wiseman, *The Voice of the Dawn: An Autohistory of the Abenaki Nation* (Hanover: University Press of New England, 2001), 30. Wickman, *Snowshoe Country,* 20–22. Strother E. Roberts, "The Dog Days of Winter: Indigenous Dogs, Indian Hunters, and Wintertime Subsistence in the Northeast," *Northeastern Naturalist* 24, no. 7 (2017): H1–H21. Archaeologists have noted that maize cultivation extended into the subarctic region despite the short growing season. Matthew Boyd and Clarence Surette, "Northernmost Precontact Maize in North America," *American Antiquity* 75, no. 1 (January 2010): 117–33.

27. The quotation of "a creation story from hell" is from Karen Ordahl Kupperman, *The Jamestown Project* (Cambridge: Harvard University Press, 2008), 1. On early colonial "seasons of misery," see Donegan, *Seasons of Misery;* Rachel B. Herrmann, " 'The Tragicall Historie': Food and Abundance in Colonial Jamestown," *William and Mary Quarterly* 68, no. 1 (January 2011): 47–71; William M. Kelso, *Jamestown: The Truth Revealed* (Charlottesville: University of Virginia Press, 2017), 185–203; Katherine A. Grandjean, *American Passage,* chap. 1; LaCombe, *Political Gastronomy,* 90–107. On negotiations between Indigenous peoples and early colonial invaders, see Camilla Townsend, *Pocahontas and the Powhatan Dilemma* (New York: Hill and Wang, 2007), x–xi, 35–37; Karen Ordahl

Kupperman, *Indians and English: Facing Off in Early America* (Ithaca: Cornell University Press, 2000), 14–15; LaCombe, *Political Gastronomy*, 90–107, 135–67. On Indigenous peoples teaching foodways to colonists in New France, see Victoria Dickerson, "Curiosity into Edibility: The Taste of New France," in *What's to Eat?: Entrées in Canadian Food History*, ed. Nathalie Cooke (Montreal: McGill–Queen's University Press, 2009), 46; Margery Fee, "Stories of Traditional Aboriginal Food, Health, and Territory," in *What's to Eat?: Entrées in Canadian Food History*, 60–62.

28. On climate and crisis in the seventeenth century, see Geoffrey Parker, *Europe in Crisis: 1598–1648* (Ithaca: Cornell University Press, 1979); Geoffrey Parker and Lesley M. Smith, *The General Crisis of the Seventeenth Century*, 2nd ed. (London and New York: Routledge, 1997); Geoffrey Parker, *Global Crisis: War, Climate Change and Catastrophe in the Seventeenth Century* (New Haven: Yale University Press, 2013). On Indigenous and European adaptations to northern climes and the Little Ice Age: Parsons, *A Not-So-New World*; Wickman, *Snowshoe Country*; Sam White, *A Cold Welcome: The Little Ice Age and Europe's Encounter with North America* (Cambridge: Harvard University Press, 2017). Both early Americanists and scholars of Indigenous environmental studies have argued that Native environmental knowledges offer crucial alternatives in our own era of climate change. See Joyce E. Chaplin, "Ogres and Omnivores: Early American Historians and Climate History," *William and Mary Quarterly* 72, no. 1 (January 2015): 25–32; Joyce E. Chaplin, "The Other Revolution," *Early American Studies* 13, no. 2 (Spring 2015): 285–308; Zilberstein, *Temperate Empire*. Important works in Indigenous environmental studies include: Kyle Whyte, "Critical Investigations of Resilience: A Brief Introduction to Indigenous Environmental Studies and Sciences," *Daedalus: Journal of the American Academy of Arts and Sciences* 147, no. 2 (2018): 136–47; Robin Kimmerer, *Braiding Sweetgrass: Indigenous Wisdom, Scientific Knowledge and the Teachings of Plants* (Minneapolis: Milkweed Editions, 2013).

29. On early modern humoral understandings of the body, see Olivia Weisser, *Ill Composed: Sickness, Gender, and Belief in Early Modern England* (New Haven: Yale University Press, 2016), 20–22; Antoinette Emch-Dériaz, "The Non-Naturals Made Easy," in *The Popularization of Medicine, 1650–1850*, ed. Roy Porter (New York: Routledge, 1992), 134–59; Ulinka Rublack and Pamela Selwyn, "Fluxes: The Early Modern Body and the Emotions," *History Workshop Journal* 53 (Spring 2002): 1–16. On colonists' environmental theories of the body in early America, see Joyce E. Chaplin, *Subject Matter: Technology, the Body, and Science on the Anglo American Frontier, 1500–1676* (Cambridge: Harvard University Press, 2001), 255–77; Kupperman, *Indians and English*, 41–76. On convergent theories of the body among Indigenous North American, west African, and European cultures, see Sharon Block, *Colonial Complexions: Race and Bodies in Eighteenth-Century America* (Philadelphia: University of Pennsylvania Press, 2018), 15–16. On environmental change, Philip Deloria notes that "change is in fact destruction" for Indigenous peoples, whose cultures are rooted in their homelands. "Places Like Houses, Banks, and Continents: An Appreciative Reply to the Presidential Address," *American Quarterly* 58,

no. 1 (March 2006): 26. Key works in the history of the body in early America include: *A Centre of Wonders: The Body in Early America*, ed. Janet Moore Lindman and Michele Lise Tarter (Ithaca: Cornell University Press, 2001); Kathleen Brown, *Foul Bodies: Cleanliness in Early America* (New Haven: Yale University Press, 2009); Greta LaFleur, *The Natural History of Sexuality in Early America* (Baltimore: Johns Hopkins University Press, 2018); Trudy Eden, *The Early American Table: Food and Society in the New World* (DeKalb: Northern Illinois University Press, 2008).

30. Alfred Crosby, *The Columbian Exchange: Biological and Cultural Consequences of 1492* (Westport, Conn.: Greenwood Publishing, 1972). Norman, " 'Fit for the Table of the Most Fastidious Epicure,'" 36–45. Sarah F. McMahon, "A Comfortable Subsistence: The Changing Composition of Diet in Rural New England, 1620–1840," *William and Mary Quarterly* 42, no. 1 (January 1985): 33, 26–65, 28–29, 33; see also Sarah F. McMahon, " 'All Things in Their Proper Season': Seasonal Rhythms of Diet in Nineteenth Century New England," *Agricultural History* 63, no. 2 (Spring 1989): 130–51. Norman, " 'Fit for the Table of the Most Fastidious Epicure,'" 36–45. Dickerson, "Curiosity into Edibility," 21–54. Louise Dechêne, *Power and Subsistence: The Political Economy of Grain in New France*, trans. Peter Feldstein (Montreal: McGill–Queen's University Press, 2018). On early modern European foodways, see Sara Pennell, *The Birth of the English Kitchen, 1600–1850* (London: Bloomsbury, 2016); Wendy Wall, *Recipes for Thought: Knowledge and Taste in the Early Modern English Kitchen* (Philadelphia: University of Pennsylvania Press, 2016); Stephen Mennell, *All Manners of Food: Eating and Taste in England and France from the Middle Ages to the Present*, 2nd ed. (Urbana: University of Illinois Press, 1996); Barbara Ketchum Wheaton, *Savoring the Past: The French Kitchen and Table from 1300 to 1789* (Philadelphia: University of Pennsylvania Press, 1983); Robert Appelbaum, *Aguecheek's Beef, Belch's Hiccup, and Other Gastronomic Interjections: Literature, Culture, and Food among the Early Moderns* (Chicago: University of Chicago Press, 2006).

31. On the history of the concept of food sovereignty, see Elizabeth Hoover, " 'You Can't Say You're Sovereign If You Can't Feed Yourself': Defining and Enacting Food Sovereignty in American Indian Community Gardening," *American Indian Culture and Research Journal* 41, no. 3: Special Issue on Indigenous Food Sovereignty (2017): 32–34. Rachel B. Herrmann describes three distinct kinds of colonial and Indigenous negotiations over hunger policy in the late eighteenth and early nineteenth centuries. All of these behaviors hinged on the strategic and symbolic importance of food. Both Native and colonial powers used "food diplomacy," the practice of cementing alliances via "the sharing of or collective abstention from" food. In "victual warfare," belligerents turned to "stealing, withholding, or destroying" food, either their own or their enemies', for strategic gain. Finally, in "victual imperialism," imperial authorities exploited anti-hunger policies, such as " 'civilization' programs," to assert imperial authority over Indigenous peoples. *No Useless Mouth*, 9–10. On Indigenous hunger in the eighteenth century see Herrmann, *No Useless Mouth*; Little, *Many Captivities of Esther Wheelwright*, 51–56; Wickman, *Snowshoe Country*, 193–233. On colonial ideas about Indigenous poverty, see Cronon, *Changes in the*

Land, 34–53; Jennifer Anderson, " 'A Laudable Spirit of Enterprise': Renegotiating Land, Natural Resources, and Power on Post-Revolutionary Long Island," *EAS* 13, no. 2 (2015): 413–42; Mt. Pleasant, "New Paradigm for Pre-Columbian Agriculture in North America." On Native food sovereignty in other parts of the continent in the eighteenth century, see Susan Sleeper-Smith, *Indigenous Prosperity and American Conquest: Indian Women of the Ohio River Valley, 1690–1792* (Chapel Hill: Omohundro Institute of Early American History and Culture and University of North Carolina Press, 2018), esp. chap. 1; Mary Elizabeth Fitts, *Fit for War: Sustenance and Order in the Mid-Eighteenth-Century Catawba Nation* (Gainesville: University of Florida Press, 2017). For overviews of food and power in early America, see Michael A. LaCombe, "Subject or Signifier?: Food in Early North America," *History Compass* 11, no. 10 (2013): 859–68; Jennifer L. Anderson and Anya Zilberstein, "Empowering Appetites: The Political Economy and Culture of Food in the Early Atlantic World," *Early American Studies* 19, no. 2 (Spring 2021): 195–214.

32. The classic study of American ideals of plenty is David M. Potter, *People of Plenty: Economic Abundance and the American Character* (Chicago: University of Chicago Press, 1954). For overviews of studies of plenty and food in American history, see Amy Bentley, "American Abundance Examined: David M. Potter's *People of Plenty* and the Study of Food," *Digest: An Interdisciplinary Study of Food and Foodways* 15 (1995): 20–24; Amy Bentley, "Sustenance, Abundance, and the Place of Food in United States Histories," in *Writing Food History: A Global Perspective,* ed. Kyri Claflin and Peter Scholliers (London and New York: Berg, 2012), 72–86; Sandra Oliver, "Ruminations on the State of American Food History," *Gastronomica: The Journal of Food and Culture* 6, no. 4 (Fall 2006): 91–98. Scholarship on food, scarcity, and power in early America and the Atlantic World includes: Anderson and Zilberstein, "Empowering Appetites"; Herrmann, *No Useless Mouth*; LaCombe, *Political Gastronomy*; LaCombe, "Subject or Signifier?"; Eden, *Early American Table*; Kelly L. Watson, *Insatiable Appetites: Imperial Encounters with Cannibals in the North Atlantic World* (New York: New York University Press, 2015); Appelbaum, *Aguecheek's Beef*; Robert Appelbaum, "Hunger in Early Virginia: Indians and English Facing Off over Excess, Want, and Need," in *Envisioning an English Empire: Jamestown and the Making of the North Atlantic World,* ed. Robert Appelbaum and John Sweet (Philadelphia: University of Pennsylvania Press, 2005), 195–216; James McWilliams, *A Revolution in Eating: How the Quest for Food Shaped America* (New York: Columbia University Press, 2007).

33. On the psychological effects of hunger, see Ancel Keys, Josef Brozek, Austin Henschel, Olaf Mickelsen, and Henry Longstreet Taylor, *The Biology of Human Starvation* (Minneapolis: University of Minnesota Press, 1950), 2:835–38, 880–904, 84. The literary historian Piero Camporesi argued that hunger and the consumption of tainted grain induced altered states in early modern peasants. Piero Camporesi, *Bread of Dreams: Food and Fantasy in Early Modern Europe,* trans. David Gentilcore (Cambridge: Polity Press, 1989). On hunger's social effects, see Robert Dirks, "Social Responses during Severe Food Shortages and Famine," *Current Anthropology* 21, no. 1 (February 1980): 21–32.

34. The first issue of *Gastronomica* neatly summed up food studies scholars' tendency to emphasize plenty: "The more we know about food, the greater our pleasure in it." Darra Goldstein, "Food Studies Come of Age," *Gastronomica: The Journal of Food and Culture* 1, no. 1 (Winter 2001): iii–iv. In the eighteenth century, reformers experimented on marginalized populations by applying animal science to feeding free and unfree laborers. Anya Zilberstein, "Bastard Breadfruit and Other Cheap Provisions: Early Food Science for the Welfare of the Lower Orders," *Early Science and Medicine* 21 (2016): 492–508. Even more notoriously, during World War II, Nazi leaders used starvation as a cheap method of exterminating populations; doctors in the occupied Netherlands and the Warsaw ghetto diligently recorded the horrific consequences of these policies. Lizzie Collingham, *The Taste of War: World War II and the Battle for Food* (London: Penguin, 2011), 180–218; Charles G. Roland, *Courage under Siege: Starvation, Disease and Death in the Warsaw Ghetto* (New York: Oxford University Press, 1992), 98–120; Zena Stein et. al., *Famine and Human Development: The Dutch Hunger Winter of 1944–45* (New York: Oxford University Press, 1975). While less violent than their Nazi equivalents, the Minnesota Starvation Experiment's studies of starvation on conscientious objector subjects during World War II would not pass institutional review today. Keys, Brozek, Henschel, Mickelsen, and Taylor, *Biology of Human Starvation*. Calls for academic considerations of hunger include Sara Millman and Robert W. Kates, "Toward Understanding Hunger," in Lucile F. Newman et al., *Hunger in History: Food Shortage, Poverty, and Deprivation* (Cambridge, Mass.: Basil Blackwell, 1990), quotation on 22; Kirsten Hastrup, "Hunger and the Hardness of Facts," *Man*, n.s., 28, no. 4 (December 1993): 727–39; Bruegel, "From the Crisis of Food to Food in Crisis," 40–52. An important field in the history of hunger is the social history of famine in early modern Europe, such as Andrew B. Appleby, *Famine in Tudor and Stuart England* (Stanford: Stanford University Press, 1978); John Bohstedt, *The Politics of Provisions: Food Riots, Moral Economy, and Market Transition in England, c. 1550–1850* (Burlington, Vt.: Ashgate, 2010); John Bohstedt, *Riots and Community Protest in England and Wales, 1790–1810* (Cambridge: Harvard University Press, 1983); Buchanan Sharp, *Famine and Scarcity in Late Medieval and Early Modern England: The Regulation of Grain Marketing, 1256–1631* (Cambridge: Cambridge University Press, 2016). Other histories of hunger include: James Vernon, *Hunger: A Modern History* (Cambridge: Belknap Press of Harvard University Press, 2007); Tom Scott-Smith, *On an Empty Stomach: Two Hundred Years of Hunger Relief* (Ithaca: Cornell University Press, 2020).

35. Important works on early American archives and power include: Marisa Fuentes, *Dispossessed Lives: Enslaved Women, Violence, and the Archive* (Philadelphia: University of Pennsylvania Press, 2016); Matt Cohen, *The Networked Wilderness: Communicating in Early New England* (Minneapolis: University of Minnesota Press, 2010), esp. 1–28. On archives and power more generally: Terry Cook, "The Archive(s) Is a Foreign Country: Historians, Archivists, and the Changing Archival Landscape," *American Archivist* 74, no. 2 (Fall/Winter 2011): 600–632; Randall C. Jimerson, "Documents and Archives in Early America," *Archivaria* 60 (Fall 2005): 235–58; Michelle Light and Tom Hyry, "Colophons and

Annotations: New Directions for the Finding Aid," *American Archivist* 65, no. 2 (Fall/Winter 2002): 216–30; Ann Laura Stoler, *Along the Archival Grain: Anxieties and Colonial Common Sense* (Princeton: Princeton University Press, 2009).

36. For ease of reading, early modern typography has been silently modernized, but spelling has been retained.

37. Clifford Geertz, "Thick Description: Toward an Interpretive Theory of Culture," in *The Interpretation of Cultures: Selected Essays* (New York: Basic Books, 1973), 18. Kyla Wazana Tompkins, " 'You Make Me Feel Right Quare': Promiscuous Reading, Minoritarian Critique, and White Sovereign Entrepreneurial Terror," *Social Text* 35, no. 4 (December 2017): 55.

38. Drew Lopenzina, *Red Ink: Native Americans Picking Up the Pen in the Colonial Period* (Albany: SUNY Press, 2012), 9–10. The explanation of triangulation comes from Chaplin, *Subject Matter*, 27–28. I use upstreaming as described in Parsons, *Not-So-New World*, introduction, n51. Brooks, *Common Pot*; Brooks, "Awikhigawôgan ta Pildowi Ôjmowôgan"; Vera B. Palmer, "The Devil in the Details: Controverting an American Indian Conversion Narrative," in *Theorizing Native Studies*, ed. Audra Simpson and Andrea Smith (Durham: Duke University Press, 2014), 266–96; Kimmerer, *Braiding Sweetgrass*.

Chapter 1. Take a Hitch Up in My Belt

1. Samuel Kirkland, "A Journal of the Reverend Samuel Kirkland, November 1764—June 1765," in *The Journals of Samuel Kirkland*, ed. Walter Pilkington (Clinton, N.Y.: Hamilton College Press, 1980), 15–17.

2. Isaac Hollister, *A Brief Narrative of the Captivity of Isaac Hollister* (New London, Conn., 1767), 3, 4, 5–6, 6–7. Emphasis in the original.

3. *The Jesuit Relations and Allied Documents: Travels and Explorations of the Jesuit Missionaries in New France, 1610–1791*, ed. Reuben Gold Thwaites (Cleveland: Burrows Brothers, 1900), 67:222–24 (hereafter JR). My translation.

4. On physiology vs. culture in early American food history, see Michael A. LaCombe, "Subject or Signifier?: Food in Early North America," *History Compass* 11, no. 10 (2013): 859–68. Robert Appelbaum has characterized the English as not recognizing themselves as part of a "culture of hunger" when they first encountered Native peoples in the Americas. Robert Appelbaum, "Hunger in Early Virginia: Indians and English Facing Off over Excess, Want, and Need," in *Envisioning an English Empire: Jamestown and the Making of the North Atlantic World*, ed. Robert Appelbaum and John Sweet (Philadelphia: University of Pennsylvania Press, 2005), 214–16. By contrast, I argue that this lack of recognition does not mean that the English lacked a hunger culture: their disavowal of hunger was just a different kind of hunger culture than Native hunger cultures, which tended to accept hunger as natural. Anthropologists, too, have cataloged the ways that hunger shapes culture; one important example is Nancy Scheper-Hughes, *Death without Weeping: The Violence of Everyday Life in Brazil* (Berkeley: University of California Press, 1993). I use

both "knowledges" and "cultures" in the plural to indicate that neither were homogeneous in any given place and time. My reading of knowledge is here informed by scholarship on agnotology, the concept of "culturally-induced ignorances," in Londa Schiebinger's words, that disrupt the transfer of knowledge, particularly in colonial contexts; an important work is Thomas M. Wickman's study of "winter knowledge" that the Wabanaki used to survive the harsh winters of Maine and the Maritimes, knowledge that English colonists valued only once they recognized the military advantage it granted the Wabanaki. Thomas M. Wickman, *Snowshoe Country: An Environmental and Cultural History of Winter in the Early American Northeast* (New York: Cambridge University Press, 2018). See also Londa Schiebinger, *Plants and Empire: Colonial Bioprospecting in the Atlanta World* (Cambridge: Harvard University Press, 2004); *Agnotology: The Making and Unmaking of Ignorance,* ed. Robert N. Proctor and Londa Schiebinger (Stanford: Stanford University Press, 2008); Paul Mapp, *The Elusive West and the Contest for Empire, 1713–1763* (Chapel Hill: Omohundro Institute of Early American History and Culture and University of North Carolina Press, 2011). Other recent histories of environments, science and medicine, and colonialism include: Anya Zilberstein, *A Temperate Empire: Making Climate Change in Early America* (New York: Oxford University Press, 2016); Christopher M. Parsons, *A Not-So-New World: Empire and Environment in Colonial North America* (Philadelphia: University of Pennsylvania Press, 2018); Kelly Wisecup, *Medical Encounters: Knowledge and Identity in Early American Literatures* (Amherst: University of Massachusetts Press, 2013); and the Spring 2015 special issue of *Early American Studies* on early American environmental history.

5. Appelbaum, "Hunger in Early Virginia," 214–16.

6. On medieval and early modern famine regulation, see Buchanan Sharp, *Famine and Scarcity in Late Medieval and Early Modern England: The Regulation of Grain Marketing, 1256–1631* (Cambridge: Cambridge University Press, 2016), esp. 2–3, 8, 222, 230; see also Richard M. Smith, "Contrasting Susceptibility to Famine in Early Fourteenth- and Late Sixteenth-Century England: The Significance of Late Medieval Rural Social Structural and Village Governmental Changes," in *Popular Culture and Political Agency in Early Modern England and Ireland: Essays in Honor of John Walter,* ed. Michael J. Braddick and Phil Withington (Woodbridge, Suffolk: Boydell Press, 2017), 35–54. On bread and wheat regulation, see James Davis, "Baking for the Common Good: A Reassessment of the Assize of Bread in Medieval England," *Economic History Review* 57, no. 3 (August 2004): 465–502.

7. Michael A. LaCombe, *Political Gastronomy: Food and Authority in the English Atlantic World* (Philadelphia: University of Pennsylvania Press, 2012), 26–32. See also David Arnold, *Famine: Social Crisis and Historical Change* (Oxford: Basil Blackwell, 1988); Keith Wrightson, *English Society: 1580–1680* (New Brunswick: Rutgers University Press, 2003); *The Politics of the Excluded, c. 1500–1850,* ed. Tim Harris (New York: Palgrave, 2001); Kevin Sharpe, "A Commonwealth of Meanings: Languages, Analogues, Ideas and Politics," in *Remapping Early Modern England: The Culture of Seventeenth-Century Politics,* ed. Kevin Sharpe (Cambridge: Cambridge University Press, 2000), 38–125.

8. On early modern famine more generally, see *Famine, Disease, and the Social Order in Early Modern Society*, ed. John Walter and Roger Schofield (Cambridge: Cambridge University Press, 1989). On food riots and their outcomes in the early modern period, see John Bohstedt, *The Politics of Provisions: Food Riots, Moral Economy, and Market Transition in England, c. 1550–1850* (Burlington, Vt.: Ashgate, 2010), 21–245; the "golden age of food riots" quotation is from 107. See also John Bohstedt, *Riots and Community Protest in England and Wales, 1790–1810* (Cambridge: Harvard University Press, 1983); David Nally, "The Biopolitics of Food Provisioning," *Transactions of the Institute of British Geographers* 36, no. 1 (January 2011): 37–53; Sharp, *Famine and Scarcity in Late Medieval and Early Modern England*, chaps. 6–8; Andrew B. Appleby, *Famine in Tudor and Stuart England* (Stanford: Stanford University Press, 1978), 155–56; Amy Bentley, "Reading Food Riots: Scarcity, Abundance and National Identity," in *Food, Drink and Identity: Cooking, Eating and Drinking in Europe since the Middle Ages*, ed. Peter Scholliers (New York: Berg, 2001), 179–93. E. P. Thompson famously argued that market relations in pre-capitalist communities created the "moral economy," in which poorer classes expected protection (e.g., from dearth) from elites. E. P. Thompson, "The Moral Economy of the English Crowd in the Eighteenth Century," *Past and Present* 50, no. 1 (1971): 76–136. Bohstedt complicates this picture, noting that elites acquiesced to the "politics of provisions" because "it was easier and cheaper to appease . . . than to crush" peasant uprisings. Bohstedt, *The Politics of Provisions*, 265. On the demographic shift of the English colonization of North America, see Bernard Bailyn, *The Peopling of British North America: An Introduction* (New York: Vintage, 1986). On the ways that colonization reconfigured English attitudes about sufficiency and excess, see Hillary Eklund, *Literature and Moral Economy in the Early Modern Atlantic: Elegant Sufficiencies* (Burlington, Vt.: Ashgate, 2015), esp. chap. 5.

9. On rhetoric of "improvement" in early modern England, see Paul Slack, *The Invention of Improvement: Information and Material Progress in Seventeenth-Century England* (New York: Oxford University Press, 2014). On changes in agriculture, see Mark Overton, *Agricultural Revolution in England: The Transformation of the Agrarian Economy, 1500–1850* (New York: Cambridge University Press, 1996); E. A. Wrigley, "The Transition to an Advanced Organic Economy: Half a Millennium of English Agriculture," *Economic History Review*, n.s. 59, no. 3 (August 2006): 435–80.

10. Sarah F. McMahon, "A Comfortable Subsistence: The Changing Composition of Diet in Rural New England, 1620–1840," *William and Mary Quarterly* 42, no. 1 (January 1985): 28–29. McMahon argued that innovations in agriculture and food preservation began to mitigate the impact of seasonality upon diet in New England after 1750; see " 'All Things in Their Proper Season': Seasonal Rhythms of Diet in Nineteenth Century New England," *Agricultural History* 63, no. 2 (Spring, 1989): 130–51. Penelope Bradshaw, *The Family Jewel, and Compleat Housewife's Companion* (London: R. Whitworth, 1754), 121, 123.

11. Religious fasting will be covered in detail in chapter 2. On religious calendars adapted to seasonal scarcity and plenty, see John Walter, "The Social Economy of Dearth in Early Modern England," in *Famine, Disease, and the Social Order in Early Modern Society*, ed.

John Walter and Roger Schofield (Cambridge: Cambridge University Press, 1989), 112–13. On providentialism, hunger and fasting, see Walsham, *Providence in Early Modern England,* esp. 142–50. Appelbaum, "Hunger in Early Virginia," 201.

12. Robert Appelbaum, *Aguecheek's Beef, Belch's Hiccup, and Other Gastronomic Interjections: Literature, Culture, and Food among the Early Moderns* (Chicago: University of Chicago Press, 2006), 239–47. Steven Shapin, "How to Eat Like a Gentleman: Dietetics and Ethics in Early Modern England," in *Right Living: An Anglo-American Tradition of Self-Help Medicine and Hygiene,* ed. Charles E. Rosenberg (Baltimore: Johns Hopkins University Press, 2003), 21–58.

13. Ancel Keys, Josef Brozek, Austin Henschel, Olaf Mickelsen, and Henry Longstreet Taylor, *The Biology of Human Starvation* (Minneapolis: University of Minnesota Press, 1950), 1:587–600. Raymund Minderer, *Medicina Militaris, or A Body of Military Medicines Experimented* (London: William Godbid, 1674), 74–75. Appleby, *Famine in Tudor and Stuart England,* 8. Keys et al. noted that "where famine and severe undernutrition prevail there are present numerous other factors which would tend to spread infectious diseases." Keys et al., *Biology of Human Starvation,* 2:1002.

14. Appelbaum has argued that the age of colonization and exploration demoted gluttony on the hierarchy of early modern European dietary dangers, because of the more dramatic perils of starvation and cannibalism. Appelbaum, *Aguecheek's Beef,* 245; see also William Ian Miller, "Gluttony," *Representations* 60 (Autumn 1997): 92–112. Daniel Sennert, *Nine Books of Physick and Chirurgery* (London: F.M., 1658), 50. John Harris, *The Divine Physician* (Norwich: T. Goddard and L. Reeve, 1709), 6. On humoral theory, see Antoinette Emch-Dériaz, "The Non-Naturals Made Easy," in *The Popularization of Medicine, 1650–1850* (New York: Routledge, 1992), 134–59. Harris, *Divine Physician,* 19; on crudities and concoction, see also Ken Albala, *Eating Right in the Renaissance* (Berkeley: University of California Press, 2002), 54. Thomas Tryon, *The Way to Health, Long Life and Happiness; Or, a Discourse of Temperance* (London: Edmund Richardson, 1698), 43. Emphasis in the original. On doglike hunger, see Philip Barrough, *The Method of Phisick, Containing the Causes, Signes, and Cures of Inward Diseases in Mans Body, From the Head to the Foot,* 3rd ed. (London: Richard Field, 1601), 110; and Peter Shaw, *A New Practice of Physick* (London: J. Osborn and T. Longman, 1726), 1:177–78.

15. Ken Albala speculates that the persistent concern about lack of appetite arose out of two factors: first, many early modern medical authorities drew on classical traditions born from hotter Mediterranean climates, which likely suppressed appetite; second, humoral theories about hunger's origins at the mouth of the stomach may have made early modern people "psychosomatically" attentive to that part of the body. Albala, *Eating Right in the Renaissance,* 54–55. Sennert, *Nine Books of Physick and Chirurgery,* 82. Barrough, *Method of Phisick,* 109. Shaw, *New Practice of Physick,* 1:170–71. Nicholas Culpeper, *Medicaments for the Poor; Or, Physick for the Common People* (Edinburgh, 1664), 10. Barrough, *Method of Phisick,* 109.

16. Minderer, *Medicina Militaris,* 19–20, 6. The botanist John Gerard's *Herball* identifies three kinds of *Carlina* thistles but does not mention appetite-suppressing qualities in any of them. John Gerard, *The Herball or Generall Historie of Plantes* (London: A. Islip, J. Norton, and R. Whitakers, 1633), 1157–60.

17. Appelbaum, "Hunger in Early Virginia," 209. Hugh Platt, *Sundrie New and Artificiall Remedies against Famine* (London, 1596). A thorough analysis of Platt's works can be found in Ayesha Mukherjee, *Penury into Plenty: Dearth and the Making of Knowledge in Early Modern England* (London: Routledge, 2014). Perhaps the most famous English hunger knowledge to emerge from the early modern period came two centuries later, in the works of Thomas Malthus. Alison Bashford and Joyce E. Chaplin, *The New Worlds of Thomas Robert Malthus* (Princeton: Princeton University Press, 2016). In the late eighteenth century, imperial authorities would turn to new forms of hunger knowledge, as described in the conclusion.

18. Mukherjee, *Penury into Plenty*, 4, 39–40. McMahon, "Comfortable Subsistence," 33. Platt, *Remedies against Famine*.

19. Platt, *Remedies against Famine*. The economist Cormac Ó'Gráda argues that survival cannibalism is probably much more common than the historical record indicates, given that it (a) happens under conditions of extreme hardship in which many people die (thus restricting the archive of direct witnesses) and (b) is extremely taboo. Moreover, he notes, archaeology has focused on excavating the remains of wealthy people, where excavating peasant sites would likely turn up more physical evidence of cannibalism. Cormac Ó'Gráda, *Eating People Is Wrong, and Other Essays on Famine, Its Past, and Its Future* (Princeton: Princeton University Press, 2015), 11–37.

20. Warren Belasco has posited that fear over food shortage, especially reduced meat consumption, is a particularly male and Western predilection, because men have traditionally played less of a role in meal preparation. *Meals to Come: A History of the Future of Food* (Berkeley: University of California Press, 2005), 16–19. On women's herbal knowledge, see Rebecca Laroche, *Medical Authority and Englishwomen's Herbal Texts, 1550–1650* (Burlington, Vt.: Ashgate, 2009); Elaine Leong and Sara Pennell, "Recipe Collections and the Currency of Medical Knowledge in the Early Modern 'Medical Marketplace,'" in *Medicine and the Market in England and Its Colonies,* ed. Mark S. R. Jenner and Patrick Wallis (Basingstroke, Hampshire: Palgrave Macmillan, 2007), 133–52; Rebecca Tannenbaum, *The Healer's Calling: Women and Medicine in Early New England* (Ithaca: Cornell University Press, 2002); Laurel Thatcher Ulrich, *A Midwife's Tale: The Life of Martha Ballard, Based on Her Diary, 1785–1812* (New York: Vintage Books, 1990), 11, 322–30, 353–64. On women's roles in food production and consumption in early modern England, see Wendy Wall, *Recipes for Thought: Knowledge and Taste in the Early Modern English Kitchen* (Philadelphia: University of Pennsylvania Press, 2016); Madeline Bassnett, *Women, Food Exchange, and Governance in Early Modern England* (New York: Palgrave Macmillan, 2016); Alexandra Shepard, "Provision, Household Management and the Moral Authority of Wives and Mothers in Early Modern England," in *Popular Culture and Political Agency in Early Modern England and Ireland: Essays in Honor of John Walter* 73–89, Ann Carter quoted on 73.

21. On British versus French fairy tales, see Robert Darnton, *The Great Cat Massacre and Other Episodes in French Cultural History* (New York: Basic Books, 1984), 42–43. A Prentice

that is troubled with a Stingy Mistress, *The London Apprentices Complaint of Victuals; Or, A Satyr against Hunger* (London: D. Brown, 1706), 4, 2, 4.

22. *London Apprentices Complaint of Victuals*, 2, 3. Emphasis in the original.

23. Steven Laurence Kaplan, *Provisioning Paris: Merchants and Millers in the Grain and Flour Trade During the Eighteenth Century* (Ithaca: Cornell University Press, 1986), 23–24; Steven Laurence Kaplan, *Bread, Politics and Political Economy in the Reign of Louis XV* (The Hague: Martinus Nijhoff, 1976), 2:677–78. Kaplan argued that rather than using food regulations to advance totalitarian ends, authorities were forced into totalitarianism by the subsistence demands of the population. *Bread, Politics, and Political Economy*, 677–78. On wheat regulation, see Kaplan, *Provisioning Paris*, and *The Bakers of Paris and the Bread Question, 1700–1775* (Durham: Duke University Press, 1996), 439–566. Kaplan has written voluminously on grain and famine in early modern France, including the above citations and the following: "The Famine Plot Persuasion in Eighteenth-Century France," *Transactions of the American Philosophical Society* 72, no. 3 (1982): 1–79; *The Stakes of Regulation: Perspectives on "Bread, Politics, and Political Economy" Forty Years Later* (London: Anthem Press, 2015).

24. Cormac Ó'Gráda and Jean-Michel Chevet, "Famine and Market in Ancien Régime France," *Journal of Economic History* 62, no. 3 (2002): 709, 727–28. Laurence Brockliss and Colin Jones, *The Medical World of Early Modern France* (Oxford: Clarendon Press, 1997), 364–68, 58–61. Jacques Dupâquier, "Demographic Crises and Subsistence Crises in France, 1650–1725," in *Famine, Disease, and the Social Order in Early Modern Society*, 189–201.

25. *Conseil tres-utile contre la famine* (Paris: Jacques Gazeau, 1545), 15. My translation.

26. On the famine conspiracy theories, see Kaplan, "Famine Plot Persuasion," 1–79; on similar tensions in a colonial context, see Joseph Horan, "The Colonial Famine Plot: Slavery, Free Trade, and Empire in the French Atlantic, 1763–1791," *International Review of Social History* 55 (December 2010): 103–21.

27. Madame Foucquet, *Les remèdes charitables de Madame Fouquet* (Lyon: Jean Certe, 1685), 464–71. My translation. Colin Jones, *The Charitable Imperative: Hospitals and Nursing in Ancien Régime and Revolutionary France* (London: Routledge, 1989), 76–78, 40–41. Sidoine-Charles-François Séguier de Saint Brisson, *Philopénes, ou du régime des pauvres* (Paris, 1764). My translation.

28. Andrew Wear, "Popularized Ideas of Health and Illness in Seventeenth-Century France," *Seventeenth-Century French Studies* 8, no. 1 (1986): 229–42. While English medical print had similar popular medical guides, the genre originated and was most widespread in France. Matthew Ramsey, "The Popularization of Medicine in France, 1650–1900," in *The Popularization of Medicine, 1650–1850*, ed. Roy Porter (London: Routledge, 1992): 97–134, esp. 103–4. Jean Claude Adrien Helveticus, *Traité des maladies les plus frequentes* (Paris: Laurent D'Houry and Pier Augustin Le Mercier, 1703), 33. My translation.

29. Paul Dubé, *Le médecin et le chirurgien des pauvres* (Paris: Edme Couterot, 1682), 2, 138–39. My translation. Nicolas Abraham de la Framboisière, *Ordonnances sur la preparation des medicaments* (Paris, 1613), 8:807. My translation.

30. *Conseil tres-utile contre la famine,* 33, 15–32. My translation.

31. Rebecca Earle, "Promoting Potatoes in Eighteenth-Century Europe," *Eighteenth-Century Studies* 51, no. 2 (Winter 2017): 147–62. Antoine-Augustin Parmentier, *Examen chymique des pommes de terre* (Paris, 1773), xx. My translation. Barbara Ketchum Wheaton, *Savoring the Past: The French Kitchen and Table from 1300 to 1789* (Philadelphia: University of Pennsylvania Press, 1983), 83. Priscilla Parkhurst Ferguson, *Accounting for Taste: The Triumph of French Cuisine* (Chicago: University of Chicago Press, 2006), 134.

32. *Le rabais du pain en vers burlesques* (Paris, 1649), 4, 7. My translation.

33. Not all historians support the peasant hardship thesis; Christopher Dyer has argued that peasant quality of life steadily improved after the medieval period. "Did the Peasants Really Starve in Medieval England?" in *Food and Eating in Medieval Europe,* ed., Martha Carlin and Joel T. Rosenthal (London: Hambledon Press, 1998), 53–71. Robert Darnton, by contrast, argued that eighteenth-century French fairytales depicted "a world of raw and naked brutality." Darnton, *Great Cat Massacre,* 15, 23–29. On Cockaigne, see Appelbaum, *Aguecheek's Beef,* 118–55. For more on the cultural history of food in early modern Europe, see Piero Camporesi, *Bread of Dreams: Food and Fantasy in Early Modern Europe,* trans. David Gentilcore (Cambridge: Polity Press, 1989); *The Magic Harvest: Food, Folklore, and Society,* trans. Joan Krakover Hall (Cambridge: Polity Press, 1989); *The Land of Hunger,* trans. Tania Croft-Murray (Cambridge: Polity Press, 1996).

34. Lisa Brooks, *The Common Pot: The Recovery of Native Space in the Northeast* (Minneapolis: University of Minnesota Press, 2008), 3–8, quotation on 3–4.

35. On hierarchy and food distribution, see LaCombe, *Political Gastronomy,* 69–107; Rachel B. Herrmann, *No Useless Mouth: Waging War and Fighting Hunger in the American Revolution* (Ithaca: Cornell University Press, 2019). On food redistribution and alliances, see Wickman, *Snowshoe Country,* 53–54; Lisa Brooks, *Our Beloved Kin: A New History of King Philip's War* (New Haven: Yale University Press, 2018), 271.

36. The practice of eating increasingly desperate and meager foods has been called the "hunger topos." See Appelbaum, *Aguecheek's Beef,* 263–64. Herman Pleij coined the term in *Dreaming of Cockaigne: Medieval Fantasies of the Perfect Life,* trans. Diane Webb (New York: Columbia University Press, 1997), 107–17. On Wabanaki foraging, see Frederick Matthew Wiseman, *The Voice of the Dawn: An Autohistory of the Abenaki Nation* (Hanover: University Press of New England, 2001), 41–42. Mary Rowlandson, *The Soveraignty and Goodness of God* (1682), in *American Captivity Narratives,* ed. Gordon M. Sayre (Boston: Houghton Mifflin, 2000), 170. Ground nuts (*Apios americana*) were eaten raw, boiled, roasted, or dried and ground into flour. Harriet V. Kuhnlein and Nancy J. Turner, *Traditional Plant Foods of Canadian Indigenous Peoples: Nutrition, Botany and Use* (Philadelphia: Gordon and Breach Science Publishers, 1991), 193. "Artichokes" were likely Jerusalem artichokes. The "lily roots" were likely the plant now known as meadow garlic (*Allium canadense*). Ground bean (*Ampicarpa bracteata*), now also known as hog-peanut, produces edible seeds underground. Kuhnlein and Turner, *Traditional Plant Foods,* 78–79, 188. Cotton Mather, "A Narrative of Hannah Swarton Containing Wonderful Passages Relating to Her Captivity and

Deliverance," in *Puritans among the Indians: Accounts of Captivity and Redemption, 1676–1724,* ed. Alden T. Vaughan and Edward W. Clark (Cambridge.: Belknap Press of Harvard University Press, 1981), 152. The Haudenosaunee boiled and ate purslane (*Portulaca oleracea*). Kuhnlein and Turner, *Traditional Plant Foods,* 228. Purslane was familiar to the English, as well, and appeared in Gerard's *Herball,* 521. Mather, "Narrative of Hannah Swarton," 150. Kuhnlein and Turner, *Traditional Plant Foods,* 174–87. Colonial accounts of eating parts of trees: "Of the Captivity of Quintin Stockwell," in *Tragedies of the Wilderness,* ed. Samuel Gardner Drake (Boston: Antiquarian Bookstore and Institute, 1841), 64; Stephen Williams, "What Befell Stephen Williams in His Captivity," in *Captive Histories: English, French, and Native Narratives of the 1704 Deerfield Raid,* ed. Evan Haefeli and Kevin Sweeney (Amherst: University of Massachusetts Press, 2006), 164. *God's Mercy Surmounting Man's Cruelty, Exemplified in the Captivity and Redemption of Elizabeth Hanson,* in *Women's Indian Captivity Narratives,* ed. Kathryn Zabelle Derounian-Stodola (New York, London: Penguin, 1998), 70; Rowlandson, *Soveraignty,* 170. On "tree-eaters," see Joseph Francois Lafitau, *Customs of the American Indians Compared with the Customs of Primitive Times,* ed. and trans. William N. Fenton and Elizabeth L. Moore (Toronto: Champlain Society, 1974), 1:62. Emphasis in the original.

37. Rebecca Huss-Ashmore and Susan L. Johnston, "Wild Plants as Famine Foods: Food Choice under Conditions of Scarcity," in *Food Preferences and Taste: Continuity and Change,* ed. Helen Macbeth (Providence: Berghahn Books, 1997), 91. On palatability of wild foods, see Timothy Johns, "Ambivalence to the Palatability Factors in Wild Food Plants," *Eating on the Wild Side: The Pharmalogic, Ecologic, and Social Implications of Using Noncultigens,* ed. Nina L. Etkin (Tucson: University of Arizona Press, 1994), 46–61; Huss-Ashmore and Johnson, "Wild Plants as Famine Foods," 85–86, 91; Kuhnlein and Turner, *Traditional Plant Foods,* 201; Platt, *Remedies against Famine.* Kuhnlein and Turner have extensive tables of the nutritional values of wild plants in *Traditional Plant Foods,* 342–483.

38. Robin Wall Kimmerer, *Braiding Sweetgrass: Indigenous Wisdom, Scientific Knowledge, and the Teachings of Plants* (Minneapolis: Milkweed Editions, 2013), 175–201, esp. 183.

39. On gender and herbal plant knowledge, including how colonists' gendered assumptions led them to disregard Indigenous women's role as tradition-bearers, and how Indigenous peoples kept certain forms of knowledge secret from colonial prying, see Carolyn Merchant, *Ecological Revolutions: Nature, Gender, and Science in New England,* 2nd ed. (Chapel Hill: University of North Carolina Press, 2010), 75–76, 82; Parsons, *A Not-So-New World,* 74–77, 81–87, 90–94. On women and Native peoples' roles in the production of natural history knowledge in the colonial period, see Susan Scott Parrish, *American Curiosity: Cultures of Natural History in the Colonial British Atlantic World* (Chapel Hill: Omohundro Institute of Early American History and Culture and University of North Carolina Press, 2006), 174–258. Examples of herbal Wabanaki digestive remedies can be found in Wiseman, *Voice of the Dawn,* 209–211. Samson Occom, "Herbs and Roots," in *The Collected Writings of Samson Occom, Mohegan: Leadership and Literature in Eighteenth-Century Native America,* ed. Joanna Brooks (New York: Oxford University Press, 2006), 44–45; for a

detailed reading of Occom's herbal knowledge in this document, see Kelly Wisecup, "Medicine, Communication, and Authority in Samson Occom's Herbal," *Early American Studies* 10, no. 3 (Fall 2012): 540–65. Kirkland, "Journal," 15–17. The anthropologists Huss-Ashmore and Johnston note that children living in societies that relied on foraging were encouraged to forage themselves, which made them familiar with wild foods from a young age. Huss-Ashmore and Johnston, "Wild Plants as Famine Foods," 87.

40. JR 67:142. *God's Mercy Surmounting Man's Cruelty,* 74, 42. Wickman, *Snowshoe Country,* 52–54.

41. JR 63:252, 67:140–42. On tobacco, see Christopher Parsons, "Of Natives, Newcomers and Nicotiana: Tobacco in the History of the Great Lakes Region," in *French and Indians in the Heart of North America,* ed. Robert Englebert and Guillaume Teasdale (East Lansing: Michigan State University Press, 2013), 21–41. On energy expenditures and food during winter hunts, see Wickman, *Snowshoe Country,* 158–92.

42. Kirkland, "Journal," 29–30, 35. Emphasis in the original.

43. Rowlandson, *Sovereignty,* 155. Rowlandson's son was still alive and she reunited with him a few months later. *God's Mercy Surmounting Man's Cruelty,* 74. Emphasis in the original. Kirkland, "Journal," 35. Emphasis in the original. Humor is a crucial part of many Native cultures and a site of resistance against colonization. Eva Gruber, *Humor in Contemporary Native North American Literature: Reimagining Nativeness* (Rochester, N.Y.: Camden House, 2008).

44. Herrmann notes that colonists tended to see Native peoples as either not hungry or too hungry. Herrmann, *No Useless Mouth,* 31. On colonists learning and refusing to learn survival knowledge from Indigenous teachings, see Wickman, *Snowshoe Country,* 170–80.

45. On how Weetamoo and Rowlandson would have perceived each other, see Brooks, *Our Beloved Kin,* 253–98. Readings of Rowlandson's narrative include: Brooks, *Our Beloved Kin*; Laurel Thatcher Ulrich, *Good Wives: Image and Reality in the Lives of Women in Northern New England, 1650–1750* (New York: Vintage Books, 1991), 227–31; Jordan Alexander Stein, "Mary Rowlandson's Hunger and the Historiography of Sexuality," *American Literature* 81, no. 3 (September 2009): 469–95; Rachel B. Herrmann, " 'Their Filthy Trash': Taste, Eating, and Work in Mary Rowlandson's Captivity Narrative," *Labor: Studies in Working-Class History of the Americas* 12, no. 1–2 (May 2015): 45–70; Herrmann makes a thorough reading of food in the narrative. Rowlandson, *Sovereignty,* 152. On the Indigenous food landscape of the Connecticut River valley, see Brooks, *Our Beloved Kin,* 271.

46. Rowlandson, *Sovereignty,* 170.

47. Rowlandson, *Sovereignty,* 170. Brooks, *Our Beloved Kin,* 275–76.

48. JR 67:224–26. My translation.

49. JR 67:222. Strother E. Roberts, "The Dog Days of Winter: Indigenous Dogs, Indian Hunters, and Wintertime Subsistence in the Northeast," *Northeastern Naturalist* 24, no. 7 (2017), H1–H21. Sébastian Rales, *A Dictionary of the Abnaki Language, In North America* (Cambridge, Mass.: Charles Folsom, 1833), 452.

50. Dubé, *Le médecin et le chirurgien des pauvres,* 2. My translation.

51. Kirkland, "Journal," 29.

52. Kirkland, "Journal," 31–32, 34, 36.

53. On difference as a colonial excuse for the "denigration" of Indigenous bodies, see Joyce E. Chaplin, *Subject Matter: Technology, the Body, and Science on the Anglo American Frontier, 1500–1676* (Cambridge: Harvard University Press, 2001), 34. Colonial scholars long theorized that there was a physiological basis for differences between Indigenous and colonial bodies—that Native peoples had a "thrifty gene" that allowed them to metabolize food differently in order to survive scarcity. However, no evidence of this gene has been found, and researchers trying to explain high rates of metabolic disorders in present-day Native populations have turned to analyzing the epigenetics of trauma. I thank Elizabeth Hoover for her guidance on this topic. See Russel Lawrence Barsh, "Chronic Health Effects of Dispossession and Dietary Change: Lessons from North American Hunter-Gatherers," *Medical Anthropology* 18, no. 2 (1999): 135–51; Ann Bullock and Ronny A. Bell, "Stress, Trauma, and Coronary Heart Disease among Native Americans," *American Journal of Public Health* 95, no. 12 (2005): 2122–23; Teresa Evans-Campbell, "Historical Trauma in American Indian/Native Alaska Communities," *Journal of Interpersonal Violence* 23, no. 3 (2008): 316–38; Les B. Whitbeck, Gary W. Adams, and Dan R. Hoyt, "Conceptualizing and Measuring Historical Trauma among American Indian People," *American Journal of Community Psychology* 33, no. 3/4 (2004): 119–30.

54. On cross-cultural survivors, see Karen Ordahl Kupperman, *The Jamestown Project* (Cambridge: Harvard University Press, 2008), 43–72.

55. Schiebinger, *Plants and Empire*, 3.

Chapter 2. Govern Well Your Appetites

1. Samuel Kirkland, "A Journal of the Reverend Samuel Kirkland, November 1764–June 1765," in *The Journals of Samuel Kirkland*, ed. Walter Pilkington (Clinton, N.Y.: Hamilton College Press, 1980), 24, 23. Emphasis in the original throughout.

2. Arthur Browne, *The Necessity of Reformation, in Order to Avert Impending Judgments* (Portsmouth, N.H.: Daniel Fowle, 1757), 17. Emphasis in the original throughout.

3. Browne, *Necessity of Reformation*, 10, 14. The roots of Browne's anxiety about "*a famine . . . of hearing the word of the Lord*" stems from a conflict between Catholic and Protestant beliefs: Protestants insisted that believers be able to read the Bible and understand worship services in their native languages, while the Catholic Mass was conducted in Latin until the Vatican II reforms in the 1960s; Protestants believed that this practice kept ordinary people from achieving true salvation by interpreting sacred texts themselves.

4. Browne, *Necessity of Reformation*, 17. This image was likely a reference to Lamentations 4:3, "Even the sea monsters draw out the breast, they give suck to their young ones."

5. On ritual and community, see Mary Douglas, *Purity and Danger: An Analysis of the Concept of Purity and Taboo* (London: Routledge and Kegan Paul, 1966). Quotation from Mary Douglas, *Natural Symbols: Explorations in Cosmology*, 2nd ed. (London: Routledge,

1996), 79. On other ways that authorities used food during this period, see Michael A. LaCombe, *Political Gastronomy: Food and Authority in the English Atlantic World* (Philadelphia: University of Pennsylvania Press, 2012). On the body politic: Maggie Kilgour, *From Communion to Cannibalism: An Anatomy of Metaphors of Incorporation* (Princeton: Princeton University Press, 1990); Cristobal Silva, *Miraculous Plagues: An Epidemiology of Early New England Narrative* (New York: Oxford University Press, 2011). My reading of discipline is shaped by Michel Foucault, *Discipline and Punish: The Birth of the Prison*, trans. Alan Sheridan, 2nd ed. (New York: Vintage Books, 1991).

6. On feasting and fasting generally, see *Oxford Symposium on Food and Cookery 1990 Proceedings: Fasting and Feasting* (London: Prospect Books, 1990). Previous scholarship on the overlaps between Native and colonial feasting and fasting includes: Douglas L. Winiarski, "Native American Popular Religion in New England's Old Colony, 1670–1770," *Religion and American Culture: A Journal of Interpretation* 15, no. 2 (Summer 2005): 147–86; Robert Appelbaum, "Hunger in Early Virginia: Indians and English Facing Off over Excess, Want, and Need," in *Envisioning an English Empire: Jamestown and the Making of the North Atlantic World*, ed. Robert Appelbaum and John Sweet (Philadelphia: University of Pennsylvania Press, 2005), 201–2. Religious studies scholars have argued for varying degrees of hybridity and syncretism between Native and colonial religious practices. See Erik Seeman, *Death in the New World: Cross-Cultural Encounters, 1492–1800* (Philadelphia: University of Pennsylvania Press, 2010); Laura M. Chmielewski, *The Spice of Popery: Converging Christianities on an Early American Frontier* (Notre Dame: University of Notre Dame Press, 2011); Linford D. Fisher, *The Indian Great Awakening: Religion and the Shaping of Native Cultures in Early America* (New York: Oxford University Press, 2012). Native Studies scholars have stressed the ways that Indigenous peoples used at least the appearances of Christianity to conserve existing cultural traditions. See Drew Lopenzina, *Red Ink: Native Americans Picking Up the Pen in the Colonial Period* (Albany: SUNY Press, 2012), esp. chaps. 2 and 5; Vera B. Palmer, "The Devil in the Details: Controverting an American Indian Conversion Narrative," in *Theorizing Native Studies*, ed. Audra Simpson and Andrea Smith (Durham: Duke University Press, 2014), 266–96.

7. John Williams, *The Redeemed Captive Returning to Zion*, 2nd ed. (Boston: T. Fleet, 1707), 31. Emphasis in the original.

8. David Hall, *Worlds of Wonder, Days of Judgment: Popular Religious Belief in Early New England* (Cambridge: Harvard University Press, 1989); Alexandra Walsham, *Providence in Early Modern England* (New York: Oxford University Press, 2001); Michael Winship, *Seers of God: Puritan Providentialism in the Restoration and Early Enlightenment* (Baltimore: Johns Hopkins University Press, 1996), chaps. 1–2. Lawrence Hammond, diary, 1687–1694, Pre-Revolutionary Diaries microfilm 5.3, Massachusetts Historical Society, Boston.

9. Winship, *Seers of God*, 22–26.

10. Lewis Bayly, *The Practice of Piety: Directing a Christian How to Walk, That He May Please God* (Boston: B. Green, 1718), 267. Emphasis in the original. Walsham, *Providence in Early Modern England*, 150–156.

11. Walsham has contended that "there was far less difference in practice than Protestants so energetically alleged." Walsham, *Providence in Early Modern England,* 148–49.

12. The Oxford English Dictionary definition of the verb "fast" refers to both limiting and complete abstention from food. But this definition does not mention any of the other sensory or ascetic practices that this chapter describes, indicating that modern definitions of fasting have contracted, rather than expanded, its meanings. "Fast, v.2," *Oxford English Dictionary Online,* accessed November 2, 2015. On Protestant and Catholic fasting in the Reformation era: Ken Albala, "The Ideology of Fasting in the Reform Era," in *Food and Faith in Christian Culture,* ed. Ken Albala and Trudy Eden (New York: Columbia University Press, 2012), 41–57; Martha L. Finch, "Pinched with Hunger, Partaking of Plenty: Fasts and Thanksgivings in Early New England," in *Eating in Eden: Food and American Utopias,* ed. Etta M. Madden and Martha L. Finch (Lincoln: University of Nebraska Press, 2006), 35–53; Douglas L. Winiarski, *Darkness Falls on the Land of Light: Experiencing Religious Awakenings in Eighteenth-Century New England* (Chapel Hill: Omohundro Institute of Early American History and Culture and University of North Carolina Press, 2017), 69–72; Caroline Walker Bynum, *Holy Feast and Holy Fast: The Religious Significance of Food to Medieval Women* (Berkeley and Los Angeles: University of California Press, 1987); Raymond A. Mentzer, "Fasting, Piety, and Political Anxiety among French Reformed Protestants," *Church History* 76, no. 2 (June, 2007): 330–62. On gluttony, see Robert Appelbaum, *Aguecheek's Beef, Belch's Hiccup, and Other Gastronomic Interjections: Literature, Culture, and Food among the Early Moderns* (Chicago: University of Chicago Press, 2006), 239–47. On the importance of seasons and cycles in early modern Europe and early America, see John Demos, *Circles and Lines: The Shape of Life in Early America* (Cambridge: Harvard University Press, 2004), 1–25.

13. John Walter, "The Social Economy of Dearth in Early Modern England," in *Famine, Disease, and the Social Order in Early Modern Society,* ed. John Walter and Roger Schofield (Cambridge: Cambridge University Press, 1989), 112–13. Robert Nelson, *A Companion for the Festivals and Fasts of the Church of England: With Collects and Prayers for Each Solemnity* (London, 1732), 439.

14. Church of England, *The Book of Common Prayer* (Edinburgh: Alexander Kincaid, 1761). Catholic Church, *Rituel du diocese de Quebec* (Paris: Simon Langlois, 1703). Ken Albala, *Food in Early Modern Europe* (Westport, Conn.: Greenwood Press, 2003), 196. On saints surviving on the Eucharist alone, see Bynum, *Holy Feast and Holy Fast,* 131–32.

15. Hall, *Worlds of Wonder,* 166–67, 212, 171–72, 185. Martha L. Finch, *Dissenting Bodies: Corporeality in Early New England* (New York: Columbia University Press, 2010), 169–75. Charles E. Hambrick-Stowe, *The Practice of Piety: Puritan Devotional Disciplines in Seventeenth-Century New England* (Chapel Hill: Omohundro Institute of Early American History and Culture and University of North Carolina Press, 1982), 100–101, 249.

16. Massachusetts Archives Collections, Boston, 11:58. Emphasis in the original throughout.

17. Massachusetts Archives Collections, 11:164, 11:194b.

18. Walsham, *Providence in Early Modern England,* 146, 148–49. Nelson, *Companion for the Festivals and Fasts of the Church of England,* 434.

19. Samuel Pike, *Public Fasting; Or, the Manner in which Christians Should Observe a Public Fast* (London, 1757), 2, 3–5, 8–9. Emphasis in the original.

20. Simon Patrick, *A Treatise of Repentance and of Fasting, Especially of the Lent-Fast* (London, 1686), 90–91. Emphasis in the original. Nelson, *Companion for the Festivals and Fasts of the Church of England*, 433–34. Emphasis in the original.

21. John Gother, *Instructions for the Whole Year, Part I, For Lent* (1695), 8–9. John Gother, *A Practical Catechism* (London: Thomas Meighan, 1735), 324.

22. Gother, *Instructions for the Whole Year*, 9; *Practical Catechism*, 324.

23. Pike, *Public Fasting*, 5, 7. Emphasis in the original.

24. Albala, *Food in Early Modern Europe*, 196. Nicolas Andry, *Le regime du caresme* (Paris: Jean Baptiste Coignard, 1710), 5. My translation. Finch, *Dissenting Bodies*, 171. Patrick, *Treatise of Repentance and of Fasting*, preface. Gother, *Instructions for the Whole Year*, 11.

25. Albala, *Food in Early Modern Europe*, 197, 200. Gother, *Instructions for the Whole Year*, 7–8. Patrick, *Treatise of Repentance and of Fasting*, preface. Emphasis in the original. Nicolas Bownde, *The Holy Exercise of Fasting* (London: John Legat, 1604).

26. Gother, *Practical Catechism*, 321. Sermons that cite Isaiah 58–59: Marston Cabot, *The Nature of Religious Fasting Opened, In Two Short Discourses Deliver'd At Thompson in Kellingley, Connecticut Colony, On A Day of Publick Fasting and Prayer, April 18, 1733* (Boston: John Eliot, 1734), 14; Benjamin Colman, *The Fast Which God Hath Chosen* (Boston: S. Kneeland and T. Green, 1734), 1; Benjamin Colman, *Righteousness and Compassion the Duty and Character of Pious Rulers* (Boston: J. Draper, 1736); John Rogers, "The Vanity of Prayer and Fasting, as Unconnected with Reformation of Manners," in *Three Sermons on Different Subjects and Occasions* (Boston: Edes and Gill, 1756). Colman, *The Fast Which God Hath Chosen*, 6. Cabot, *The Nature of Religious Fasting Opened*, 4. Browne, *Necessity of Reformation*, 6, 12. Emphasis in the original.

27. Jan Frans van Dijkhuizen, "Partakers of Pain: Religious Meanings of Pain in Early Modern England," in *The Sense of Suffering: Constructions of Physical Pain in Early Modern Culture*, ed. Jan Frans van Dijkhuizen and Karl A. E. Enenkel (Leiden: Brill, 2009), 190, 215–16. See also John Yamamoto-Wilson, *Pain, Pleasure and Perversity: Discourses of Suffering in Seventeenth-Century England* (Burlington, Vt.: Ashgate, 2013).

28. Devotional manuals citing Paul in 1 Corinthians 9:27: Patrick, *Treatise of Repentance and of Fasting*, 105; *Early Piety the Duty & Interest of Youth, As It was Shown, in A Sermon Preached at Sherbourn, on May 10, 1727* (Boston: D. Henchman, 1728), 34. Patrick, *Treatise of Repentance and of Fasting*, 106. Emphasis in the original. Pike, *Public Fasting*, 7. Bayly, *Practice of Piety*, 267. Joseph Sewall, *Nineveh's Repentance and Deliverance* (Boston: J. Draper, 1740). Colman, *Fast Which God Hath Chosen*. Emphasis in the original. Bayly, *Practice of Piety*, 256. Emphasis in the original. Gother, *Practical Catechism*, 271–73. *Early Piety the Duty & Interest of Youth*, 32.

29. Benjamin Wadsworth, *True Piety the Best Policy for Times of War* (Boston: B. Green, 1722), 5, 8, 17, 22–23. Emphasis in the original. Ann Little, *Abraham in Arms: War and Gender in Colonial New England* (Philadelphia: University of Pennsylvania Press, 2007), 167–71.

30. Evan Haefeli and Kevin Sweeney, *Captors and Captives: The 1704 French and Indian Raid on Deerfield* (Amherst: University of Massachusetts Press, 2004), 286. Williams, *Redeemed Captive,* 31. Emphasis in the original.

31. David Hall has characterized the relationship between clerical and popular religion as one of "consensus and resistance, of common ground, but also differences." Hall, *Worlds of Wonder,* 12. See also Hall, *The Faithful Shepherd: A History of the New England Ministry in the Seventeenth Century,* 2nd ed. (Cambridge: Harvard University Press, 2006). For a history of Deerfield in the seventeenth and eighteenth centuries, see Richard Melvoin, *New England Outpost: War and Society in Colonial Deerfield* (New York: Norton, 1989).

32. Solomon Williams, *The Power and Efficacy of the Prayers of the People of God* (Boston: S. Kneeland and T. Green, 1742), 19, 25. Emphasis in the original. For a biography of Eunice Williams/Marguerite Kanenstenhawi, see John Demos, *The Unredeemed Captive: A Family Story from Early America* (New York: Alfred Knopf, 1994); see also Audra Simpson, "Captivating Eunice: Membership, Colonialism, and Gendered Citizenships of Grief," *Wicazo Sa Review* 24, no. 2, Native Feminism (Fall 2009): 105–29.

33. *The Jesuit Relations and Allied Documents: Travels and Explorations of the Jesuit Missionaries in New France, 1610–1791,* ed. Reuben Gold Thwaites (Cleveland: Burrows Brothers, 1900), 70:94–98 (hereafter JR). My translation.

34. JR 70:98, 100. My translation. Emphasis in the original. Despite the cannibalistic undertones Roubaud saw in the ceremony, no ritual cannibalism has ever been documented among Wabanaki people. Roubaud was a colorful and shifty character who would, within a few years, be defrocked, marry, and become a spy for the British. These facts raise questions about Roubaud's reliability as a historical source, but his accounts line up convincingly enough with other sources cited in the next note that I have decided to quote him here.

35. John Gyles, *Memoir of Odd Adventures, Strange Deliverances, etc. in the Captivity of John Gyles,* in *Puritans Among the Indians: Accounts of Captivity and Redemption, 1676–1724,* ed. Alden T. Vaugh and Edward W. Clark (Cambridge: Belknap Press of Harvard University Press, 1981), 120. JR 67:202. My translation. The Wendat and Haudenosaunee also consumed dogs for ritual purposes. Marion Schwartz, *A History of Dogs in the Early Americas* (New Haven: Yale University Press, 1997), 82–83.

36. While the English did not see parallels between Indigenous and English religious practices, scholars of Native and colonial religious interactions have pointed to similarities, as in Winiarski, "Native American Popular Religion in New England's Old Colony," 164. On the gender stratification of Wabanaki feasts, see Ann M. Little, *The Many Captivities of Esther Wheelwright* (New Haven: Yale University Press, 2016), 65–66. On overlaps between Indigenous and English concepts of masculinity, see Little, *Abraham in Arms,* 13–14; on English rhetoric that feminized Indigenous men, see Kathleen M. Brown, "The Anglo-American Gender Frontier," in *Negotiators of Change: Historical Perspectives on Native American Women,* ed. Nancy Shoemaker (New York: Routledge, 1995), 36. Other Indigenous peoples, such as Cherokees, practiced similar rituals of war leaders calling up

recruits for raids, and spiritual preparations that included sexual abstinence. But the Cherokee, unlike the Wabanaki, practiced ritual fasting and purging on the eve of war rather than feasting. See Susan Abram, "Real Men: Masculinity, Spirituality, and Community in Late Eighteenth-Century Cherokee Warfare," in *New Men: Manliness in Early America*, ed. Thomas A. Foster (New York: New York University Press, 2011), 71–91, esp. 74–80; Tyler Boulware, " 'We Are MEN: Native American and Euroamerican Projections of Masculinity During the Seven Years' War," in *New Men*, 51–70.

37. *God's Mercy Surmounting Man's Cruelty, Exemplified in the Captivity and Redemption of Elizabeth Hanson*, in *Women's Indian Captivity Narratives*, ed. Kathryn Zabelle Derounian-Stodola (New York: Penguin, 1998), 71.

38. JR 67:164. My translation. Sébastian Rales, *A Dictionary of the Abnaki Language, in North America* (Cambridge, Mass.: Charles Folsom, 1833), 481. My translation from the French.

39. "Of the Captivity of Quintin Stockwell," in *Tragedies of the Wilderness*, ed. Samuel Gardner Drake (Boston: Antiquarian Bookstore and Institute, 1841), 64.

40. JR 67:164. "Of the Captivity of Quintin Stockwell," 64. *God's Mercy Surmounting Man's Cruelty*, 74, 42. On scarcity in Wabanaki communities in the late seventeenth and early eighteenth centuries, see Little, *Many Captivities of Esther Wheelwright*, 51–56.

41. JR 25:162; 23:316; 31:216–18; 25:164–66. My translation. My thanks to Tom Wickman for sharing research with me that shaped this section.

42. Where earlier scholarship tended to see Native conversion to Christianity as a passive process, more recent scholarship has stressed the ways that Native people actively created their terms of engagement with Christianity. See Fisher, *Indian Great Awakening*, and the end of this chapter. JR 63:252. My translation.

43. JR 62:176. My translation. For a biography of Tekakwitha, see Allan Greer, *Mohawk Saint: Catherine Tekakwitha and the Jesuits* (New York: Oxford University Press, 2005); see also Nancy Shoemaker, "Kateri Tekakwitha's Torturous Path to Sainthood," in *Negotiators of Change*, 49–71.

44. JR 63:218. My translation. Nancy Shoemaker notes that many Haudenosaunee rituals "involved fasting, feasting, or cannibalism," and "all show an obsession with food" and the possibility of food scarcity. Shoemaker, "Kateri Tekakwitha's Torturous Path," 65.

45. JR 62:175, 179. On the history of self-discipline in early modern Europe, see Patrick Vandermeersch, "Self-Flagellation in the Early Modern Era," in *Sense of Suffering*, 253–66. JR 63:216–18. My translation. On overlaps between Catholic and Haudenosaunee traditions, see Shoemaker, "Kateri Tekakwitha's Torturous Path," 61–66.

46. On Tekakwitha as Mohawk spiritual leader, see Vera B. Palmer, "The Devil in the Details: Controverting an American Indian Conversion Narrative," in *Theorizing Native Studies*, ed. Audra Simpson and Andrea Smith (Durham: Duke University Press, 2014), 268, 269, 282–83, 286–87, 290–91. Bynum argued that medieval female saints refused food in order to deny male control over their bodies within a patriarchal society. Bynum, *Holy Feast and Holy Fast*. In some ways Tekakwitha's story is similar, in that Tekakwitha and

other Indigenous women used their distinctive spiritual practices to resist colonial male authority in the form of Jesuit priests. However, Palmer's work makes clear that a matrilineal Mohawk context is necessary for a fuller understanding of Tekakwitha's life.

47. The definitive biography of Edwards is George M. Marsden, *Jonathan Edwards: A Life* (New Haven: Yale University Press, 2003).

48. Jonathan Edwards, *Fast Days in Dead Times*, in *Sermons and Discourses, 1734–1738, Works of Jonathan Edwards Online* (Jonathan Edwards Center, Yale University, 2008) (hereafter *WJE*), 19:62, 83, 63, 72–73. Donald S. Whitney, *Finding God in Solitude: The Personal Piety of Jonathan Edwards (1703–1758) and Its Influence on His Pastoral Ministry* (New York: Peter Lang, 2014), 76, 110–12.

49. Edwards to Deborah Hatheway, June 3, 1741, *WJE* 16:94. Bayly, *Practice of Piety,* 257–60. Emphasis in the original.

50. Edwards to Hatheway, June 3, 1741, *WJE* 16:94. Jonathan Edwards, *The Great Awakening, WJE* 4:521.

51. Edwards, Diary, *Letters and Personal Writings, WJE* 16:754, 756, 766. Marsden, *Jonathan Edwards*, 133. Whitney, *Finding God in Solitude,* 75. Hopkins, *Life and Character,* 40, 42.

52. Edwards, *The Life of David Brainerd, WJE* 7:277, 276, 512. Emphasis in the original. JR 63:252. Sarah Rivett, *Unscripted America: Indigenous Languages and the Origins of a Literary Nation* (New York: Oxford University Press, 2017), 156–59; see also Laura M. Stevens, *The Poor Indians: British Missionaries, Native Americans, and Colonial Sensibility* (Philadelphia: University of Pennsylvania Press, 2004), 137–48.

53. Rachel Wheeler, " 'Friends to Your Souls': Jonathan Edwards' Indian Pastorate and the Doctrine of Original Sin," *Church History* 72 (December 2003): 744–46; Rachel Wheeler, *To Live upon Hope: Mohicans and Missionaries in the Eighteenth-Century Northeast* (Ithaca: Cornell University Press, 2008), 207–9; on Edwards's time in Stockbridge more generally, see 206–22. Edwards, "Warring with the Devil," *WJE* 25:679. On the Mohican history of Stockbridge before Edwards's arrival, see Lopenzina, *Red Ink*, 258–82.

54. Edwards, "God Is Infinitely Strong," *WJE* 25:644. There were moments when Edwards did seem to see overlaps between his theology and existing spiritual metaphors for Mohican and Mohawk people, such as the rich ecological imagery of his 1754 sermon "Christ Is to the Heart Like a River to a Tree Planted by It." *WJE* 25:601–5. On this point, see Rivett, *Unscripted America*, 177–80. On Edwards's reactions to borderlands conflicts, see Wheeler, *To Live upon Hope*, 212; and Kenneth P. Minkema, "Jonathan Edwards's Life and Career: Society and Self," in *Understanding Jonathan Edwards: An Introduction to America's Theologian,* ed. Gerald R. McDermott (New York: Oxford University Press, 2009), 18–19. For more on Edwards's life during his missionary years, see Marsden, *Jonathan Edwards*, 373–431.

55. Though usually safer than contracting the smallpox virus naturally, inoculation was still a dangerous process. Many medical practitioners required patients to undergo restricted diets and oral doses of mercury before inoculation with the live smallpox virus from the pustules of infected individuals. For an already weakened, fasting and sleep-

deprived person like Edwards, the preparatory treatments alone, much less the only partially controlled exposure to the virus, could be deadly. Elizabeth Fenn, *Pox Americana: The Great Smallpox Epidemic of 1775–82* (New York: MacMillan, 2001), 33–35.

56. On Occom's life, see Fisher, *Indian Great Awakening*, 122–26; Lopenzina, *Red Ink*, 207–51; Edward E. Andrews, *Native Apostles: Black and Indian Missionaries in the British Atlantic World* (Cambridge: Harvard University Press, 2013), chap. 5; *The Collected Writings of Samson Occom, Mohegan: Leadership and Literature in Eighteenth-Century Native America*, ed. Joanna Brooks (New York: Oxford University Press, 2006), 3–40; Joanna Brooks, "Hard Feelings: Samson Occom Contemplates His Christian Mentors," in *Native Americans, Christianity, and the Reshaping of the American Religious Landscape*, ed. Joel W. Martin and Mark A. Nicholas (Chapel Hill: University of North Carolina Press, 2010), 23–37; Joanna Brooks, *American Lazarus: Religion and the Rise of African American and Native American Literatures* (New York: Oxford University Press, 2007), chap. 2. Where Julius H. Rubin emphasizes Occom's Christian identity first and foremost, I join Lopenzina, Brooks, Fisher, and other scholars in seeing Occom's Mohegan and pan-tribal connections as the foundation of his life and work. Julius H. Rubin, *Tears of Repentance: Christian Indian Identity and Community in Colonial Southern New England* (Lincoln: University of Nebraska Press, 2013), chap. 4.

57. Occom, "Preface to A Choice Collection of Hymns and Spiritual Songs" (1774), *Collected Writings*, 233. Emphasis in the original. Occom, "The Remarkable and Strange State Situation and Appearance of Indian Tribes in this Great Continent" (1783), *Collected Writings*, 59.

58. The community was also racially separatist, only allowing "pure" Native, not Black Indigenous individuals, to own land. Linford Fisher, "Religion, Race, and the Formation of Pan-Indian Identities in the Brothertown Movement, 1700–1800," in *Native Diasporas: Indigenous Identities and Settler Colonialism in the Americas*, ed. Gregory D. Smithers and Brooke N. Newman (Lincoln: University of Nebraska Press, 2014), 158–60, 174. Brooks, introduction to "Journals," *Collected Writings of Samson Occom*, 244. For more on the founding of Brothertown, see Lopenzina, *Red Ink*, 301–22. Lopenzina argues that "while the town of Brothertown bore the stamp of assimilation to colonial norms in much of its rhetorical and material design, there is reason enough to consider Brothertown . . . as [a] vital exampl[e] of how elements of both [I]ndigenous and colonial tradition might be syncretically situated within a template of survivance in Native space." Lopenzina, *Red Ink*, 317.

59. Brooks, "Hard Feelings," 31–35.

60. Occom, Journals, November 8–12, 1785, *Collected Writings of Samson Occom*, 310. Fisher notes that Brothertown was "a socially divisive movement and involved far fewer people than contemporary observers and later historians have assumed," and that most Native people in southern New England "continued on as they had before the migration." Fisher, *Indian Great Awakening*, 181. The federal government would force the Brothertown community to move west again between 1818 and the 1830s.

61. Joyce E. Chaplin, *Subject Matter: Technology, the Body, and Science on the Anglo American Frontier, 1500–1676* (Cambridge: Harvard University Press, 2001), 255–77.

62. Cabot, *Nature of Religious Fasting Opened,* 7. Emphasis in the original.

63. Kirkland, "Journal," 24.

64. Occom, Journals, November 9–12, 1785, *Collected Writings,* 310.

Chapter 3. Nothing Which Hunger Will Not Devour

1. Samuel Kirkland, "A Journal of the Reverend Samuel Kirkland, November 1764—June 1765," in *The Journals of Samuel Kirkland,* ed. Walter Pilkington (Clinton, N.Y.: Hamilton College Press, 1980), 30–31. Emphasis in the original.

2. Classic theoretical considerations of food choice include: Claude Levi-Strauss, "The Culinary Triangle," in *Food and Culture: A Reader,* ed. Caroline Counihan and Penny van Esterik (London: Routledge, 1997), 40–48; Claude Levi-Strauss, *The Raw and the Cooked,* trans. John and Doreen Weightman (New York: Harper and Row, 1969); Mary Douglas, *Purity and Danger: An Analysis of the Concept of Purity and Taboo* (London: Routledge and Kegan Paul, 1966).

3. On the increasing restrictiveness of European diet, see Ken Albala, "Wild Food: The Call of the Domestic," in *Wild Food: Proceedings of the Oxford Symposium on Food and Cookery 2004,* ed. Richard Hosking (Totnes: Prospect Books, 2006), 9–19. Most cultures only consume a small proportion of the possible animals they could eat. William Ian Miller, *The Anatomy of Disgust* (Cambridge: Harvard University Press, 1997), 45–46. Stereotypes about other cultures eating "unclean" animals have recurred throughout history. Harriet Ritvo, *The Platypus and the Mermaid and Other Figments of the Classifying Imagination* (Cambridge: Harvard University Press, 1997), 203–9.

4. On food and colonial narratives of supremacy, see Joyce E. Chaplin, *Subject Matter: Technology, the Body, and Science on the Anglo American Frontier, 1500–1676* (Cambridge: Harvard University Press, 2001), 8–10, 149–52, 209–12; and Trudy Eden, *The Early American Table: Food and Society in the New World* (DeKalb: Northern Illinois University Press, 2008), chaps. 1–2. Disgust theorists agree that hunger will in the end overwhelm the disgust response— in the end it is better to eat than to starve—but this phenomenon has received very little analysis. Valerie Curtis, *Don't Look, Don't Touch, Don't Eat: The Science Behind Revulsion* (Chicago: University of Chicago Press, 2013), 42–43; Colin McGinn, *The Meaning of Disgust* (New York: Oxford University Press, 2011), 127–30.

5. Captivity narratives are an "imperial genre," concerned with colonists' experiences of unfreedom when the vast majority of "captives" in early America were Indigenous or of African descent. Ann Laura Stoler, "Intimidations of Empire: Predicaments of the Tactile and Unseen," in *Haunted by Empire: Geographies of Intimacy in North American History,* ed. Ann Laura Stoler (Durham: Duke University Press, 2006), 18; see also Jill Lepore, *The Name of War: King Phillip's War and the Origins of American Identity* (New York: Knopf, 1998), 125–49. Important studies of colonists' captivity in the northeastern borderlands include: John Demos, *The Unredeemed Captive: A Family Story from Early America* (New York: Vintage, 1994); Ann M. Little, *The Many Captivities of Esther Wheelwright* (New Haven: Yale

University Press, 2016). On the rhetorical and political agendas of colonial captivity narratives, see Audra Simpson, "Captivating Eunice: Membership, Colonialism, and Gendered Citizenships of Grief," *Wicazo Sa Review* 24, no. 2 (Fall 2009): 105–29; Teresa A. Toulouse, *The Captive's Position: Female Narrative, Male Identity, and Royal Authority in Colonial New England* (Philadelphia: University of Pennsylvania Press, 2007); Lorrayne Carroll, *Rhetorical Drag: Gender Impersonation, Captivity, and the Writing of History* (Kent, Ohio: Kent State University Press, 2007); Pauline Turner Strong, *Captive Selves, Captivating Others: The Politics and Poetics of Colonial American Captivity Narratives* (Boulder, Colo.: Westview Press, 1999); June Namias, *White Captives: Gender and Ethnicity on the American Frontier* (Chapel Hill: University of North Carolina Press, 1993). On the rhetoric and historical memory of missionary accounts such as the Jesuit Relations, see Emma Anderson, *The Death and Afterlife of the North American Martyrs* (Cambridge: Harvard University Press, 2013); Drew Lopenzina, "Le Jeune Dreams of Moose: Altered States among the Montagnais in the Jesuit Relations of 1634," *Early American Studies* 13, no. 1 (Winter 2015): 3–37; Vera B. Palmer, "The Devil in the Details: Controverting an American Indian Conversion Narrative," in *Theorizing Native Studies*, ed. Audra Simpson and Andrea Smith (Durham: Duke University Press, 2014): 266–97; Laura M. Stevens, *The Poor Indians: British Missionaries, Native Americans, and Colonial Sensibility* (Philadelphia: University of Pennsylvania Press, 2006).

6. Sara Ahmed describes how "disgust is deeply ambivalent, involving desire for, or an attraction towards, the very objects that are felt to be repellent." Sara Ahmed, *The Cultural Politics of Emotion* (New York: Routledge, 2004), 84. On affect, intimacy, and power in early America, see Stoler, ed., *Haunted by Empire*; Nicole Eustace, *Passion Is the Gale: Emotion, Power, and the Coming of the American Revolution* (Chapel Hill: Omohundro Institute of Early American History and Culture and University of North Carolina Press, 2008); Lisa Lowe, *The Intimacies of Four Continents* (Durham: Duke University Press, 2015); Joanna Brooks, "Hard Feelings: Samson Occom Contemplates His Christian Mentors," in *Native Americans, Christianity, and the Reshaping of the American Religious Landscape*, ed. Joel W. Martin and Mark A. Nicholas (Chapel Hill: University of North Carolina Press, 2010), 23–37; Jessica Marie Johnson, *Wicked Flesh: Black Women, Intimacy, and Freedom in the Atlantic World* (Philadelphia: University of Pennsylvania Press, 2000)

7. On power in the making of archives, see Marisa Fuentes, *Dispossessed Lives: Enslaved Women, Violence, and the Archive* (Philadelphia: University of Pennsylvania Press, 2016); Matt Cohen, *The Networked Wilderness: Communicating in Early New England* (Minneapolis: University of Minnesota Press, 2010), 1–28; Lowe, *Intimacies of Four Continents*.

8. Carolyn Korsmeyer has coined the term "terrible eating," contending that "even the most refined and delicate of meals presupposes a violent backdrop," the death of someone (plant or animal) for someone else to eat. Carolyn Korsmeyer, *Making Sense of Taste: Food and Philosophy* (Ithaca: Cornell University Press, 1999), 194. I have refined this definition to include the many kinds of violence terrible eating may inflict on bodies and social norms. See also Carolyn Korsmeyer, *Savoring Disgust: The Foul and the Fair in Aesthetics*

(Ithaca: Cornell University Press, 2011). The architectural theorist David Gissen has theorized the concept of "subnature," the way people have categorized certain aspects of the built environment—pigeons, mud, dust—as "fearsome," beyond "the limits in which contemporary life might be staged." Gissen instead calls for an embrace of the subnatural, because of its potential as "another possible form of nature in which we can be something more or less than is currently possible within our conceptions of nature." David Gissen, *Subnature: Architecture's Other Environments: Atmospheres, Matter, Life* (New York: Princeton Architectural Press, 2009), 23. My thanks to Ashley Rose Young for introducing me to Gissen's work.

9. William Ian Miller, *The Anatomy of Disgust* (Cambridge: Harvard University Press, 1997), 18. Sianne Ngai, *Ugly Feelings* (Cambridge: Harvard University Press, 2007), 338; on disgust within critical theory more broadly, see 332–54. For a review of the philosophical literature on disgust, see Nina Strohminger, "Disgust Talked About," *Philosophy Compass* 9, no. 7 (2014): 478–93. On the biology and psychology of disgust, see Curtis, *Don't Look, Don't Touch, Don't Eat, Food Preferences and Taste: Continuity and Change*, ed. Helen Macbeth (Providence: Berghahn Books, 1997).

10. On changing manners in the early modern period, see Norbert Elias, *The Civilizing Process: The History of Manners* (Cambridge, Mass.: Blackwell, 1994). On how early colonialism changed European foodways, see Robert Appelbaum, *Aguecheek's Beef, Belch's Hiccup, and Other Gastronomic Interjections: Literature, Culture, and Food among the Early Moderns* (Chicago: University of Chicago Press, 2006); Sara Pennell, *The Birth of the English Kitchen, 1600–1850* (London: Bloomsbury, 2016). Gervase Markham, *The English Housewife,* ed. Michael R. Best (Montreal: McGill–Queen's University Press, 1986), 8. On how Indigenous peoples defended their foodways against various colonial invaders, see Virginia DeJohn Anderson, *Creatures of Empire: How Domesticated Animals Transformed Early America* (New York: Oxford University Press, 2004); Christopher M. Parsons, *A Not-So-New World: Empire and Environment in Colonial North America* (Philadelphia: University of Pennsylvania Press, 2018); Thomas M. Wickman, *Snowshoe Country: An Environmental and Cultural History of Winter in the Early American Northeast* (New York: Cambridge University Press, 2018).

11. "Disgust, n.," *Oxford English Dictionary Online,* June 2018, http://www.oed.com/view/Entry/54422?rskey=50Sxi1&result=1&isAdvanced=false (accessed July 9, 2018). "Dégoût, n.," *Dictionnaire Électronique de l'Académie Française,* 9th ed., June 2018, https://academie.atilf.fr/consulter/d%C3%A9go%C3%BBt?page=1 (accessed July 9, 2018). Sébastian Rales, *A Dictionary of the Abnaki Language, In North America* (Cambridge, Mass.: Charles Folsom, 1833), 429. My translations from the French.

12. Ngai points out that "the language of repulsion is much more narrow and restricted" than that of desire. Ngai, *Ugly Feelings,* 338. Nevertheless, philosophers have conceived of disgust expansively, noting that while in English and French the word "disgust" is etymologically linked with taste, this is not always so in other languages. The German word for disgust, *ekel,* does not allude to taste at all. Disgust extends far beyond the gustatory. Miller, *Anatomy of Disgust,* 1–2. Biologists have argued that most common disgust trig-

gers are also potential carriers of disease (feces, corpses, etc.); thus, the disgust reflex operates as a sort of immune system, preventing contact with disease vectors. See Curtis, *Don't Look, Don't Touch, Don't Eat*. On cultural and individual food choice, see Macbeth, ed., *Food Preferences and Taste*.

13. For a history of changing concepts of hygiene in early America, see Kathleen Brown, *Foul Bodies: Cleanliness in Early America* (New Haven: Yale University Press, 2009), 2, 4; on increasing English disgust with Native bodily habits, see 156–57, 188. On hygiene across the Atlantic, see Susan North, *Sweet and Clean? Bodies and Clothes in Early Modern England* (New York: Oxford University Press, 2020). On how ideas of cleanliness create "unity in experience," see Douglas, *Purity and Danger*, 3. On how the classification of food-stuffs, or "gastronomic taxonomy," intersected with other taxonomic projects of European science, see Ritvo, *Platypus and the Mermaid*, 195.

14. On food as a "trope of the genre" of captivity narratives, see Ann Little, *Abraham in Arms: War and Gender in Colonial New England* (Philadelphia: University of Pennsylvania Press, 2007), 114, 112–18; see also Rachel B. Herrmann, " 'Their Filthy Trash': Taste, Eating, and Work in Mary Rowlandson's Captivity Narrative," *Labor: Studies in Working-Class History of the Americas* 12, no. 1–2 (May 2015): 45–70.

15. On colonial exchange and theft of Indigenous foods, see Michael A. LaCombe, *Political Gastronomy: Food and Authority in the English Atlantic World* (Philadelphia: University of Pennsylvania Press, 2012), 90–108. On English colonial foodways throughout the period, see Sarah F. McMahon, "A Comfortable Subsistence: The Changing Composition of Diet in Rural New England, 1620–1840," *William and Mary Quarterly* 42, no. 1 (January 1985): 26–65.

16. On the decrease of wild foods in early modern European diets, see Albala, "Wild Food," 9–19. On the English preference for beef, see Ritvo, *Platypus and the Mermaid*, 203–9; see also chap. 2 on religious food prohibitions. On Indigenous consumption of dogs, see Strother E. Roberts, "The Dog Days of Winter: Indigenous Dogs, Indian Hunters, and Wintertime Subsistence in the Northeast," *Northeastern Naturalist* 24, no. 7 (2017): H1–H21.

17. "A Narrative of the Captivity of Mrs. Johnson," in *North Country Captives: Selected Narratives of Indian Captivity from Vermont and New Hampshire*, ed. Colin Calloway (Hanover, N.H.: University Press of New England, 1992), 57, 61.

18. "A Narrative of the Captivity of Mrs. Johnson," 61, 62. The consumption of horse-meat had been banned in Britain since the suppression of the pagans, as eating horse was associated with paganism, a category into which English observers also placed Native peoples. Ritvo, *Platypus and the Mermaid*, 204–6. English people saw horses as "noble," "af-fectionate," and "humble," as well as beautiful and useful animals; this identification of positive human characteristics with horses would have made it disturbing to eat horse flesh. Harriet Ritvo, "Learning from Animals: Natural History for Children in the Eighteenth and Nineteenth Centuries," in *Noble Cows and Hybrid Zebras: Essays on Animals and History* (Charlottesville: University of Virginia Press, 2010), 40. On the naming of and closeness with livestock in early modern England, see Erica Fudge, "The Animal Face of

Early Modern England," *Theory Culture and Society* 30, no. 7–8 (2013): 185–88. Naming animals was a way for pet owners to "express psychological closeness," but this closeness is difficult to measure in Scoggin's case. Katherine C. Grier, *Pets in America: A History* (Chapel Hill: University of North Carolina Press, 2006), 67–69.

19. "Narrative of the Captivity of Mrs. Johnson," 61, 62, 80, 81.

20. Haudenosaunee raiding parties targeted women and children because they were much more open to acculturation than were adult men. Evan Haefeli and Kevin Sweeney, *Captors and Captives: The 1704 French and Indian Raid on Deerfield* (Amherst: University of Massachusetts Press, 2004), 155–63, 222–23. On colonial children who were adopted into Indigenous communities, see Demos, *Unredeemed Captive*; Little, *Many Captivities of Esther Wheelwright*. Today's disgust theorists have argued that small children are inherently less prone to disgust than adults, because disgust must be learned. There are three reasons why a person might reject any given food: (1) "undesirable sensory properties" of the food (smell, etc.), (2) "anticipated consequences" of eating the food, or (3) "conceptual" concerns about the food (cruelty, contamination, etc.). While young children react to food's sensory properties, the other two categories of "food rejection" must be learned throughout childhood. Paul Rozin, Jonathan Haidt, Clark McCauley, and Sumio Imada, "Disgust: Preadaption and the Cultural Evolution of a Food-based Emotion," in *Food Preferences and Taste*, 66–67.

21. Markham, *English House-Wife*, 64. Hannah Woolley, *The Gentlewomans Companion* (London, 1673), 213. On early modern European kitchens, see Barbara Ketchum Wheaton, *Savoring the Past: The French Kitchen and Table from 1300 to 1789* (Philadelphia: University of Pennsylvania Press, 1983), 16–18; on handwashing, see Brown, *Foul Bodies*, 33–34.

22. *The Jesuit Relations and Allied Documents: Travels and Explorations of the Jesuit Missionaries in New France, 1610–1791*, ed. Reuben Gold Thwaites (Cleveland: Burrows Brothers, 1900), 67:140 (hereafter JR). On European conceptions of food, morality, and gentility, see Steven Shapin, "How to Eat Like a Gentleman: Dietetics and Ethics in Early Modern England," in *Right Living: An Anglo-American Tradition of Self-Help Medicine and Hygiene*, ed. Charles E. Rosenberg (Baltimore: Johns Hopkins University Press, 2003), 21–58.

23. JR 65:44, 46, 48.

24. JR 65:44. On early modern sleep habits, see Sasha Handley, *Sleep in Early Modern England* (New Haven: Yale University Press, 2016).

25. On European dismissal of Indigenous emotions, see Lisa Brooks, *Our Beloved Kin: A New History of King Philip's War* (New Haven: Yale University Press, 2018), 282. On colonial notions of Indigenous uncleanliness as a justification for colonialism, see Brown, *Foul Bodies*, 188. On archival violence, see Fuentes, *Dispossessed Lives*, esp. 1–12.

26. Mary Rowlandson, *The Soveraignty and Goodness of God*, in *American Captivity Narratives*, ed. Gordon M. Sayre (Boston: Houghton Mifflin, 2000), 150. My reading of this scene is informed by Brooks, *Our Beloved Kin*, 270–71, and Little, *Abraham in Arms*, 122–23. The Wabanaki also had taboos around food and gender, specifically with regard to menstruat-

ing, pregnant, or postpartum women. Alice N. Nash, "The Abiding Frontier: Family, Gender and Religion in Wabanaki History, 1600–1763" (Ph.D. diss., Columbia University, 1997), 83, 236–39. Nash notes that the missionary Chrestien LeClercq recorded a number of food taboos in the M'ikmaq community he missionized in *New Relation of Gaspesia: With the Customs and Religion of the Gaspesian Indians* (Toronto: Champlain Society, 1910), 226–29. Nash argued that these taboos seem to have been evidence of "an almost frantic search for order and stability in a changing world" upended by colonization. "Abiding Frontier," 83. Because these taboos operated within a community as opposed to cross-culturally, I have chosen not to discuss them in text. On the move from communal to individual place settings in early modern Europe, see Richard L. Bushman, *The Refinement of America: Persons, Houses, Cities* (New York: Knopf, 1992), 74–75; Elias, *Civilizing Process*, 85–88; on the common pot, see Lisa Brooks, *The Common Pot: The Recovery of Native Space in the Northeast* (Minneapolis: University of Minnesota Press, 2008).

27. On the hierarchical relations of Weetamoo and Rowlandson's relationship, see Brooks, *Our Beloved Kin*, 270–71. Douglas, *Purity and Danger*, 50. Weetamoo and her family seem to have found Rowlandson generally dirty and revolting and urged her to bathe; see Brown, *Foul Bodies*, 79–80.

28. David Fowler to Eleazar Wheelock, June 15, 1765, in *The Letters of Eleazar Wheelock's Indians*, ed. James Dow McCallum (Brattleboro, Vt.: Stephen Daye Press, 1932), 94. David Fowler to Eleazar Wheelock, January 21, 1766, in *Letters of Eleazar Wheelock's Indians*, 99. On Fowler's letters to Wheelock, see Laura Murray, " 'Pray Sir, Consider a Little': Rituals of Subordination and Strategies of Resistance in the Letters of Hezekiah Calvin and David Fowler to Eleazar Wheelock, 1764–1768," *Studies in American Indian Literatures* 4, no. 2/3 (Summer/Fall 1992): 57–74.

29. Fowler to Wheelock, June 15, 1765, 94, 95. Fowler to Wheelock, January 21, 1766, 98. Ritvo noted that eighteenth- and nineteenth-century writers saw pigs as "defective in morality as well as taste"—their own undiscriminating taste in food, that is, not the taste of their flesh. Ritvo, "Learning from Animals," 41.

30. On the "perpetual identity crisis" facing Fowler and other Indigenous missionaries to Haudenosaunee communities, see Edward E. Andrews, *Native Apostles: Black and Indian Missionaries in the British Atlantic World* (Cambridge: Harvard University Press, 2013), chap. 5, quotation on 152. See also Linford Fisher, *The Indian Great Awakening: Religion and the Shaping of Native Cultures in Early America* (New York: Oxford University Press, 2012), 149; Murray, "'Pray Sir, Consider a Little,'" 58. On interactions between Native religions and Christianity, see Fisher, *The Indian Great Awakening*; Emma Anderson, *The Betrayal of Faith: The Tragic Journey of a Colonial Native Convert* (Cambridge: Harvard University Press, 2007); Rachel Wheeler, *To Live upon Hope: Mohicans and Missionaries in the Eighteenth-Century Northeast* (Ithaca: Cornell University Press, 2008); Laura M. Chmielewski, *The Spice of Popery: Converging Christianities on an Early American Frontier* (Notre Dame: University of Notre Dame Press, 2011).

31. Fowler to Wheelock, June 15, 1765, 94. Fowler to Wheelock, January 21, 1766, 99.

32. There was likely an outside audience for Fowler's letters: Wheelock regularly circulated his students' letters with potential donors. Murray, "'Pray Sir, Consider a Little,'" 50.

33. Kirkland, "Journal," 30. Rowlandson, *Soveraignty*, 149. Emphasis in the original. My thanks to Julie Kim for drawing my attention to this part of Rowlandson's narrative as evidence of Native recognition of colonial disgust. Other scholars have noted the reflexive nature of Indigenous commentary on colonial ideas about Indigenous peoples; see Philip Deloria, *Playing Indian* (New Haven: Yale University Press, 1998), 8.

34. Colonial beliefs in the inefficiency of Indigenous land use centered on the concept of agricultural "improvement" of land. See Cronon, *Changes in the Land*, 55, 77–81; Chaplin, *Subject Matter*, 201–42; Jennifer Anderson, " 'A Laudable Spirit of Enterprise': Renegotiating Land, Natural Resources, and Power on Post-Revolutionary Long Island," *EAS* 13, no. 2 (2015): 413–42.

35. Sidney Mintz, "The Place of Fermentation in a Thinkable World Food System," *Cured, Fermented and Smoked Foods: Proceedings of the Oxford Symposium on Food and Cookery 2010*, ed. Helen Saberi (Totnes: Prospect Books, 2011), 15, 16, 20, 27. Emphasis in the original. Mintz argued that many sedentary Indigenous cultures rely on "core" staple grains (rice, corn, wheat, etc.) for the bulk of their caloric intake, and then add nutritional value, flavor, and variety with the use of condiments, or "fringe" foods. Sidney Mintz, "The Anthropology of Food: Core and Fringe in Diet," *India International Centre Quarterly* 12, no. 2, Food Culture (June 1985): 193–204. Gissen's concept of subnature can be productively read to understand cultural constructions of fermentation, making something delicious out of controlled decay. Gissen, *Subnature*.

36. Joseph François Lafitau, *Customs of the American Indians Compared with the Customs of Primitive Times*, ed. and trans. William N. Fenton and Elizabeth L. Moore (Toronto: Champlain Society, 1974), 2:62. Kirkland, "Journal," 22.

37. Joseph Johnson to Wheelock, February 10, 1768, 128. Fowler to Wheelock, January 21, 1766, 99.

38. Markham, *English Housewife*, 101. Recipe book, ca. 1700–1750, 102, 20, 184, MC 675, folder 1.2v, American Institute of Wine and Food Recipe Books, ca., 1690–1830, Schlesinger Library, Radcliffe Institute, Cambridge, Mass. Markham, *English Housewife*, 103. Hannah Glasse, *The Art of Cookery* (London, 1747), 198. Kirkland, "Journal," 30.

39. *"Mothers represented the affectionate mode in an essentially authoritarian system of child-rearing."* Laurel Thatcher Ulrich, *Good Wives: Image and Reality in the Lives of Women in Northern New England, 1650–1750* (New York: Vintage Books, 1991), 154. Emphasis in the original. Rowlandson, *Soveraignty*, 162, 147.

40. Rowlandson, *Soveraignty*, 175, 176. Rowlandson's reference to the Prodigal Son comes from Luke 15:11–32; the section also contains references to Psalm 60:3, "Thou hast shewed thy people hard things: thou hast made us to drink the wine of astonishment," and Proverbs 28:3, "A poor man that oppresseth the poor is like a sweeping rain which leaveth no food."

41. Nicolas quoted in Parsons, *Not-So-New World*, 63. Rowlandson, *Soveraignty*, 147.

42. Kirkland, "Journal," 30. Emphasis in the original.

Chapter 4. Eaten Up

1. Cadwallader Colden, *The History of the Five Indian Nations of Canada* (London: T. Osborne, 1747), 153. On Teganissorens, see Daniel K. Richter, *The Ordeal of the Longhouse: The Peoples of the Iroquois League in the Era of European Colonization* (Chapel Hill: Omohundro Institute of Early American History and Culture and University of North Carolina Press, 1992).

2. Thomas Brown, *A Plain Narrative of the Uncommon Sufferings, and Remarkable Deliverance of Thomas Brown* (Boston: Fowle and Draper, 1760), 23.

3. John Gother, *Instructions for Confession and Communion* (London: Thomas Meighan, 1726), 76–77. Cotton Mather, *A Companion for Communicants* (Boston: Samuel Green, 1690), 12.

4. Cormac Ó'Gráda, *Eating People Is Wrong, and Other Essays on Famine, Its Past, and Its Future* (Princeton: Princeton University Press, 2015), 11–38. On cannibalism and butchery, see William M. Kelso, *Jamestown: The Truth Revealed* (Charlottesville: University of Virginia Press, 2017), 185–203.

5. This chapter takes an expansive view of ritual cannibalism, by defining communion as the ritualistic consumption of actual or metaphorical human flesh. See Carla Cevasco, "This Is My Body: Communion and Cannibalism in Colonial New England and New France," *New England Quarterly* 89, no. 4 (December 2016): 556–86. On reasons for ritual cannibalism, see Peggy Reeves Sanday, *Divine Hunger: Cannibalism as a Cultural System* (Cambridge: Cambridge University Press, 1986). 6, 25–26, 125; on endocannibalism vs. exocannibalism, 7. Other important theoretical works on cannibalism include Maggie Kilgour, *From Communion to Cannibalism: An Anatomy of Metaphors of Incorporation* (Princeton: Princeton University Press, 1990); Frank Lestrigant, *Cannibals: The Discovery and Representation of the Cannibal from Columbus to Jules Verne*, trans. Rosemary Morris (Berkeley: University of California Press, 1997); Catalin Avramescu, *An Intellectual History of Cannibalism*, trans. Alistair Ian Blyth (Princeton: Princeton University Press, 2009).

6. On conflicts over communion, see Richard Sugg, *Mummies, Cannibals, and Vampires: The History of Corpse Medicine from the Renaissance to the Victorians* (London: Routledge, 2011); Avramescu, *Intellectual History of Cannibalism*, esp. chap. 5; Cevasco, "This Is My Body," 556–86; Kilgour, *From Communion to Cannibalism*. On the consistency of colonial narratives of Indigenous cannibalism, see Thomas S. Abler, "Iroquois Cannibalism: Fact Not Fiction," *Ethnohistory* 27, no. 4 (Autumn 1980): 309–16. Recognizing that colonial stereotypes of Indigenous cannibals have served as an important justification for colonization, some scholars have gone so far as to argue that all ritual cannibalism is a fabrication. William Arens claimed that Europeans invented ritual cannibalism as an excuse for colonization. William Arens, *The Man-Eating Myth: Anthropology and Anthropopha* (Oxford: Oxford University Press, 1979). Rebuttals to Arens have emphasized both the presence of ritual cannibalism in some Native traditions and the importance of ritual cannibalism in early modern Europe.

7. There is an enormous scholarship on cannibalism in the early Atlantic. Important recent works include: Kelly L. Watson, *Insatiable Appetites: Imperial Encounters with Cannibals in the North Atlantic World* (New York: New York University Press, 2015); Rachel B.

Herrmann, ed., *To Feast on Us as Their Prey: Cannibalism and the Early Modern Atlantic* (Fayetteville: University of Arkansas Press, 2019).

8. On cannibalism overtaking gluttony as a European fear during colonization, see Robert Appelbaum, *Aguecheek's Beef, Belch's Hiccup, and Other Gastronomic Interjections: Literature, Culture, and Food among the Early Moderns* (Chicago: University of Chicago Press, 2006), 239–86. Joachim de la Chétardie, *Homélie XXIV pour le jeudy de la 2e semaine de carême, sur le mauvais riche* (Paris: Raymond Mazieres, 1708), 38.

9. Mark Nicholls, "George Percy's 'Trewe Relacyon': A Primary Source for the Jamestown Settlement," *Virginia Magazine of History and Biography* 113, no. 3 (2005): 248, 249. Rachel Herrmann has contended that historians should not take this and other documentary evidence as proof that cannibalism really happened, citing political discord within the colony and in England. Rachel Herrmann, " 'The Tragicall Historie': Food and Abundance in Colonial Jamestown," *William and Mary Quarterly* 68, no. 1 (January 2011): 47–71. Nevertheless, material evidence has reinforced the documentary record. In 2012, archaeologists at Historic Jamestowne revealed that they had excavated a skeleton from a fourteen-year-old girl with knife marks on the bones and argued that this constituted evidence of butchery. Kelso, *Jamestown*, 185–203.

10. Brown, *Narrative*, 24. Isaac Hollister, *A Brief Narrative of the Captivity of Isaac Hollister* (New London, CT, 1767), 6–7. These accounts, Kelly Watson has argued, reveal "the lengths [English colonists] will go to ensure their success in the New World," alongside an "Anglo-American masculine ideal that emphasized strength, sacrifice, and piety." Watson, *Insatiable Appetites*, 151.

11. In Britain until the late nineteenth century, cannibalism among the survivors of shipwrecks was generally legal, so long as the survivors drew lots to decide who would be killed or consumed the flesh of already-deceased people. This legal precedent changed in the 1880s, when the survivors of a wrecked yacht named the *Mignonette* faced a murder trial after drawing lots and consuming one of their number. A. W. Brian Simpson, *Cannibalism and the Common Law: The Story of the Tragic Last Voyage of the* Mignonette *and the Strange Legal Proceedings to Which It Gave Rise* (Chicago: University of Chicago Press, 1984). On colonial justifications of survival cannibalism, see Watson, *Insatiable Appetites*, 174; Richard Slotkin, *Regeneration through Violence: The Mythology of the American Frontier, 1600–1860* (Norman: University of Oklahoma Press, 1973), 124–26.

12. *An Abstract of the Douay Catechism* (Douay: Mairesse, 1716), 57. *The Grounds and Principles of Religion, Contained in a Shorter Catechism* (1646), 25. John Gother, *Instructions and Devotions for Hearing Mass* (London, 1699), 87. John Gother, *A Papist Misrepresented and Represented* (1685), 7. Mather, *Companion for Communicants*, 8, 12.

13. Mather, *Companion for Communicants*, 17, 113, 100, 105. Emphasis in the original. Thomas Doolittle, *A Treatise Concerning the Lord's Supper* (Boston: B. Green, and J. Allen, 1700), 25.

14. Mather, *Companion for Communicants*, 116. Emphasis in the original. Edward Taylor, *The Poems of Edward Taylor*, ed. Donald E. Stanford (New Haven: Yale University Press, 1960), 232, 231, 233, 234. Gother, *Instructions for Confession and Communion*, 80.

15. For a summary of Paracelsian thought, see Allen C. Debus, *The English Paracelsians* (London: F. Watts, 1965). On Taylor and the Paracelsian embrace of medicinal cannibalism, see Karen Gordon-Grube, "Evidence of Medicinal Cannibalism in Puritan New England: 'Mummy' and Related Remedies in Edward Taylor's 'Dispensatory,'" *Early American Literature* 28, no. 3 (1993): 185, 186–88, 190–91. On corpse medicine more generally, see Karen Gordon-Grube, "Anthropophagy in Post-Renaissance Europe: The Tradition of Corpse Medicine," *American Anthropologist* 90, no. 2 (June 1988): 407; Lynn Noble, *Medicinal Cannibalism in Early Modern English Literature and Culture* (New York: Palgrave Macmillan, 2011), 3; Piero Camporesi, *The Juice of Life: The Symbolic and Magic Significance of Blood*, trans. Robert R. Barr (New York, Continuum, 1995), 29–30; Sugg, *Mummies, Cannibals, and Vampires*, 14–16, 43, 78. Gother, *Instructions for Confession and Communion*, 88.

16. Sugg, *Mummies, Cannibals, and Vampires*, 198, 173–76. Gordon-Grube, "Evidence of Medicinal Cannibalism in Puritan New England," 203–4. Noble, *Medicinal Cannibalism*, 90–100. Taylor, *Poems*, 19.

17. Taylor, *Poems*, 231.

18. *The Jesuit Relations and Allied Documents: Travels and Explorations of the Jesuit Missionaries in New France, 1610–1791*, ed. Reuben Gold Thwaites (Cleveland: Burrows Brothers, 1900), 8:28–30 (hereafter JR). My translation.

19. JR 35:21. Editor's translation from the Latin.

20. For a review of the literature on the windigo in a variety of fields, and a survey of a variety of windigo stories, see Anthony Wonderly, *At the Font of the Marvelous: Exploring Oral Narrative and Mythic Imagery of the Iroquois and Their Neighbors* (Syracuse: Syracuse University Press, 2009), 69–97. On the relationship of windigo narratives to hunger, see Shawn Smallman, *Dangerous Spirits: The Windigo in Myth and History* (Toronto: Heritage, 2014), 25–26. See also Robin Wall Kimmerer, *Braiding Sweetgrass: Indigenous Wisdom, Scientific Knowledge, and the Teachings of Plants* (Minneapolis: Milkweed Editions, 2013), 304–5 and 375–77. For other varieties of Indigenous cannibalistic monsters, see Carolyn Podruchny, "Werewolves and Windigos: Narratives of Cannibal Monsters in French-Canadian Voyageur Oral Tradition," *Ethnohistory* 51, no. 4 (Fall 2004): 683. I am here upstreaming by using late nineteenth-century ethnography to discuss traditions from the seventeenth and eighteenth centuries. Of course, there are inherent flaws in this body of evidence, some of which is recorded second- or third-hand through multiple colonial narrators and at a great chronological distance. Nevertheless, the symptoms that the informants here described closely mirror the progression of cannibalistic illness as described in the seventeenth century Jesuit texts, so I have made the decision to consider the nineteenth-century sources, recognizing that they represent (however incompletely) the preserved traditions of Wabanaki elders in the nineteenth century. The seventeenth- and eighteenth-century archive itself is, according to critical archive theory, no less flawed than later ethnography. A similar method is seen in Jessica Yirush Stern, *The Lives in Objects: Native Americans, British Colonists, and Cultures of Labor and Exchange in the Southeast* (Chapel Hill: University of North Carolina

Press, 2017), 175–76, n44. The ethnographer who collected the Chenoo stories, Charles Leland, listed the following Wabanaki and colonial informants: "Tomah Josephs, Passamaquoddy, Indian Governor at Peter Dana's Point, Maine. The Rev. Silas T. Rand, Baptist Missionary among the Micmac Indians at Hantsport, Nova Scotia. This gentleman lent me his manuscript collection of eighty-five stories, all taken down from verbal Indian narration. . . . John Gabriel, and his son Peter J. Gabriel, Passamaquoddy Indians, of Point Pleasant, Maine. Noel Josephs, of Peter Dana's Point, alias *Che gach goch*, the Raven. Joseph Tomah, Passamaquoddy, of Point Pleasant. Louis Mitchell, Indian member of the Legislature of Maine. To this gentleman I am greatly indebted for manuscripts, letters, and oral narrations of great value. Sapiel Selmo, keeper of the Wampum Record, formerly read every four years at the kindling of the great fire at Canawagha. Marie Saksis, of Oldtown, a capital and very accurate narrator of many traditions. Miss Abby Alger, of Boston, by whom I was greatly aided in collecting the Passamaquoddy stories, and who obtained several for me among the St. Francis or Abenaki Indians. Edward Jack, of Fredericton, for several Micmac legends and many letters containing folk-lore, all taken down by him directly from Indians. Mrs W. Wallace Brown. Mr. Brown was agent in charge of the Passamaquoddies in Maine. . . . Noel Neptune, Penobscot, Oldtown, Maine." Charles G. Leland, *The Algonquin Legends of New England, Or Myths and Folk Lore of the Micmac, Passamaquoddy, and Penobscot Tribes* (London: Sampson Low, Marston, Seaerle and Rivington, 1884), x.

21. Leland, *Algonquin Legends*, 233, 238, 242.

22. Leland, *Algonquin Legends*, 252–53. On windigo stories and their relationship to family and gender roles, see Smallman, *Dangerous Spirits*, 28, 35–62.

23. Wickman, *Snowshoe Country*, 53–55, 187, 190–92. Alice N. Nash, "The Abiding Frontier: Family, Gender and Religion in Wabanaki History, 1600–1763" (Ph.D. diss., Columbia University, 1997), 79–83.

24. Wickman, *Snowshoe Country*, 193–233. Podruchny, "Werewolves and Windigos," 678, 680, 684.

25. Leland, *Algonquin Legends*, n252. On windigo traditions in response to colonialism, see Carol Devens, *Countering Colonization: Native American Women and Great Lakes Missions, 1630–1900* (Berkeley: University of California Press, 1992), 44; and Kenneth M. Morrison, *The Solidarity of Kin: Ethnohistory, Religious Studies, and the Algonkian-French Religious Encounter* (Albany: SUNY Press, 2002), 59–78, esp. 69–71.

26. JR 46:262–64. My translation.

27. Smallman, *Dangerous Spirits*, 24–25. For examples of windigo dreams from the upper Midwest in the early nineteenth century, see George Nelson, "George Nelson's Letter-Journal," in *"The Orders of the Dreamed": George Nelson on Cree and Northern Ojibwa Religion and Myth, 1823* (St. Paul: Minnesota Historical Society Press, 1988), 90–94. On Native and colonial understandings of dreams, see Drew Lopenzina, "Le Jeune Dreams of Moose: Altered States among the Montagnais in the Jesuit Relations of 1634," *Early American Studies* 13, no. 1 (Winter 2015): 3–37. JR 42:154. My translation.

28. JR 10:226–28. My translation.

29. JR 22:252–56. My translation. For more on how Jesuit missionaries reacted to cannibalism among the Haudenosaunee in New France, see Watson, *Insatiable Appetites*, chap. 4, esp. 134–35.

30. Jonathan Carver, "Captain Jonathan Carver's Narrative of His Capture," in *Tragedies of the Wilderness; or True and Authentic Narratives of Captives Who Have Been Carried Away by the Indians*, ed. Samuel Gardner Drake (Boston: Antiquarian Bookstore and Institute, 1841), 174. JR 70:126. Emphasis in the original. My translation.

31. On the documentary evidence for Haudenosaunee ritual cannibalism, see Abler, "Iroquois Cannibalism: Fact Not Fiction," 309–16. An anthropologist, Sanday lists a variety of reasons for ritual cannibalism, including mourning, warfare, and rebalancing the social order. Sanday, *Divine Hunger*, especially 6, 25–26, 125; see also Sugg, *Mummies, Cannibals, and Vampires*, 5, 129.

32. On eating culture, see Kyla Wazana Tompkins, *Racial Indigestion: Eating Bodies in the 19th Century* (New York: New York University Press, 2012), esp. introduction. The quotation about Ata-entsic comes from Joseph François Lafitau, *Customs of the American Indians Compared with the Customs of Primitive Times*, ed. and trans. William N. Fenton and Elizabeth L. Moore (Toronto: Champlain Society, 1974), 1:168. Brebeuf's description of the Wendat ritual is in JR 10:226–28. My translation.

33. For an analysis of Brebeuf's death from Haudenosaunee, Wendat, and Jesuit perspectives, see Anderson, "Blood, Fire, and 'Baptism,'" 125–58.

34. Samuel Checkley, *Prayer a Duty, When God's People Go Forth to War* (Boston: B. Green, 1745), 8. Emphasis added. Jeremiah 30:16: Therefore all they that devour thee shall be devoured; and all thine adversaries, every one of them, shall go into captivity; and they that spoil thee shall be a spoil, and all that prey upon thee will I give for a prey. Colden, *History of the Five Indian Nations of Canada*, 153. JR 70:98, 100. Emphasis in the original. JR 67:202.

35. JR 70:128, 124. "A Narrative of the Captivity of Mrs. Johnson," in *North Country Captives: Selected Narratives of Indian Captivity from Vermont and New Hampshire*, ed. Colin Calloway (Hanover: University Press of New England, 1992), 61.

36. Mary Rowlandson, *The Soveraignty and Goodness of God*, in *American Captivity Narratives*, ed. Gordon M. Sayre (Boston: Houghton Mifflin, 2000), 155. *God's Mercy Surmounting Man's Cruelty, Exemplified in the Captivity and Redemption of Elizabeth Hanson*, in *Women's Indian Captivity Narratives*, ed. Kathryn Zabelle Derounian-Stodola (New York: Penguin, 1998), 74. Emphasis in the original.

37. "A Particular Account of the Captivity and Redemption of Mrs. Jemima Howe," in *Tragedies of the Wilderness; or True and Authentic Narratives of Captives*, ed. Samuel Gardner Drake (Boston: Antiquarian Bookstore and Institute, 1841), 159–60.

38. On the divisiveness of certain wartime practices such as cannibalism, see Thomas S. Abler, "Scalping, Torture, Cannibalism, and Rape: An Ethnohistorical Analysis of Conflicting Cultural Values in War," *Anthropologica* 34, no. 1 (1992): 3–20. Avramescu, *Intellectual History of Cannibalism*, 75. Dudley Bradstreet Diary, May 27, 1745, Pre-

Revolutionary Diaries microfilm 2.23, Massachusetts Historical Society, Boston. John Norton, *The Redeemed Captive* (Boston, 1748), 10. The same Frenchman, Norton reported, then made a tobacco pouch of the watchman's skin. On Catholic "seduction" in British captivity narratives, see Teresa A. Toulouse, *The Captive's Position: Female Narrative, Male Identity, and Royal Authority in Colonial New England* (Philadelphia: University of Pennsylvania Press, 2007), chap. 7.

39. JR 42:154. JR 10:228. My translation.

40. For Native Studies interpretations of colonialism as windigo, see Kimmerer, *Braiding Sweetgrass*, 303–9, 374–79; Jack D. Forbes, *Columbus and Other Cannibals: The Wétiko Disease of Exploitation, Imperialism, and Cannibalism*, rev. ed. (New York: Seven Stories Press, 2008). Brazilian artists, writers, and critics have adopted the metaphor of Indigenous cannibalism as a post-colonial critique on this literature; see Carlos Jáuregui, *Canibalia: Canibalismo, Calinabismo, Antropofagia Cultural y Consumo en América Latina* (Madrid: Iberoamericana, 2008).

41. Ó'Gráda, *Eating People Is Wrong*, 11–38. On European conceptions of Haudenosaunee hunger, see Herrmann, *No Useless Mouth*, chaps. 1 and 2.

42. JR 46:262. My translation. Sanday described hunger having an "antisocial power." *Divine Hunger*, 102.

43. Leland, *Algonquin Legends*, 234. Nash, "Abiding Frontier," 79–83. Kimmerer, *Braiding Sweetgrass*, 375–76.

Chapter 5. Give Us Some Provision

1. Samuel Kirkland, "A Journal of the Reverend Samuel Kirkland, November 1764—June 1765," in *The Journals of Samuel Kirkland*, ed. Walter Pilkington (Clinton, N.Y.: Hamilton College Press, 1980), 31.

2. Anonymous Soldier's Diary, November 3, 1758, Octavo vol. 2, French and Indian War Collection, American Antiquarian Society, Worcester, Mass. (hereafter AAS).

3. Anonymous Soldier's Diary, November 3, 1758. Luke Knowlton, Diary (transcript—original has been lost), September 20, 1759, box 1, folder 5, Miscellaneous Documents, 1754–1763, French and Indian War Collection, AAS.

4. Massachusetts State Archives, vol. 29, p. 339, Massachusetts Archives Collection, Boston (hereafter MSA).

5. On the constructions of hierarchies of race, gender, class, and power in early America, see Kathleen Brown, *Foul Bodies: Cleanliness in Early America* (New Haven: Yale University Press, 2009); Kathleen Brown, *Good Wives, Nasty Wenches, and Anxious Patriarchs* (Chapel Hill: Omohundro Institute of Early American History and Culture and University of North Carolina Press, 1996); Rhys Isaac, *Landon Carter's Uneasy Kingdom: Revolution and Rebellion on a Virginia Plantation* (Oxford: Oxford University Press, 2004). For a broader articulation of these hierarchies as they related to colonialism and anthropocentrism, see Sylvia Wynter, "Unsettling the Coloniality of Being/Power/Truth/ Freedom:

Towards the Human, after Man, Its Overrepresentation—An Argument," *CR: The New Centennial Review* 3, no. 3 (Fall 2003): 257–337.

6. Food, diplomacy, and politics in seventeenth- and eighteenth-century North America have received scholarly attention, but the role of food in Wabanaki diplomacy in particular has not. As I will argue below, the distinctiveness of Wabanaki culture and politics created a distinctive negotiating environment. Key works on Native-colonial diplomacy and food are Rachel B. Herrmann, *No Useless Mouth: Waging War and Fighting Hunger in the American Revolution* (Ithaca: Cornell University Press, 2019); and Michael A. LaCombe, *Political Gastronomy: Food and Authority in the English Atlantic World* (Philadelphia: University of Pennsylvania Press, 2012). Herrmann's concept of "food diplomacy," or the use of food and hunger in diplomatic relations, is relevant here. *No Useless Mouth*, 9. On the construction of narratives of the legality of colonial land claims, see Jean O'Brien, *Firsting and Lasting: Writing Indians Out of Existence in New England* (Minneapolis: University of Minnesota Press, 2010), chap. 2. Literature on European-Native diplomatic exchange has tended to replicate a colonial narrative of gift-giving Indians and ruthless capitalist colonists; examples include Richard White, *The Roots of Dependency: Subsistence, Environment, and Social Change among the Choctaws, Pawnees, and Navajos* (Lincoln: University of Nebraska Press, 1983); Colin Calloway, *New Worlds for All: Indians, Europeans, and the Remaking of Early America* (Baltimore: Johns Hopkins University Press, 1997). For a rebuttal of these arguments, see Jessica Yirush Stern, *The Lives in Objects: Native Americans, British Colonists, and Cultures of Labor and Exchange in the Southeast* (Chapel Hill: University of North Carolina Press, 2017).

On British imperial medical policy in the late eighteenth century, see Erica Charters, "The Caring Fiscal-Military State during the Seven Years War, 1756–1763," *Historical Journal* 52, no. 4 (December 2009): 921–41; Erica Charters, *Disease, War, and the Imperial State: The Welfare of the British Armed Forces during the Seven Years' War* (Chicago: University of Chicago Press, 2014). Important scholarship on late eighteenth-century imperial warfare includes: Fred Anderson, *Crucible of War: The Seven Years' War and the Fate of Empire in British North America, 1754–1766* (New York: Knopf, 2000); Guy Chet, *Conquering the American Wilderness: The Triumph of European Warfare in the Colonial Northeast* (Amherst: University of Massachusetts Press, 2003); Christian Ayne Crouch, *Nobility Lost: French and Canadian Martial Cultures, Indians and The End of New France* (Ithaca: Cornell University Press, 2014); John Grenier, *The First Way of War: American War Making on the Frontier, 1607–1814* (New York: Cambridge University Press, 2005); Wayne E. Lee, *Barbarians and Brothers: Anglo-American Warfare, 1500–1865* (Oxford University Press, 2011).

7. Scholars have described the distinctiveness of Wabanaki subsistence patterns and social and political organization, which were critical aspects of Wabanaki resistance to colonization. Important examples include: Colin G. Calloway, *The Western Abenakis of Vermont, 1600–1800: War, Migration, and the Survival of an Indian People* (Norman, Okla.: University of Oklahoma Press, 1994); Thomas M. Wickman, *Snowshoe Country: An Environmental and Cultural History of Winter in the Early American Northeast* (New York:

Cambridge University Press, 2018); Alice N. Nash, "The Abiding Frontier: Family, Gender and Religion in Wabanaki History, 1600–1763" (Ph.D. diss., Columbia University, 1997); Ann M. Little, *The Many Captivities of Esther Wheelwright* (New Haven: Yale University Press, 2016), 1–83. There is plenty of scholarship on Wabanaki diplomacy, but it has not been examined through a food studies lens. Major scholarship on Wabanaki diplomacy includes: Ian Saxine, *Properties of Empire: Indians, Colonists, and Land Speculators on the New England Frontier* (New York: New York University Press, 2019); Kenneth M. Morrison, *The Embattled Northeast: The Elusive Ideal of Alliance in Abenaki-Euramerican Relations* (Berkeley: University of California Press, 1984); Harold E. L. Prins, "The Crooked Path of Dummer's Treaty: Anglo-Wabanaki Diplomacy and the Quest for Aboriginal Rights," in *Papers of the Thirty-Third Algonquian Conference,* ed. H. C. Wolfart (Winnipeg: University of Manitoba Press, 2002), 360–77; Emerson W. Baker and John G. Reid, "Amerindian Power in the Early Modern Northeast: A Reappraisal," *William and Mary Quarterly* 61, no. 1 (January 2004): 77–106; David L. Ghere and Alvin H. Morrison, "Searching for Justice on the Maine Frontier: Legal Concepts, Treaties, and the 1749 Wicasset Incident," *American Indian Quarterly* 25, no. 3 (Summer, 2001): 378–99; David L. Ghere, "Mistranslations and Misinformation: Diplomacy on the Maine Frontier, 1725 to 1755," *American Indian Culture and Research Journal* 8, no. 4 (1984): 3–26.

8. Philip Deloria reads assertions of settler colonial "indigeneity" in colonists' use of Native-inspired costumes during protests against British authority in the eighteenth century. Philip Deloria, *Playing Indian* (New Haven: Yale, 1998), 10–38.

9. Baker and Evans, "Amerindian Power in the Northeast," 79; Wickman, *Snowshoe Country,* 2–11.

10. Nash, "Abiding Frontier," 18. Wickman, *Snowshoe Country,* 54–55, 21–22.

11. MSA 29:254. Jonathan Belcher to Mr. Grant, May 21, 1733, *Collections of the Massachusetts Historical Society,* Sixth Series (Boston: Massachusetts Historical Society, 1893), 6:296.

12. Quotation from Wickman, *Snowshoe Country,* 181. Mary Black-Rogers, "Varieties of 'Starving': Semantics and Survival in the Subarctic Fur Trade, 1750–1850," *Ethnohistory* 33, no. 4 (Fall 1986): 353–83. On these kinds of rhetoric in Haudenosaunee-British-American negotiations, see Herrmann, *No Useless Mouth,* chaps. 1 and 2. On Indigenous performance in early America, see *Native Acts: Indian Performance, 1603–1832,* ed. Joshua David Bellin and Laura L. Mielke (Lincoln: University of Nebraska Press, 2012); Deloria, *Playing Indian,* esp. introduction and chap. 1.

13. *The Conference with the Eastern Indians . . . 1726* (Boston: S. Kneeland, 1754), 4. Ghere, "Mistranslations and Misinformation," 4–5, 10. Morrison, *Embattled Northeast,* 170–71. Prins, "Crooked Path of Dummer's Treaty." On translation, see Lisa Brooks, "Awikhigawôgan ta Pildowi Ôjmowôgan: Mapping a New History," *William and Mary Quarterly* 75, no. 2 (April 2018): 262–67; Sarah Rivett, *Unscripted America: Indigenous Languages and the Origins of a Literary Nation* (New York: Oxford, 2017), 89–114, esp. 100–101.

14. Nash, "Abiding Frontier," 165, 162; Saxine, *Properties of Empire,* 15.

15. The English recorded his name variously as Loren, Laurence, Saguaarum, or combinations of these names. On reading treaty conference proceedings for Indigenous voices, see Daniel K. Richter, *Facing East from Indian Country: A Native History of Early America* (Cambridge: Harvard University Press, 2001), 110–11. On Penobscot orality, oral tradition, and history, see Annette Kolodny, " 'This Long Looked For Event': Retrieving Early Contact History from Penobscot Oral Traditions," *Native American and Indigenous Studies* 2, no. 1 (Spring 2015), esp. 107–9.

16. Richter, *Facing East from Indian Country*, 134, 135, 137. *At a Conference Held at Deerfield in the County of Hampshire* (Boston: S. Kneeland and T. Green, 1735), 8. Tom Arne Midtrød, *The Memory of All Ancient Customs: Native American Diplomacy in the Colonial Hudson Valley* (Ithaca: Cornell University Press, 2016), 42–43. *An Account of Conferences Held, and Treaties Made* (London: A. Millar, 1756), 27. On wampum, see Lisa Brooks, *The Common Pot: The Recovery of Native Space in the Northeast* (Minneapolis: University of Minnesota Press, 2008), chap. 2; Marc Shell, *Wampum and the Origins of American Money* (Champaign: University of Illinois Press, 2013); David Graeber, "Wampum and Social Creativity among the Iroquois," in *Toward an Anthropological Theory of Value: The False Coin of Our Own Dreams* (New York: Palgrave Macmillan, 2001): 117–49.

17. MSA 29:82, 83, 95. *At a Conference Held at Deerfield*, 5, 6, 7.

18. MSA 29:339, 344, 345. *A Conference, Held at the Fort at St. George's in the County of York* (Boston: J. Draper, 1742), 3–4, 9.

19. Brooks, *Common Pot*. Wickman, *Snowshoe Country*, 181. However, ceremonial food exchanges did not always have the intended English effect of highlighting Native dependency, with Native leaders just as often having the opportunity to emphasize colonial dependency on Indigenous goodwill and resources. See LaCombe, *Political Gastronomy*, esp. chap. 4; Herrmann, *No Useless Mouth*, chaps. 1 and 2.

20. MSA 31:633, 634–35. On gentility and eating, see Richard L. Bushman, *The Refinement of America: Persons, Houses, Cities* (New York: Knopf, 1992), 74–78.

21. The most thorough consideration of Indigenous-European disputes over animals in the northeast, though limited to the seventeenth century, is Virginia DeJohn Anderson, *Creatures of Empire: How Domestic Animals Transformed Early America* (New York: Oxford, 2004), esp. chap. 6; see also Andrea L. Smalley, *Wild by Nature: North American Animals Confront Colonization* (Baltimore: Johns Hopkins University Press, 2017). *A Conference . . . at Falmouth in Casco-Bay, July 1732* (Boston: B. Green, 1732), 16, 17. Emphasis in the original. Strother E. Roberts, "The Dog Days of Winter: Indigenous Dogs, Indian Hunters, and Wintertime Subsistence in the Northeast," *Northeastern Naturalist* 24, no. 7 (2017): H1–H21.

22. *A Conference, Held at the Fort at St. George's*, 6, 15. Anderson calls Native destruction of English livestock "a guerilla campaign of opposition to English expansion." *Creatures of Empire*, 195–96, 228–30, quotation on 229.

23. *A Conference . . . at Falmouth in Casco-Bay, July 1732*, 11.

24. MSA 29:340–41. On English-French tensions in the region, see Laura M. Chmielewski, *The Spice of Popery: Converging Christianities on an Early American Frontier* (Notre Dame: University of Notre Dame Press, 2011); Saxine, *Properties of Empire.*

25. Contrary to previous generations of historians' depiction of guileless Native people and ruthless English traders, Jessica Yirush Stern has found that Creeks and Cherokees wanted a more open trade than regulation-minded English. Stern, *The Lives in Objects,* 2. MSA 29:368. *A Conference, Held at the Fort at St. George's in the County of York . . . 1742,* 6. MSA 29:372. Little, *Many Captivities of Esther Wheelwright,* 51–56.

26. Scholars of food and diplomacy have also considered alcohol, even if it does not fall neatly into the category of foodstuff. On alcohol, violence, and land speculation, see David Preston, *The Texture of Contact: European and Indian Settler Communities on the Frontiers of Iroquoia* (Lincoln: University of Nebraska Press, 2009), 130–31, 162–63, 269–78. On alcohol and trauma, Peter C. Mancall, *Deadly Medicine: Indians and Alcohol in Early America* (Ithaca: Cornell University Press, 1995), 8, 76–79; see also Joanna Brooks, "Hard Feelings: Samson Occom Contemplates His Christian Mentors," in *Native Americans, Christianity, and the Reshaping of the American Religious Landscape,* ed. Joel W. Martin and Mark A. Nicholas (Chapel Hill: University of North Carolina Press, 2010), esp. 26–29. Examining colonial perspectives on Shawnee alcohol use, Sami Lakomäki, Ritva Kylli, and Timo Ylimaunu note that British officials rejected Shawnee regulation of their own alcohol consumption, believing that only colonists were "entitled to ban or allow alcohol in the Indian country." Sami Lakomäki, Ritva Kylli, and Timo Ylimaunu, "Drinking Colonialism: Alcohol, Indigenous Status, and Native Space on Shawnee and Sámi Homelands," *Native American and Indigenous Studies* 4, no. 1 (Spring 2017): 19.

27. Mancall, *Deadly Medicine,* 47–49, 63–79, 82–84. On the alcohol trade, see also Preston, *Texture of Contact.* On tobacco, see Marcy Norton, *Sacred Gifts, Profane Pleasures: A History of Tobacco and Chocolate in the Atlantic World* (Ithaca: Cornell University Press, 2008); James Warren Springer, "An Ethnohistoric Study of the Smoking Complex in Eastern North America," *Ethnohistory* 28, no. 3 (Summer 1981): 217–35. In general, the Wabanaki did not smoke tobacco during negotiations, but Springer notes an exception: a French missionary account of the Wabanaki at Sillery learning the Calumet Dance from the Meskwaki during alliance negotiations in the 1710s. Springer, "Ethnohistoric Study of the Smoking Complex," 227.

28. MSA 29:39. MSA 29:253–54. MSA 29:349. Emphasis in the original. *Conference . . . at Falmouth in Casco-Bay, July 1732,* 6.

29. *Conference . . . at Falmouth in Casco-Bay, July 1732,* 10, 13. MSA 29:337–38, 340. He repeated nearly identical demands to limit alcohol distribution in a 1740 conference. MSA 29:368, 371. *At a Conference Held at St. George's in the County of York . . . 1753* (Boston: Samuel Kneeland, 1753), 22.

30. MSA 31:186, 188, 190, 193. MSA 29:52, 336. Emphasis removed from the original. *A Conference, Held at the Fort at St. George's in the County of York . . . 1742,* 4.

31. *Documents Relative to the Colonial History of the State of New-York,* ed. E. B. O'Gallaghan (Albany: Weed, Parsons, 1855), 9:966–67. On the larger context of this incident, see

Ghere and Morrison, "Searching for Justice on the Maine Frontier," 382–83; Ghere, "Mistranslations and Misinformation," 10–11; Prins, "Crooked Path of Dummer's Treaty," 373–74.

32. MSA 29:254.

33. On the Seven Years' War and the continuing struggle for Wabanaki land rights, see Saxine, *Properties of Empire,* chap. 8 and conclusion, quotation on 165.

34. On desertion: Thomas Agostini, " 'Deserted His Majesty's Service': Military Runaways, the British-American Press, and the Problem of Desertion during the Seven Years' War," *Journal of Social History* 40, no. 4 (Summer 2007): 957–85, quotation on 959; Fred Anderson, *A People's Army: Massachusetts Soldiers and Society in the Seven Years' War* (Chapel Hill: Omohundro Institute of Early American History and Culture and University of North Carolina Press, 1984), 162–63, 187–88, 192–94.

35. On these changes in British military strategy, see Gina M. Martino, *Women at War in the Borderlands of the Early American Northeast* (Chapel Hill: University of North Carolina Press, 2018), 121; Chet, *Conquering the American Wilderness,* 73–75.

36. Charters, *Disease, War, and the Imperial State,* 4, 5, 12; Charters, "Caring Fiscal-Military State During the Seven Years War." Chet, *Conquering the American Wilderness,* chap. 5, esp. 101, 132–35. Chet argued that the British army's logistical innovations led to its success in the Seven Years' War, but I join Charters in highlighting how pervasive problems with provisioning stoked rebellion against British military authorities. In addition to Loudon's centralized supply system, local purveyors also supplied soldiers, including with alcohol; a rum distillery in Albany served soldiers there. Justin Divirgilio, "Rum Punch and Cultural Revolution: The Impact of the Seven Years' War in Albany," *New York History* 86, no. 4 (Fall 2005): 435–49. On Haudenosaunee food interactions with the British in borderlands forts during the American Revolution see Herrmann, *No Useless Mouth,* chap. 2.

37. P. J. Marshall, *The Making and Unmaking of Empires: Britain, India, and America c. 1750–1783* (New York: Oxford University Press, 2007), chap. 3, quotation on 98. In England, relations between militia and regulars were similarly tense. Matthew McCormack, *Embodying the Militia in Georgian England* (New York: Oxford University Press, 2015), 109; on debates regarding the uses of the militia in England, see chap. 1. Many historians have seen the roots of the American Revolution in these disagreements between colonial and British authorities and in the day-to-day frustrations of colonial troops with British military policy. Anderson, *Crucible of War;* Anderson, *People's Army;* Alan Rogers, *Empire and Liberty: American Resistance to British Authority, 1755–1763* (Berkeley: University of California Press, 1974); Douglas Edward Leach, *Roots of Conflict: British Armed Forces and Colonial Americans, 1677–1763* (Chapel Hill: University of North Carolina Press, 1989). For a counterpoint, see Woody Holton, "How the Seven Years' War Turned Americans into (British) Patriots," in *Cultures in Conflict: The Seven Years' War in North America,* ed. Warren R. Hofstra (Lanham, Md.: Rowman and Littlefield, 2007), 138. British Seven Years' War veterans who remained in North America would become important members of the Loyalist cause

during the Revolution. Stephen Brumwell, *Redcoats: The British Soldier and War in the Americas, 1755–1783* (New York: Cambridge University Press, 2002), 310–14. This section concerns colonial soldiers, but Indigenous men also served in and as allies to the British military. For examples, see Brian D. Carroll, " 'Savages' in the Service of Empire: Native American Soldiers in Gorham's Rangers, 1744–1762," *New England Quarterly* 85, no. 3 (September 2012): 383–429; Brumwell, *Redcoats*, 162–91.

38. Charters, *Disease, War, and the Imperial State*, 5.

39. Thomas Venn, *Military and Maritime Discipline* (London: R. Pawlet, 1672). Sieur de Birac, M. de Lamont, and Chevalier de la Valière, *The Art of War* (London: J. Morphew, 1707), 138. Richard Lambart Cavan, *A New System of Military Discipline* (Philadelphia: R. Aitken, 1776), 256, 257. John Darker, *A Breviary of Military Discipline* (London: D. Brown, 1692). On eighteenth-century trends in European military discipline, see Crouch, *Nobility Lost*, 19, n9.

40. Anderson, *People's Army*, 69, 90–98, 99–101. J. S., *Fortification and Military Discipline* (London: Robert Morden, 1688), plate 18. Emphasis in the original.

41. J. S., *Fortification and Military Discipline*, 62. John Pringle, *Observations on the Diseases of the Army*, 5th ed. (London: A. Millar, D. Wilson, T. Durham, and T. Payne, 1765). Capt. Silas Brown Orderly Book, September 2, 1760, reel 13, vol. 13.6, Pre-Revolutionary Diaries microfilm, Massachusetts Historical Society (hereafter MHS), Boston; Capt. David Holmes Orderly Book, July 3, 1760, MHS 13.9.

42. Holmes Orderly Book, August 26, 1758, MHS 13.8. Richard Kane, *A System of Camp-Discipline, Military Honours, Garrison-Duty, and other Regulations for the Land Forces*, 2nd ed. (London: J. Millan, 1757), 28. Capt. Josiah Perry Orderly Book, July 12, 1758, April 19, 1760, February 19, 1760, misc. boxes P, AAS. Holmes, August 19, 1759, MHS 139. On sutlers, see Holly A. Mayer, *Belonging to the Army: Camp Followers and Community during the American Revolution* (Columbia : University of South Carolina Press, 1996), chap. 3.

43. There is relatively little scholarship on camp followers and even less on their specific roles in provisioning; exceptions include: Paul E. Kopperman, "The British High Command and Soldiers' Wives in America, 1755–1783," *Journal of the Society for Army Historical Research* 60, no. 241 (Spring 1982), esp. 15–16, 27–28; Scott N. Hendrix, "In the Army: Women, Camp Followers and Gender Roles in the British Army in the French and Indian Wars, 1755–1765," in *A Soldier and A Woman: Sexual Integration in the Military*, ed. Gerard J. De Grott and C. M. Peniston-Bird (New York: Longman, 2000), 33–48; Peter Way, "Venus and Mars: Women and the British-American Army in the Seven Years' War," in Julie Flavell and Stephen Conway, eds., *Britain and America Go to War: The Impact of War and Warfare on Anglo-America, 1754–1815* (Gainesville: University Press of Florida, 2004), 41–68; Mayer, *Belonging to the Army*, 8–10, 138–40; and "From Forts to Families: Following the Army into Western Pennsylvania, 1758–1766," *Pennsylvania Magazine of History and Biography* 130, no. 1 (January 2006): 5–43; John A. Lynn II, *Women, Armies, and Warfare in Early Modern Europe* (New York: Cambridge, 2008), chap. 3, esp. 124–25; Barton Hacker, "Women and Military Institutions in Early Modern Europe: A Reconnaissance," *Signs* 6,

no. 4 (Summer 1981): 643–71, quotation on 644; Brumwell, *Redcoats*, 122–27; see also Walter Hart Blumenthal, *Women Camp Followers of the American Revolution* (Philadelphia: George S. MacManus Company, 1952).

44. Kopperman, "British High Command and Soldiers' Wives in America," 22–26.

45. Kane, *System of Camp-Discipline*, 10, 25.

46. Lieut. Dudley Bradstreet Diary, June 10 and June 26, 1745, MHS 2.23. Anonymous, July 20, 1759, MHS 13.2. As noted in chapter 1, colonial men were much less likely to have extensive knowledge of wild plants compared to Indigenous peoples of all genders or colonial women. Charters claims that there was nothing to forage in the northeastern borderlands in the winter, which elides the wide array of foods that Native peoples foraged in the colder months. Charters, *Disease, War, and the Imperial State*, 25. Perry Orderly Book, May 28, 1759. On the challenges facing colonial agriculture in Canada, see Christopher M. Parsons, *A Not-So-New World: Empire and Environment in Colonial North America* (Philadelphia: University of Pennsylvania Press, 2018).

47. Raymund Minderer, *Medicina Militaris, or A Body of Military Medicines Experimented* (London: William Godbid, 1674), 65, 75. Kane, *System of Camp-Discipline*, 12. Pringle, *Observations on the Diseases of the Army*, 110, 113. Bradstreet Diary, May 30, 1745, MHS 2.23.

48. Stephen R. Bown, *Scurvy: How a Surgeon, a Mariner, and a Gentleman Solved the Greatest Medical Mystery in the Age of Sail* (New York: Thomas Dunne Books, St. Martin's Press, 2003), chap. 4. Charters, *Disease, War, and the Imperial State*, 24–40.

49. Cartier was vague about the type of tree that the Indigenous peoples showed him, meaning that the original "spruce beer" may not have been made from spruce at all. Unfortunately for spruce beer boosters, while fresh spruce might be a source of vitamin C and therefore a true antiscorbutic, the processes of boiling and fermenting would have destroyed the vitamin content. Charters, *Disease, War, and the Imperial State*, 26–28. John Hawks, *Orderly Book and Journal of Major John Hawks* (Society of Colonial Wars in the State of New York, 1911), 2. Holmes Orderly Book, August 17, 1759, MHS 13.9.

50. Perry Orderly Book, July 21, August 3, 1759.

51. On working-class consumption of sugar in Britain, see Sidney Mintz, *Sweetness and Power: The Place of Sugar in Modern History* (New York: Viking, 1985), 112–131.

52. On changes in European and colonial alcohol consumption, see David W. Conroy, *In Public Houses: Drink and the Revolution of Authority in Colonial Massachusetts* (Chapel Hill: Omohundro Institute of Early American History and Culture and University of North Carolina Press, 1995), 25–27; Mack P. Holt, "Europe Divided: Wine, Beer, and the Reformation in Sixteenth-Century Europe," in *Alcohol: A Social and Cultural History*, ed. Mack P. Holt (Oxford: Berg, 2006), 25–40. On the rise of spirits, see Jessica Warner, *Craze: Gin and Debauchery in an Age of Reason* (New York: Four Walls Eight Windows, 2002); Matthew Warner Osborn, *Rum Maniacs: Alcoholic Insanity in the Early American Republic* (Chicago: University of Chicago Press, 2014), 17; Jordan Buchanan Smith, "The Invention of Rum" (Ph.D. diss., Georgetown University, 2018); Sarah Hand Meacham, *Every Home a*

Distillery: Alcohol, Gender, and Technology in the Colonial Chesapeake (Baltimore: Johns Hopkins University Press, 2009).

53. Holt, "Europe Divided," 25–40. On British medical opinion about alcohol, see Paul E. Kopperman, " 'The Cheapest Pay': Alcohol Abuse in the Eighteenth-Century British Army," *Journal of Military History* 60, no. 3 (July 1996): 461–68. Conroy, *In Public Houses,* 24–25, 27, 30–35, 40, 51, 57, 160. On "intemperance," see John Harris, *The Divine Physician* (Norwich: T. Goddard and L. Reeve, 1709), 18. On alcohol abuse, see Mancall, *Deadly Medicine*; Osborn, *Rum Maniacs*; William Rorabaugh, *The Alcoholic Republic: An American Tradition* (New York: Oxford, 1979); Rebecca Lemon, *Addiction and Devotion in Early Modern England* (Philadelphia: University of Pennsylvania Press, 2018). On taverns and the development of civil society in early America, see Conroy, *In Public Houses*; Vaughn Scribner, *Inn Civility: Urban Taverns and Early American Civil Society* (New York: New York University Press, 2019); Benjamin Carp, *Rebels Rising: Cities and the American Revolution* (New York: Oxford University Press, 2007), chap. 2.

54. Kopperman, " 'Cheapest Pay,' " 461–68. Charters, *Disease, War, and the Imperial State,* 26. Cornelius Stowell, Book and Diary, March 23, 1759, Octavo vol. 1, French and Indian War Collection, AAS. Hawks, *Orderly Book,* 71. Nathaniel Bangs Orderly Book, April 10, 1759, MHS 13.5. Kopperman, "British High Command and Soldiers' Wives in America," 18.

55. Bangs, May 10, 1759, MHS 13.5. Bradstreet Diary, May 25, June 20, July 3, August 18, 1745, MHS 2.23. Bradstreet also wrote of a man "who went into an house to plunder and killd himself with Drink." Ibid., May 5, 1745, MHS 2.23. Perry Orderly Book, July 7, 1759. Kopperman notes that a major obstacle to alcohol regulations in the army was the "alcoholic culture" of eighteenth-century Britain and the army itself. On military alcohol abuse and regulation, see Kopperman, " 'Cheapest Pay,' " 459–60; see also Mayer, *Belonging to the Army,* 109–10.

56. Anderson, *People's Army,* 80–83, 84, 88. William J. Tharion et al., "Energy Requirements of Military Personnel," *Appetite* 44 (2005): 47–65.

57. Capt. Silas Brown Orderly Book, September 1, September 18, 1760, MHS 13.6. Kane, *System of Camp-Discipline,* 40. Kopperman, "British High Command and Soldiers' Wives," 17–18. On food theft more generally, see Laurel Thatcher Ulrich, "It 'went away she knew not how': Food, Theft and Domestic Conflict in Seventeenth-Century Essex County," in *Foodways in the Northeast,* ed. Peter Benes (Boston: Boston University, 1984), 94–104; and LaCombe, *Political Gastronomy,* chap. 4.

58. Anonymous Diary, May 1, 2, 6, 8, 1745, MHS 13.1. As they ravaged French stores, it is likely that they raped French women; the threat of sexual violence hangs around the soldier's statement that "we found one More Camp with 2 Pritty Guirls In it." Ibid., May 8, MHS 13.1. Obadiah Harris diary, October 2, 1758, August 21, 1758, quoted in Anderson, *People's Army,* 86–87, see also 83–90. Kane, *System of Camp-Discipline,* 40.

59. Anderson, *Crucible of War,* 297–377.

60. Knowlton Diary, September 20, October 20, October 28, November 1, November 2, 1759.

61. Knowlton Diary, October 28, November 1–9, 1759.
62. Knowlton Diary, November 10–18, 1759.

Conclusion

1. Samuel Kirkland, "A Journal of the Reverend Samuel Kirkland, November 1764–June 1765," in *The Journals of Samuel Kirkland,* ed. Walter Pilkington (Clinton, N.Y.: Hamilton College Press, 1980), 5–6.

2. On Haudenosaunee food sovereignty during this period, see Rachel Herrmann, *No Useless Mouth: Waging War and Fighting Hunger in the American Revolution* (Ithaca: Cornell University Press, 2019), chap. 2. On Kirkland's career throughout the late eighteenth century, see Alan Taylor, *The Divided Ground: Indians, Settlers, and the Northern Borderland of the American Revolution* (New York: Penguin Random House, 2006).

3. On the eighteenth-century imperial obsession with population, see Joanna Innes, *Inferior Politics: Social Problems and Social Policies in Eighteenth-Century Britain* (Oxford: Oxford University Press, 2009), chap. 4. On increasing state control over reproduction, see *Lisa Forman Cody, Birthing the Nation: Sex, Science, and the Conception of Eighteenth-Century Britons* (New York: Oxford University Press, 2005); Felicity A. Nussbaum, *Torrid Zones: Maternity, Sexuality, and Empire in Eighteenth-Century English Narratives* (Baltimore: Johns Hopkins University Press, 1995); Ruth Perry, "Colonizing the Breast: Sexuality and Maternity in Eighteenth-Century England," *Journal of the History of Sexuality* 2, no. 2, special issue, part 1: The State, Society, and the Regulation of Sexuality in Modern Europe (October 1991): 204–34. Michel Foucault argued that this political moment saw the birth of biopolitics, or the control of life, death, and population by the modern state. Michel Foucault, *The History of Sexuality,* vol. 1 (London: Palgrave, 1978), 142. Historians of the early Atlantic have contested this argument by pointing to authorities' earlier attempts to control health and reproduction, particularly among oppressed populations. Ernest B. Gilman, "The Subject of the Plague," *Journal for Early Modern Cultural Studies* 10, no. 2: Rhetorics of Plague, Early and Late (Fall/Winter 2010): 23–44; Sasha Turner, *Contested Bodies: Pregnancy, Childrearing, and Slavery in Jamaica* (Philadelphia: University of Pennsylvania Press, 2017); Zachary Dorner, *Merchants of Medicine: The Commerce and Coercion of Health in Britain's Long Eighteenth Century* (Chicago: University of Chicago Press, 2020); Catherine Mark and José G. Rigau-Pérez, "The World's First Immunization Campaign: The Spanish Smallpox Vaccine Expedition, 1803–1813," *Bulletin of the History of Medicine* 83, no. 1 (Spring 2009): 63–92; and the special issue of *American Quarterly* 71, no. 3, Origins of Biopolitics in the Americas (September 2019).

4. On the emerging concept of "abundant, healthy food" as "central to governance," see Rebecca Earle, "Promoting Potatoes in Eighteenth-Century Europe," *Eighteenth-Century Studies* 51, no. 2 (Winter 2017): 154; see also David Nally, "The Biopolitics of Food Provisioning," *Transactions of the Institute of British Geographers* 36, no. 1 (January 2011): 37–53; Nicholas Crawford, " 'In the Wreck of a Master's Fortune': Slave Provisioning and the

Planter Debt in the British Caribbean," *Slavery and Abolition* 27, no. 2 (January 2016): 353–74; Joseph Horan, "The Colonial Famine Plot: Slavery, Free Trade, and Empire in the French Atlantic, 1763–1791," *International Review of Social History* 55 (December 2010): 103–21. On food aid as imperialism, see Hermann, *No Useless Mouth.*

5. Thomas Malthus, *An Essay on the Principle of Population,* ed. Joyce Chaplin (New York: Norton, 2017). On the colonial roots of Malthus's analysis, see Alison Bashford and Joyce E. Chaplin, *The New Worlds of Thomas Robert Malthus* (Princeton: Princeton University Press, 2016); on eighteenth-century overlaps between animal husbandry and provisioning humans, see Anya Zilberstein, "Bastard Breadfruit and Other Cheap Provisions: Early Food Science for the Welfare of the Lower Orders," *Early Science and Medicine* 21 (2016): 492–508.

6. Tom Scott-Smith, *On an Empty Stomach: Two Hundred Years of Hunger Relief* (Ithaca: Cornell University Press, 2020); Nick Cullather, *The Hungry World: America's Cold War Battle against Poverty in Asia* (Cambridge: Harvard University Press, 2010); James Vernon, *Hunger: A Modern History* (Cambridge: Belknap Press of Harvard University Press, 2007), 17–40, 159–95.

7. Warren Belasco, *Meals to Come: A History of the Future of Food* (Berkeley: University of California Press, 2006), esp. 3–92. Garrett Broad, *More Than Just Food: Food Justice and Community Change* (Berkeley: University of California Press, 2016), esp. 3–10. On hunger and Nazi policy in the Holocaust, see Lizzie Collingham, *The Taste of War: World War II and the Battle for Food* (London: Penguin, 2011), 180–213. Amartya Sen, "The Food Problem: Theory and Policy," *Third World Quarterly* 4 (1982), quotation on 449.

8. Herrmann, *No Useless Mouth,* 201–2. Elizabeth Hoover and Devon A. Mihesuah, "Introduction," *Indigenous Food Sovereignty in the United States: Restoring Cultural Knowledge, Protecting Environments, and Regaining Health,* ed. Devon A. Mihesuah and Elizabeth Hoover (Norman: University of Oklahoma Press, 2019), 7–12. Valarie Blue Bird Jernigan, Kimberly R. Huyser, Jimmy Valdes, and Vanessa Watts Simonds, "Food Insecurity among American Indians and Alaska Natives: A National Profile Using the Current Population Survey—Food Security Supplement," *Journal of Hunger and Environmental Nutrition* 12, no. 1 (2017): 1–10. Devon A. Mihesuah, "Decolonizing Our Diets by Recovering Our Ancestors' Gardens," *American Indian Quarterly* 27, no. 3/4, special issue: Urban American Indian Women's Activism (Summer–Autumn, 2003): 807–39.

9. Harvey Levenstein, *Paradox of Plenty: A Social History of Eating in Modern America* (New York: Oxford University Press, 1993), 53–64, 144–60; Collingham, *Taste of War,* 384–411. David M. Potter, *People of Plenty: Economic Abundance and the American Character* (Chicago: University of Chicago Press, 1954). On the raced and gendered origins of social assistance programs, see Marjorie L. DeVault and James P. Pitts, "Surplus and Scarcity: Hunger and the Origins of the Food Stamp Program," *Social Problems* 31 (1984): 545–57; Linda Gordon, *Pitied but Not Entitled: Single Mothers and the History of Welfare, 1890–1935* (Cambridge: Harvard University Press, 1994). On "the hard work of being poor," see Seth Rockman, *Scraping By: Wage Labor, Slavery, and Survival in Early Baltimore* (Baltimore: Johns Hopkins

University Press, 2008), chap. 3. Melissa Chadburn, "The Food of My Youth," *New York Review of Books,* July 9, 2018, https://www.nybooks.com/daily/2018/07/09/the-food-of-my-youth/. Raphael Richmond quoted in Eli Saslow, "Waiting for the 8th," *Washington Post,* December 15, 2013, https://www.washingtonpost.com/sf/national/2013/12/15/waiting-for-the-8th/.

10. Elizabeth Hoover, " 'You Can't Say You're Sovereign If You Can't Feed Yourself,'" in *Indigenous Food Sovereignty in the United States,* quotation on 66. See also Elizabeth Hoover, *From "Garden Warriors" to "Good Seeds": Indigenizing the Local Food Movement* (Minneapolis: University of Minnesota Press, forthcoming); Sean Sherman with Beth Dooley, *The Sioux Chef's Indigenous Kitchen* (Minneapolis: University of Minnesota Press, 2017).

11. John Norden, *A Pensive Soules Delight, Or, The Devout Mans Helpe* (London: Will Stansby, 1615), 295. Priya Krishna, "How Native Americans Are Fighting a Food Crisis," *New York Times,* April 13, 2020, https://www.nytimes.com/2020/04/13/dining/native-americans-coronavirus.html.

12. Elizabeth Hoover, "Native Food Systems in the Time of COVID-19," *From Garden Warriors to Good Seeds: Indigenizing the Local Food Movement,* May 3, 2020, https://gardenwarriorsgoodseeds.com/2020/05/03/native-food-systems-in-the-time-of-covid-19/. Gabriel Pietrorazio, "The Seneca Nation Is Building Food Sovereignty, One Bison at a Time," *Civil Eats,* January 14, 2021, https://civileats.com/2021/01/14/from-bison-to-syrup-the-seneca-nation-is-making-strides-in-food-sovereignty. Jack Healy, "Tribal Elders Are Dying from the Pandemic, Causing a Cultural Crisis for American Indians," *New York Times,* January 12, 2021, https://www.nytimes.com/2021/01/12/us/tribal-elders-native-americans-coronavirus.html.

13. Kyle Powys Whyte, "Food Justice and Collective Food Relations," in *Food, Ethics, and Society: An Introductory Text with Readings,* ed. Anne Barnhill, Mark Budolfson, and Tyler Doggett (New York: Oxford University Press, 2016); Kyle Powys Whyte, "Critical Investigations of Resilience: A Brief Introduction to Indigenous Environmental Studies and Sciences," *Daedalus: Journal of the American Academy of Arts and Sciences* 147, no. 2 (2018): 137. See also Daniel R. Wildcat, *Red Alert!: Saving the Planet with Indigenous Knowledge* (Golden, Colo.: Fulcrum Publishing, 2009).

14. Hoover, "Native Food Systems in the Time of COVID-19."

15. Cheryl Savageau, *Mother/Land* (Cambridge: Salt Publishing, 2006), 18. See also Thomas M. Wickman, *Snowshoe Country: An Environmental and Cultural History of Winter in the Early American Northeast* (New York: Cambridge University Press, 2018), 267–68.

16. Robin Wall Kimmerer, *Braiding Sweetgrass: Indigenous Wisdom, Scientific Knowledge, and the Teachings of Plants* (Minneapolis: Milkweed Editions, 2013), 377.

INDEX

Abenaki, 10, 142, 218n20
agriculture: British military and, 161;
   colonialism and, 4, 11, 12, 17, 84, 95,
   214n34; corn and maize, 17, 39,
   48–49, 90, 95, 150, 186n26; in
   European hunger cultures, 25–26,
   30, 35; food sovereignty and, 143,
   154, 176; in Indigenous hunger
   cultures, 4, 14–15, 39–40, 43, 47,
   177–78; technological innovations in,
   26–27, 174–75, 193n10
alcohol: British soldiers and, 138, 139,
   155, 156, 158–60, 162–67, 169,
   227n49, 228n55; intemperance and,
   163–64; rum and liquors, 163–65,
   225n36; Wabanaki treaty negotiations and, 146, 148, 150–54, 224n26
Algonquian, 22–23, 40, 71, 90, 122–25
American Revolution, 169, 225–26n37
Anderson, Virginia DeJohn, 223n22

Andry, Nicolas: *The Lenten Diet*, 65
Anglicanism, 59, 60–65
antihunger policies, 17, 25–27, 34, 40,
   173–75, 188n31
archives and hunger studies: cannibalism in, 122, 135; disgust narratives
   and, 91–92, 100–101, 105, 108,
   110–11; methodology for study,
   18–20; Wabanaki dependence in, 144
Arens, William, 215n6
Arosen, François-Xavier, 70
Azure, Jamie, 177

Bangs, Nathaniel, 164
Barrough, Philip, 29, 30
Bayly, Lewis, 60, 67, 80
Beaver Wars, 123
Belasco, Warren, 195n20
Belcher, Jonathan, 138–39, 143, 145,
   146, 152, 153

climate change, 177, 187nn28–29. *See also* Little Ice Age

Colman, Benjamin, 66, 67

colonization and colonialism, 3; agriculture and, 4, 11, 12, 17, 84, 95, 214n34; cannibalism and, 114–22, 129–36, 215n6, 216n11; dependency on Indigenous hunger knowledge, 24–25, 95–96, 100, 105, 110–11, 147, 172–73; disgust and, 91–92, 94–100, 105, 110–11; fasting and, 69–70, 82; fragility and vulnerability of, 3–5, 11, 13–14, 141, 144, 154, 169–70; methodology in reading, 19–21. *See also* English colonists; French colonists; missionizing

common pot ethic, 40–41, 43, 52, 147

communion. *See* Eucharist debates and cannibalism

cooking and food preparation: disgust narratives and, 92–93, 98–99, 102–4; fermentation and rot, 107–8; seasonality and, 27; wild foods and, 42

corn, 14, 17, 39, 48–49, 90, 95, 150, 186n26

COVID-19 pandemic, 177–78

Crépieul, François de, 75–76, 91, 95–96, 99–100, 103

Culpeper, Nicholas, 30

Dablon, Claude, 127

Darker, John: *A Breviary of Military Discipline*, 158

Deerfield, Massachusetts, raid (1704), 60, 69

desertion from military service, 138, 155–56, 166–69

The Discount on Bread in Burlesque Verse, 38

disgust narratives: cannibalism and, 132; colonial, 90–92, 94–100, 105, 110–11, 172; of cooking and food

preparation, 92–93, 98–99, 102–4; of fermentation and rot, 105–8; history and definitions of, 92–95, 208n4, 209n6, 210–11n12; hunger cultures as context for, 89–92; Indigenous, 90–92, 95–105, 110–11, 213n33; Kirkland and, 2, 89; as resistance to assimilation, 108–11

dogs, 15, 38, 47–49, 72, 100, 102, 148–49, 204n35

Doolittle, Thomas, 119–20

Douay Catechism, 119

Douglas, Mary, 56, 94

Dubé, Paul, 36–37, 49

Dudley, Joseph, 151

Dummer, William, 149, 154

Dummer's War or Father Rale's War (1722–25), 13, 68

Dyer, Christopher, 197n33

dysentery, 28, 161

Edwards, Jonathan, 57, 78–83, 85, 206n54, 207n55

English colonists: cannibalism and, 133, 216n11; disgust of, 95–100; hunger cultures of, 24–30, 191n4; hunger knowledges of, 25, 30–33, 172, 195n17; King Philip's War and, 59; reciprocity and, 136, 140; Seven Years' War and, 55–56

Enlightenment, 59, 174

enslaved people, 11, 15, 130, 174

Eucharist debates and cannibalism, 111, 113, 115, 118–19, 121–22, 133–36, 215n5

fairy tales, 32, 39. *See also* Chenoo stories; windigo stories

famine: defined, 6; diseases and, 194n13; English hunger cultures and, 25–26; English hunger